Late Georgian and Regency England 1760–1837

CONFERENCE ON BRITISH STUDIES
BIBLIOGRAPHICAL HANDBOOKS

Editor: PETER STANSKY
Consultant Editor: G. R. ELTON

Other books in the series

Late Georgian and Regency England 1760–1837

ROBERT A. SMITH

Professor of History, Emory University

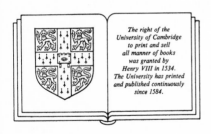

The right of the
University of Cambridge
to print and sell
all manner of books
was granted by
Henry VIII in 1534.
The University has printed
and published continuously
since 1584.

CAMBRIDGE UNIVERSITY PRESS

CAMBRIDGE

LONDON   NEW YORK   NEW ROCHELLE

MELBOURNE   SYDNEY

For the Conference on British Studies

Published by the Press Syndicate of the University of Cambridge
The Pitt Building, Trumpington Street, Cambridge CB2 1RP
32 East 57th Street, New York, NY 10022, USA
296 Beaconsfield Parade, Middle Park, Melbourne 3206, Australia

First published 1984

Printed in Great Britain at the University Press, Cambridge

Library of Congress catalogue card number: 83-26213

British Library Cataloguing in Publication Data

Smith, Robert A.
Late Georgian and Regency England. 1760–1837—(Conference on British studies
bibliographical handbooks)
1. Great Britain—History—1714–1837—Bibliography
I. Title   II. Series
016.94107′3   Z2018

ISBN 0 521 25538 4

TM

CONTENTS

PREFACE

The purpose of this handbook is to provide an up-to-date guide to the best of the voluminous literature on later eighteenth and early nineteenth century England. All subjects except strictly literary history and criticism are included; the selection has been made from a survey of all work published before 1 January 1981, with an occasional later book or article added. Much excellent material, old and new, has had to be omitted to keep the volume within the limit of about 2,500 entries and to create a useful rather than an exhaustive bibliography for students and non-specialists in the period. Towards these ends I have followed two principles: the omission of all but the most basic printed sources and the most indispensable secondary works included in entries 5 and 49 which provide exhaustive guides to the literature for the years 1760–89 published before 1950 and for the years between 1789 and 1837 published before 1970; and the exclusion of most books and articles on subjects beginning before 1837 but principally concerned with the early Victorian period which were included in Josef Altholz's *Victorian England* in this series.

As a result, this handbook concentrates on the more recent literature on most subjects. The articles particularly have been chosen to represent work or revision currently in progress rather than material and interpretations already incorporated in more general works. Many titles might well have gone into other sections than the one selected. I have generally followed the subject placement already established in previous volumes (i.e. elementary education under Social History; university education under Intellectual History; economic and political thought under Intellectual History rather than Economic or Political History) with extensive cross-referencing for the more ambiguous cases. I have also included more extensive listings for some areas particularly important between 1760 and 1837 than they have received in previous volumes, particularly Science and Technology and the Fine Arts. I have kept editorial comments to a minimum beyond an occasional indication of subject when it is not clear from the title. I have also frequently indicated particularly useful bibliographies in individual works as guides to further literature. The result, I hope, is a balanced presentation of the literature on all aspects of one of the most creative and dynamic periods of English history.

I want to thank the Emory University Research Fund for a small grant towards the preliminary verification of titles. Leslie Bessant and Patricia Bradley both helped with this task. But my greatest debt, as usual, is to my wife who has helped fundamentally at every stage of compilation, and to my sons Thomas and Jonathan who have also been incorporated into this project.

Atlanta, Georgia   ROBERT A. SMITH

ABBREVIATIONS

AgH	*Agricultural History*
AgHR	*Agricultural History Review*
AHR	*American Historical Review*
BHMed	*Bulletin of the History of Medicine*
BIHR	*Bulletin of the Institute of Historical Research*
BusH	*Business History*
BusHR	*Business History Review*
EcHR	*Economic History Review*
ECS	*Eighteenth-century Studies*
EHR	*English Historical Review*
ExEcH	*Explorations in Economic History*
HJ	*Historical Journal*
HPolEc	*History of Political Economy*
HLQ	*Huntington Library Quarterly*
JBS	*Journal of British Studies*
JEcH	*Journal of Economic History*
JEurEcH	*Journal of European Economic History*
JHI	*Journal of the History of Ideas*
JHMed	*Journal of the History of Medicine and the Allied Sciences*
JMH	*Journal of Modern History*
JPolEc	*Journal of Political Economy*
MedH	*Medical History*
PP	*Past and Present*
TRHS	*Transactions of the Royal Historical Society*
VCH	*Victoria County History*
W&MQ	*William and Mary Quarterly*

EXPLANATORY NOTES

1 When no place of publication is given for a book, its place of publication is London. When a book appeared both in England and elsewhere, the English place of publication is normally given.
2 In most cases, collected works and correspondences are listed under the editor, not the author. Both, however, are indexed.

I. BIBLIOGRAPHIES

1 Albion, Robert Greenhalgh. *Naval and maritime history: an annotated bibliography.* 4th edn, Mystic, Conn., 1972. Arranged by subject.

2 American Historical Association. *Recently published articles.* 1976–. Now appearing three times a year; a comprehensive listing, without annotation, by country. Continues the listing begun as 'Other recent publications' in the *AHR* in 1936 and continued under various titles until separate publication began in 1976.

3 Brewer, James Gordon. *Enclosures and the open fields: a bibliography.* Reading, 1972. Annual lists of writings in agricultural history are published in *AgH* and *AgHR*.

4 *British national bibliography.* 1951–. British books since 1950 in a very detailed subject arrangement. Published weekly with an annual cumulative volume.

5 Brown, Lucy Margaret and Ian Ralph Christie (comps.). *Bibliography of British history, 1789–1851.* Oxford, 1977. Comprehensive on most subjects to *c.* 1970; emphasizes source materials and guides to further information. See also (49).

6 Bruce, Anthony Peter Charles (comp.). *An annotated bibliography of the British army, 1660–1914.* New York, 1975. See also (23) and (62).

7 Chaloner, William Henry and R. C. Richardson (comps.). *British economic and social history: a bibliographical guide.* Manchester, 1976.

8 Charles, Dorothy, et al. (comps.). *The bibliographic index: a cumulative bibliography of bibliographies.* New York, 1945–. Begins with publications of 1937: now appears quarterly with annual cumulative volumes; lists all bibliographies, including those in books and articles, as they appear.

9 Crane, Ronald Salmon, et al. (comps.). 'English literature of the Restoration and eighteenth century', published annually in *Philological Quarterly*, 1926–. Useful for social and intellectual history. The bibliographies from 1926–50 have been republished in two vols., ed. Louis A. Lander and Arthur Friedman (Princeton, NJ, 1950–2); those from 1951 to 1960 in two vols., ed. Gwin J. Kolb and Curt A. Zimansky (Princeton, NJ, 1962); those from 1961 to 1970 in two vols., ed. Curt A. Zimansky (Princeton, NJ, 1972).

10 Crombie, Alistair Cameron and Michael A. Hoskin (comps.). *History of science: an annual review of literature, research and teaching.* Cambridge, 1962–. See also (50), (63) and (129).

11 *Economic History Review.* 'List of publications in the economic history of Great Britain and Ireland', 1927–. Published annually, now usually in the last number for the year. Includes monographs and articles, and has become increasingly comprehensive, including most areas of social history as well as economic history.

12 Elton, Geoffrey Rudolph (comp.). *The Royal Historical Society's annual bibliography of British and Irish history.* 1976–. Listing by period and subject of publications for each year since 1975; not definitive.

13 Ferguson, Eugene Shallcross (comp.). *Bibliography of the history of technology.* Cambridge, Mass., 1968. Subsequent publications are listed annually in *Technology and culture.*

14 Frow, Ruth, et al. (comps.). *The history of British trade unionism: a select bibliography.* 1969.

15 Gipson, Lawrence Henry. *A bibliographical guide to the history of the British Empire, 1748–1776.* New York, 1969. *A guide to manuscripts relating to the history of the British Empire, 1748–1776.* New York, 1970. (Vols. 14 and 15 of his *The British Empire before the American Revolution.*) The first volume includes some 6,000 printed sources and secondary works; the second is an equally full discussion of the manuscript sources.

16 Green, Richard. *Anti-Methodist publications issued during the eighteenth century: a chronologically arranged and annotated bibliography.* 1902. More than 600 entries issued 1732–1810.

17 —— *The works of John and Charles Wesley. A bibliography: containing an exact account of all the publications issued by the brothers Wesley.* 1896; 2nd edn, 1906.

18 Gross, Charles (comp.). *A bibliography of British municipal history, including gilds and parliamentary representation.* 1897; reprinted, with a preface by Geoffrey Haward Martin, Leicester, 1966. See also (41), which is replacing this.

19 Hancock, Philip David (comp.). *A bibliography of works relating to Scotland, 1916–1950.*

Edinburgh, 1959–60, 2 vols. A list of articles on Scottish history is published annually in the *Scottish Historical Review*.

20 Harte, Negley Boyd. 'Trends in publications on the economic and social history of Great Britain and Ireland, 1925–74', *EcHR* 2nd ser., 30 (1977), 20–41.

21 Hecht, Joseph Jean. 'The reign of George III in recent historiography', in Elizabeth Chapin Furber (ed.), *Changing views on British history: essays on historical writing since 1939*. Cambridge, Mass., 1966, pp. 206–33. Discussion of major works and trends to 1965. Continued in (54).

22 Higgs, Henry (comp.). *Bibliography of economics, 1751–1775*. Cambridge, 1935. See also (139).

23 Higham, Robin D. S. (ed.). *A guide to the sources of British military history*. Berkeley, Calif., 1971. Bibliographical essays on every aspect of the army and navy. See also (6) and (62).

24 Historical Association, London. *Annual bulletin of historical literature*. 1912–. Begins with publications of 1911; selective survey in the form of critical essays on leading books and articles appearing each year. The latest volume (LXVI), covering publications of 1980, was published in 1982.

25 Hogg, Peter C. *The African slave trade and its suppression: a classified and annotated bibliography of books, pamphlets and periodical articles.* 1973.

26 Howard-Hill, Trevor Howard. *Bibliography of British literary bibliographies*. Oxford, 1969. Especially useful for social and intellectual history.

27 Humphreys, Arthur Lee. *A handbook to county bibliography, being a bibliography of bibliographies relating to the counties and towns of Great Britain and Ireland*. 1917.

28 *International bibliography of the historical sciences*. Paris, 1930–. Begins with publications of 1926; Vols. 45–6 (Munich, 1980) covers publications of 1976–7. All countries, all subjects.

29 Jacobs, Phyllis May. 'Registers of the universities, colleges, and schools of Great Britain and Ireland', *BIHR*, 37 (1964), 185–232. See also (174).

30 Jenkins, Rhys T. and William Rees (comps.). *Bibliography of the history of Wales*. 2nd edn, Cardiff, 1962. Supplements published in the *Bulletin of the Board of Celtic Studies*.

31 Johnston, Edith Mary (comp.). *Irish history: a select bibliography.* (Historical Association, London. Helps for Students of History, 73.) 1969. Annotated. See also (44).

32 Kaminkow, Marion J. *A new bibliography of British genealogy with notes*. Baltimore, Md, 1965. See also (168).

33 Kanner, Barbara (ed.). *The women of England, from Anglo-Saxon times to the present: interpretative bibliographical essays.* Hamden, Conn., 1979.

34 Knafla, L. A. 'Crime and criminal justice: a critical bibliography', in J. S. Cockburn (ed.), *Crime in England, 1550–1800*. Princeton, NJ, 1977, pp. 270–93.

35 Lancaster, Joan Cadogan, William Kellaway and R. Taylor (comps.). *Bibliography of historical works issued in the United Kingdom, 1946–1956*. 1957. *1957–1960*. 1962. *1961–1965*. 1967. *1966–1970*. 1972. *1971–1975*. 1977. Unannotated listing of all historical works on all subjects and countries published during the respective years.

36 *A London bibliography of the social sciences, being the subject catalogue of the British Library of Political and Economic Science of the London School of Economics, The Goldsmiths' Library of Economic Literature of the University of London, the Library of the Royal Statistical Society, and the Royal Anthropological Institute.* 1931–2, 4 vols.; regular supplements, 1934–. Latest volume (35) covers 1980; largest subject index of its kind.

37 London County Council Library. *Members' library catalogue*. Vol. 1: *London history and topography.* 1939. Best bibliography of the subject.

38 London University. Courtauld Institute of Art. *Bibliography of the history of British art*. Cambridge, 1936–56, 6 vols. Projected as an annual bibliography beginning with publications of 1934, but had reached only 1948 with the sixth vol. For subsequent publications, see (66).

39 Madden, Lionel and Diana Dixon (comps.). *The nineteenth century periodical press in Britain: a bibliography of modern studies, 1901–1971.* (Supplement to *Victorian Periodicals Newsletter*, 8, 1975.) Toronto, 1975.

40 Manchester Joint Committee on the Lancashire Bibliography. *The Lancashire bibliography*. Manchester, 1968–. Seven vols. published to 1974 by various hands; model county bibliography.

41 Martin, Geoffrey Haward and Sylvia MacIntyre (comps.). *A bibliography of British and Irish municipal history*. Vol. 1 : *General works*. Leicester, 1972. Publications to the end of 1966; will eventually replace (18) on a much more extensive scale.

42 Matthews, William (comp.). *British autobiographies: an annotated bibliography of British autobiographies published or written before 1951*. Berkeley, Calif., 1955; reprinted, Hamden, Conn., 1968.

43 —— *British diaries: an annotated bibliography of British diaries written between 1442 and 1942*. Berkeley, Calif., 1950. Includes unpublished diaries. See also (68).

44 Moody, Theodore William (ed.). *Irish historiography, 1936–70*. Dublin, 1971. Bibliographical essays. See also (31). An annual bibliography of current publications appears in *Irish Historical Studies*.

45 Morton, Leslie Thomas (comp.). *A medical bibliography: an annotated checklist of texts illustrating the history of medicine*. 3rd edn, 1970. See also (57).

46 National Library of Medicine. United States Department of Health, Education and Welfare. *Bibliography of the history of medicine*. Washington, DC, 1965–. Issued annually.

47 Nichols, David. *Nineteenth-century Britain, 1815–1914*. New Haven, Conn., 1978. Selective critical bibliography.

48 Norwood, Frederick A. 'Methodist historical studies, 1930–1959', *Church History*, 28 (1959), 391–417; 29 (1960), 74–88. 'Methodist historical studies, 1960–70: a bibliographical article', *ibid.* 40 (1971), 182–99.

49 Pargellis, Stanley McCrory and Dudley Julius Medley (comps.). *Bibliography of British history: the eighteenth century, 1714–1789*. Oxford, 1951; reprinted, Totowa, NJ, 1977. Comprehensive to the late 1940s; especially strong on source material, published and unpublished. See also (5).

50 Rider, Kenneth John (comp.). *The history of science and technology: a select bibliography for students*. 2nd edn, 1970. See also (10), (63) and (129).

51 Roth, Cecil (comp.). *Magna bibliotheca anglo-judaica: a bibliographical guide to Anglo-Jewish history*. New edn, rev. and enlarged, 1937. Continued in Ruth Pauline Lehmann (comp.). *Anglo-Jewish bibliography, 1937–70*. 1973.

52 Slocum, Robert Bigney (comp.). *Biographical dictionaries and related works: an international bibliography of collective biographies, bibliographies, collections of epitaphs, selected genealogical works*. Detroit, Mich., 1967.

53 Smith, Joseph. *A descriptive catalogue of Friends' books, or books written by members of the Society of Friends ... from their first rise to the present times*. 1867, 2 vols. A third, supplemental vol., 1893.

54 Smith, Robert Arthur. 'Reinterpreting the reign of George III', in Richard Schlatter (ed.). *Recent trends in British history*. New Brunswick, NJ, 1984. Descriptive and critical essay on work published since 1965.

55 Starr, Edward Caryl (comp.). *A Baptist bibliography, being a register of printed material by and about Baptists, including works written against the Baptists*. Philadelphia, Pa., 1947–76, 25 vols.

56 Surman, Charles Edward (comp.). *A bibliography of Congregational church history, including numerous cognate Presbyterian/Unitarian records and a few Baptist*. Edington, Wilts., 1947.

57 Thornton, John Leonard, et al. (comps.). *A select bibliography of medical biography*. 1961.

58 Todd, Janet M. *Mary Wollstonecraft: an annotated bibliography*. New York, 1976.

59 Todd, William Burton. *A bibliography of Edmund Burke*. 1964. Burke's own writings; for the secondary work on him, see Clara I. Gandy, 'A bibliographical survey of writings on Edmund Burke, 1945–1975', *British Studies Monitor*, 8 (1978), 3–21.

60 Watson, George (ed.). *The new Cambridge bibliography of English literature*. Cambridge, 1969–74, 5 vols. Vol. 2: *1660–1800*; Vol. 3: *1800–1900*. The current edition omits the sections on social and political background in the previous edition, but retains comprehensive sections on all non-literary prose, periodicals, travel, sports, letters and diaries, and the history of all branches of scholarship.

61 Weed, Katherine Kirtley and Richmond Pugh Bond (comps.). *Studies of British newspapers and periodicals from their beginning to 1800: a bibliography.* Chapel Hill, NC, 1946.

62 White, Arthur Sharpin (comp.). *A bibliography of regimental histories of the British army.* 1965. See also (6) and (23).

63 Whitrow, Magda (comp.). *ISIS cumulative bibliography: a bibliography of the history of science formed from ISIS critical bibliographies 1–90, 1913–65.* 1971–6, 3 vols. From 1965 published annually in *ISIS.* See also (10), (50) and (129).

64 Wood, John A., et al. (comps.). *A bibliography of parliamentary debates of Great Britain.* (House of Commons Library, Document 2.) 1956. Best guide to the subject. See also (167), (603) and (682).

65 *Writings on British history, 1901–.* 1937–. Virtually comprehensive, although unannotated, bibliography of all books and articles published anywhere on British history since 1901. Volumes published so far are *1901–1933,* ed. Hugh Hale Bellot and Alexander Taylor Milne, 1968–70, 5 vols.; *1934–1945,* ed. Alexander Taylor Milne, 1937–60, 8 vols.; *1946–1948,* ed. Donald James Munro, 1973; *1949–51,* ed. Donald James Munro, 1975; *1952–1954,* ed. John Merriman Sims, 1975; *1955–1957,* ed. John Merriman Sims and Phyllis May Jacobs, 1977; *1958–1959,* ed. Heather J. Creaton, 1977; *1960–1961,* ed. Charles H. E. Philpin and Heather J. Creaton, 1978; *1962–1964,* ed. Heather J. Creaton, 1980.

II. CATALOGUES, GUIDES, INDEXES AND GENERAL REFERENCE WORKS

66 *The art index ... 1929–.* New York, 1933–.

67 Averly, G., et al. (comps.). *Eighteenth century British books: a subject catalogue extracted from the British Museum general catalogue of printed books.* Folkestone, Kent, 1978, 4 vols.

68 Batts, John Stuart. *British manuscript diaries of the nineteenth century: an annotated listing.* Totowa, NJ, 1976. Describes more than 3,000 diaries. See also (43).

69 Baylen, Joseph O. and Norbert J. Gossman (eds.). *Biographical dictionary of modern British radicals.* Vol. 1: *1770–1830.* Atlantic Highlands, NJ, 1979.

70 Beaven, Alfred Beaven (comp.). *The aldermen of the City of London, temp. Henry III – 1908.* 1900–13, 2 vols. Biographical notices, including many of men not included in the *Dictionary of National Biography* (162).

71 Bellamy, Joyce Margaret and John Saville (eds.). *Dictionary of labour biography.* 1970–. Each volume self-contained, A through Z; 4 vols. published through 1977.

72 Bilboul, Roger R. and Francis L. Kent (comps.). *Retrospective index to theses of Great Britain and Ireland, 1716–1950.* Vol. 1: *Social science and the humanities.* Oxford, 1975. For theses see also (107), (122), (125) and (130).

73 Bindoff, Stanley Thomas and James T. Boulton (comps.). *Research in progress in English and history in Britain, Ireland, Canada, Australia, and New Zealand.* 1976.

74 Boehm, Eric H. (comp.). *Historical abstracts 1775–1945. A quarterly of abstracts of historical articles appearing currently in periodicals the world over.* Santa Barbara, Calif. and Vienna, 1955–.

75 Boehm, Eric H. and Lelit Adolphus (comps.). *Historical periodicals: an annotated world list of historical and related serial publications.* Santa Barbara, Calif., 1961. Lists over 4,500 periodicals. For earlier journals see Pierre Carron and Marc Jaryc (comps.). *World list of historical periodicals and bibliographies.* Oxford, 1939.

76 Bond, Maurice Francis (comp.). *Guide to the records of Parliament.* 1971.

77 Brewster, John W. and Joseph A. McLeod (comps.). *Index to book reviews in historical periodicals.* Metuchen, NJ, 1976–. From 1972.

78 *British humanities index.* 1962–. Quarterly: indexes many local and specialist journals. A continuation of parts of the older *Subject index to periodicals,* 1915–62.

79 British Library. *Catalogue of additions to the manuscripts in the British Museum 1783–.* 1849–. The most recently published volume includes manuscripts acquired through 1945; the earlier volumes have been reprinted by photolithography, 1967–.

80   British Library. *Catalogue of prints and drawings in the British Museum.* Division 2: *Political and personal satires.* Comp. by Frederic George Stephens, Edward Hawkins and Mary Dorothy George. 1870–1954, 11 vols. Vols. 5–11 (1771–1832), comp. by Mary Dorothy George.

81   British Library. *Catalogue of the Newspaper Library, Colindale.* 1975, 8 vols. London newspapers and journals from 1801; English provinces, Scotland and Ireland from about 1700; many Commonwealth and foreign papers.

82   British Library. *General catalogue of printed books. Photolithographic edition to 1955.* 1959–66, 263 vols. *Ten year supplement 1956–1965.* 1968, 50 vols. *Five year supplement 1966–1970.* 1971–2, 26 vols. *Five year supplement 1971–1975.* 1978, 13 vols.

83   British Library. *Subject index of modern books added to the British Museum.* 1902–. Covers five-year periods; the most recent, for 1951–5, published in 1974, 6 vols.; that for 1956–60 appeared in 1965.

84   Brooke, John. *The prime ministers' papers 1801–1902: a survey of the privately preserved papers of those statesmen who held the office of prime minister during the nineteenth century.* 1968.

85   Burke, Sir John Bernard. *A genealogical and heraldic history of the commoners of Great Britain and Ireland.* 1833–8, 4 vols.; reprinted, Baltimore, Md, 1977. The earliest edn of what became Burke's *Landed gentry*; the families included vary from edition to edition.

86   —— *A genealogical and heraldic history of the peerage and baronetage of the British Empire.* 1826–. Burke's *Peerage.*

87   —— *Genealogical and heraldic history of the extinct and dormant baronetcies of England, Ireland, and Scotland.* 1841; new edn, 1866.

88   —— *Genealogical history of the dormant, abeyant, forfeited and extinct peerages of the British Empire.* 1831; new edn, 1883. See also (157).

89   Buttress, Frederick Arthur (comp.). *Agricultural periodicals of the British Isles, 1681–1900, and their location.* Cambridge, 1950.

90   Canney, Margaret and David Knott (comps.). *Catalogue of the Goldsmiths' Library of Economic Literature.* Vol. 1: *Printed books to 1800.* Cambridge, 1970. Vol. 2: *Printed books 1801–1850.* Cambridge, 1975.

91   Cheney, Christopher Robert (comp.). *Handbook of dates for students of English history.* 1945; reprinted 1961. A basic guide to dating; has useful perpetual calendar.

92   Clark, George Sidney Roberts Kitson and Geoffrey Rudolph Elton (comps.). *Guide to the research facilities in history in the universities of Great Britain and Ireland.* 2nd edn, Cambridge, 1965. Brief descriptions of their collections and research possibilities.

93   Cokayne, George Edward. *Complete baronetage, 1611–1800.* Exeter, 1900–6, 5 vols.

94   —— *The complete peerage of England, Scotland, Ireland, Great Britain, and the United Kingdom.* New edn, rev. and enlarged by Vicary Gibbs, et al., 1910–59, 13 vols. in 14. Definitive for holders of titles and their wives; the notes for this period less reliable than for earlier ones.

95   Collins, Arthur. *The peerage of England.* Ed. Sir Samuel Egerton Brydges. 1812, 9 vols.; reprinted 1970. Most complete edition of a work first published in 1709; valuable for families of peers.

96   Colvin, Howard Montagu (comp.). *A guide to the sources of English architectural history.* Rev. edn, Newport, Isle of Wight, 1967.

97   Crone, John Smyth (comp.). *A concise dictionary of Irish biography.* Rev. edn, Dublin, 1937.

98   Dixon, Diana (comp.). *Local newspapers and periodicals of the nineteenth century: a checklist of holdings in provincial libraries.* Leicester, 1973, 2 vols.

99   Dr Williams's Library. *Early nonconformity, 1566–1800: a catalogue of books in Dr Williams's Library.* Boston, Mass., 1968, 5 vols. Author catalogue; major collection for non-conformity.

100   Dyos, Harold James, et al. (eds.). *Urban history year book.* Leicester, 1974–. Includes reports on conferences, reviews, bibliographies and register of work in progress.

101   Emmison, Frederick George. *Archives and local history.* 2nd edn, Chichester, Sussex, 1974. How to use a local record office.

102   Emmison, Frederick George and Irvine Gray. *County records (quarter sessions, petty sessions, clerk of the peace and lieutenancy).* (Historical Association, London. Helps for Students of History, 62.) Rev. edn, 1967. How to use this type of record.

103 Ford, Percy and Grace Ford. *A guide to parliamentary papers: what they are; how to find them; how to use them.* Oxford, 1955.

104 Foster, Joseph (comp.). *Alumni oxonienses ... 1715–1886.* 1887–8, 4 vols. Alphabetical listing with minimal biographical information.

105 Gibson, Jeremy Sumner Wycherly. *Wills and where to find them.* Chichester, Sussex, 1974.

106 Gilbert, Martin. *British history atlas.* 1968.

107 Gilchrist, Donald Bean and Edward Attwood Henry (comps.). *Dissertations accepted by American universities.* New York, 1934–54/5, 22 vols. Continued as *Index to American doctoral dissertations,* 1957–. For theses see also (72), (122), (125) and (130).

108 Gold, William (ed.). *Lives of the Georgian age, 1714–1837.* New York, 1978. 300 short biographies by experts.

109 Goss, Charles William Frederick. *The London directories, 1677–1855: a bibliography with notes on their origin and development.* 1932. For provincial directories see (150).

110 Great Britain, Ministry of Defence, Naval Library, London. *Author and subject catalogues.* 1967, 5 vols. One of the largest collections of books on naval and maritime affairs. See also (149).

111 Grove, Sir George. *The new Grove dictionary of music and musicians.* Ed. Stanley Sadie, 1980, 20 vols.

112 *Guide to the contents of the Public Record Office.* 1963–8, 3 vols. Vol. 1 describes the legal records; Vol. 2, state papers and departmental records; Vol. 3, documents transferred 1960–6 and corrections to Vols. 1 and 2. Replaces the old guide by Montagu Spencer Giuseppi. See also (136) and (158).

113 Halkett, Samuel and John Laing. *Dictionary of anonymous and pseudonymous English literature.* New and enlarged edn by James Kennedy, et al., Edinburgh, 1920–34, 7 vols.; two additional vols. by Dennis E. Rhodes and Anna E. C. Simoni, 1956–62.

114 Harris, John Frederick (comp.). *A country house index: an index to over 2000 country houses illustrated in 107 books of country views published between 1715 and 1872, together with a list of British country house guides and country house art collection catalogues for the period 1726–1870.* Shalfleet Manor, Isle of Wight, 1971.

115 Harrison, Royden John, et al. (comps.). *The Warwick guide to British labour periodicals, 1790–1970.* 1977.

116 Historical Manuscripts Commission. *A guide to the reports of the Royal Commission on Historical Manuscripts.* Part 1: *Topographical* [1870–1911], 1914. *Index of places 1911–1957,* ed. A. C. S. Hall, 1973; Part 2: *Index of persons 1870–1911,* ed. Francis Bickley, 1935–8, 2 vols. *Index of persons 1911–1957,* ed. A. C. S. Hall, 1966, 3 vols.

117 Historical Manuscripts Commission. *Record repositories in Great Britain.* 5th edn, 1973. Arranged under places and regions.

118 Historical Manuscripts Commission. *List of accessions to repositories.* 1954–. Published annually. From 1971 entitled *Accessions to repositories and reports added to the National Register of Archives.* There is an index to the *Lists* for 1954–8, published in 1967.

119 Hoskins, William George. *Local history in England.* 2nd edn, 1972. Essentially a guide for amateurs, but by a master of the subject.

120 Houghton, Walter Edwards (comp.). *The Wellesley index to Victorian periodicals, 1824–1900.* Toronto, 1966–. List of all articles in selected monthlies and quarterlies; attributions of authorship; bibliographies of authors; list of pseudonyms. See also (179).

121 *Indexes to bills and reports, 1801–52.* Vol. 1: *General index. Bills.* Vol. 2: *Reports of select committees.* Vol. 3: *Accounts and papers, reports of commissioners, estimates, etc.* 1853, 3 vols. Vol. 3 reprinted, 1938. Indexes to the parliamentary papers.

122 Institute of Historical Research. 'Annual list of historical research for university degrees in the United Kingdom', *BIHR, Theses Supplement,* 1933–53. Superseded in 1954 by annual lists of 'Theses completed' and 'Theses in progress'. See also (72), (107), (125) and (130).

123 Irish University Press. *Checklist of British parliamentary papers in the Irish University Press 1000-volume series, 1801–1899.* Shannon, 1972. See also (156).

124 Irwin, Raymond and Ronald Staveley (comps.). *The libraries of London.* 2nd edn, 1961; reprinted with corrections, 1964. Library resources in London.

125 Jacobs, Phyllis May (comp.). *History theses 1901–70: historical research for higher degrees in the universities of the United Kingdom.* 1976. See also (72), (107), (122) and (130).

126 Jones, Philip Edmund and Raymond Smith (comps.). *A guide to the records in the Corporation of London Records Office and the Guildhall Library Muniment Room.* 1951.

127 Kendall, Maurice George (ed.). *The sources and nature of the statistics of the United Kingdom.* 1952–7, 2 vols. Reprints of articles from the *Journal of the Royal Statistical Society,* which serve as general guides to all British statistics.

128 Kitching, Christopher J. *The central records of the Church of England.* 1976.

129 Knight, David M. *Sources for the history of science, 1660–1914.* Ithaca, NY, 1975. See also (10), (50) and (63).

130 Kuehl, Warren Frederick (comp.). *Dissertations in history: an index to dissertations completed in history departments of United States and Canadian universities, 1873–1970.* Lexington, Ky, 1965–72, 2 vols. See also (72), (107), (122) and (125).

131 Lawton, Richard (ed.). *The census and social structure: an interpretative guide to nineteenth century censuses for England and Wales.* 1978. Essays on the methods and content of the censuses.

132 LeNeve, John and Sir Thomas Duffus Hardy (comps.). *Fasti ecclesiae anglicanae, or, a calendar of the principal ecclesiastical dignitaries in England and Wales, and of the chief officers in the Universities of Oxford and Cambridge.* Oxford, 1854, 3 vols. A new edition, sponsored by the Institute for Historical Research, is under way; five volumes of the section for 1541–1857, ed. Joyce Madeleine Horn, et al., 1969– have so far been published.

133 Library of Congress. *The national union catalogue of manuscript collections.* Ann Arbor, Mich., 1962. Describes holdings in various repositories in USA.

134 Library of Congress. *The national union catalogue: pre-1956 imprints.* Chicago, 1968–80, 685 vols. Continued as *The national union catalogue: a cumulative author list,* 1956– in several chronological series.

135 Library of Congress. *The Library of Congress catalogue. Books: subjects.* Ann Arbor, Mich., 1955–. From publications of 1950; cumulative in various chronological series.

136 Lists and Index Society. *Select catalogue of unpublished Search Room lists in the Public Record Office.* 1965. Lists, guides and indexes which the society has since been publishing in photographic copies. See also (112) and (158).

137 Lloyd, Sir John Edward and Robert Thomas Jenkins (eds.). *The dictionary of Welsh biography down to 1940.* 1959.

138 Lobel, Mary Doreen (comp.). *Historic towns: maps and plans of towns and cities in the British Isles, with historical commentaries, from earliest times to 1800.* Oxford, 1969.

139 McCulloch, John Ramsay. *The literature of political economy: a classified catalogue of select publications ... with historical, critical and biographical notices.* 1845; reprinted, 1938 and New York, 1964. See also (22).

140 Marshall, George William. *The genealogist's guide to printed pedigrees.* 1879; 4th edn, Guildford, Surrey, 1903. Supplemented by John Beach Whitmore, *A genealogical guide ... in continuation of Marshall's ...* 1947–53, 4 parts. An important index of pedigrees, including those in county and local histories.

141 Mathias, Peter and Alan William Halliday Pearsall (comps.). *Shipping: a survey of historical records.* Newton Abbot, Devon, 1971.

142 Milne, Alexander Taylor (comp.). *Catalogue of the manuscripts of Jeremy Bentham in the Library of University College, London.* 2nd edn, 1962.

143 —— (comp.). *A centenary guide to the publications of the Royal Historical Society, 1868–1968, and of the former Camden Society, 1838–1897.* 1968.

144 Mitchell, Brian Redman (comp.). *European historical statistics 1750–1970.* 1975.

145 Mitchell, Brian Redman and Phyllis Deane (comps.). *Abstract of British historical statistics.* Cambridge, 1962. Indispensable.

146 Mullins, Edward Lindsay Carson (comp.). *A guide to the historical and archaeological publications of societies in England and Wales, 1901–1933.* 1968. Indexes authors and titles.

147 —— (comp.). *Texts and calendars: an analytical guide to serial publications.* 1958. List of source materials published by the national government and by national and local historical societies.

148 Musgrave, Sir William. *Obituary prior to 1800 (as far as relates to England, Scotland and Ireland).* Ed. Sir George J. Armytage. (Harleian Society, Vols. 44–9.) 1899–1901, 6 vols. Essentially an index to the obituaries in the *Gentleman's Magazine* and the *London Magazine.*

149 National Maritime Musuem. *Catalogue of the Library.* 1968–. Guide, under subject arrangement, to over 50,000 volumes on all maritime subjects. See also (110).

150 Norton, Jane Elizabeth (comp.). *Guide to the national and provincial directories of England and Wales, excluding London, published before 1856.* 1950. For London directories, see (109).

151 Ollard, Sidney Leslie, et al. (eds.). *A dictionary of English church history.* 3rd edn, rev., 1948.

152 Ormond, Richard and Malcolm Rogers (eds.). *Dictionary of British portraiture.* Vol. 2: *The later Georgians to the early Victorians.* Comp. Elaine Kilmory. 1980.

153 Owen, Dorothy Mary (comp.). *The records of the Established Church in England, excluding parochial records.* 1970.

154 Palmer, Samuel, et al. (comps.). *Index to 'The Times' newspapers.* Corsham, Wilts., 1868–1943; reprinted, New York, 1965–6, 83 vols. From 1790.

155 Pannell, John Percival Masterman. *The techniques of industrial archaeology.* Newton Abbot, Devon, 1966.

156 Parsons, Kenneth A. C. (comp.). *A checklist of British parliamentary papers (bound set), 1801–1950.* Cambridge, 1958. See also (123).

157 Pine, Leslie Gilbert (comp.). *The new extinct peerage, 1884–1971: containing extinct, abeyant, dormant and suspended peerages with genealogies and arms.* 1972. See also (88).

158 Public Record Office. *Lists and indexes.* 1892–1936, 55 vols. *Supplementary series,* 1961–. Detailed lists and indexes of record material. For others, see (136).

159 Shaw, William Arthur. *The knights of England: a complete record ... of the knights of all the orders of chivalry in England, Scotland and Ireland, and of knights bachelors.* 1906, 2 vols.; reprinted, 1971.

160 Shorter, Edward. *The historian and the computer: a practical guide.* New York, 1971; reprinted, 1975.

161 Steinberg, Sigfrid Henry and I. H. Evans (eds.). *Steinberg's dictionary of British history.* 2nd edn, 1971.

162 Stephen, Sir Leslie and Sir Sidney Lee (eds.). *The dictionary of national biography from the earliest times to 1900.* 1888–1903, 63 vols. *Supplement.* 1901, 3 vols. Both reissued, 1908–9, 22 vols. Still fundamental, but increasingly obsolescent. An errata volume appeared in 1940; some addenda and corrigenda appear from time to time in *BIHR.* See also *The concise dictionary of national biography,* an epitome.

163 Stewart, James Douglas, et al. (comps.). *British union catalogue of periodicals ... in British libraries.* 1955–8, 4 vols.

164 Sturges, Rodney Paul. *Economists' papers, 1750–1950: a guide to archive and other manuscript sources for the history of British and Irish economic thought.* Durham, NC, 1975.

165 Tate, William Edward. *The parish chest: a study of the records of parochial administration in England.* 3rd edn, 1969. Best guide to these records.

166 Temperley, Harold William Vazeille and Dame Lillian Margery Penson. *A century of diplomatic blue books, 1814–1914.* Cambridge, 1938; reprinted, New York, 1966. Lists them and discusses policy towards publication of diplomatic papers.

167 Thomas, Peter David Garner. 'Sources for the debates of the House of Commons, 1768–1774', *BIHR.* (Special supplement, 4.) 1959. See also (64), (603) and (682).

168 Thomson, Theodore Radford (comp.). *A catalogue of British family histories.* 3rd edn, 1976. See also (32).

169 Todd, William Burton. *A directory of printers and others in allied trades, London and vicinity, 1800–1840.* 1972.

170 Treasure, Geoffrey Russell Richards (ed.). *Who's who in history.* Vol. 4: *England 1714–1789.* New York, 1969. Vol. 5: *England 1789–1837.* New York, 1975.

171 Valentine, Alan Chester. *The British establishment, 1760–1784: an eighteenth century biographical dictionary.* Norman, Okla., 1970, 2 vols. Not always accurate in details.

172 Venn, John Archibald (comp.). *Alumni cantabrigienses.* Part 2: *1752–1900.* Cambridge, 1940–54, 6 vols.

173 Wagner, Sir Anthony Richard. *English genealogy.* 2nd edn, Oxford, 1972. Introduction to the study of the subject.

174 Wallis, Peter John. *Histories of old schools: a revised list for England and Wales.* Newcastle-upon-Tyne, 1966. Includes only schools in existence by 1700. See also (29).

175 Ward, William Smith. *Index and finding list of serials published in the British Isles*

1789–1832. Lexington, Ky, 1953. Ward has a 'Supplementary list' in *Bulletin of the New York Public Library,* 77 (1973–4), 291–7.

176 Williams, Judith Blow (comp.). *A guide to the printed materials for English social and economic history, 1750–1850.* New York, 1926, 2 vols. Notes on contents of works listed; especially useful for pamphlets, trade journals, annual reports and such material.

177 Williams, Trevor Illtyd (ed.). *A biographical dictionary of scientists.* 1969.

178 Winfield, Sir Percy Henry. *The chief sources of English legal history.* Cambridge, Mass., 1925. Lectures with selected bibliographies; best introduction to the subject.

179 Wolff, Michael, et al. (comps.). *The Waterloo directory of Victorian periodicals 1824–1900.* Waterloo, Ont., 1976. Lists 25,000 periodicals. See also (120).

180 Zupko, Ronald Edward. *A dictionary of English weights and measures: from Anglo-Saxon times to the nineteenth century.* Madison, Wis., 1968.

III. GENERAL SURVEYS

181 Beales, Derek Edward Dawson. *From Castlereagh to Gladstone, 1815–1885.* 1969.

182 Briggs, Asa. *The age of improvement, 1783–1865.* 1959; 2nd impression with corrections, 1960. American title: *The making of modern England, 1783–1865: the age of improvement.* New York, 1965. One of the best treatments of the period.

183 Derry, John Wesley. *Reaction and reform, 1793–1868: England in the early nineteenth century.* 1963. American title: *A short history of nineteenth-century England.* New York, 1963.

184 *English historical documents.* Vol. 10: *1714–1783.* Ed. David Bayne Horn and Mary Ransome. 1957. Vol. 11: *1783–1832.* Ed. Arthur Aspinall and Ernest Anthony Smith. 1959. Representative selection of sources in most areas, with excellent general and subject bibliographies.

185 Finlayson, Geoffrey Beauchamp Alistair Mowbray. *England in the eighteen thirties: decade of reform.* 1969. American title: *Decade of reform: England in the eighteen thirties.* New York, 1970. Brief but comprehensive.

186 Fremantle, Alan Frederick. *England in the nineteenth century.* 1929–30, 2 vols. Covers the years 1801–10 only; fragment of a work planned on a vast scale.

187 Gash, Norman. *Aristocracy and people: Britain 1815–1865.* 1979. Important survey and reinterpretation.

188 Green, Vivian Hubert Howard. *The Hanoverians, 1714–1815.* 1948.

189 Halévy, Elie. *A history of the English people in the nineteenth century.* Vol. 1: *England in 1815.* Vol. 2: *The liberal awakening 1815–1830.* Vol. 3: *The triumph of reform 1830–1841.* Trans. E. I. Watkin. 2nd rev. edn, 1949–52, 6 vols. Classic and still indispensable.

190 Harris, Ronald Walter. *England in the eighteenth century, 1689–1793: a balanced constitution and new horizons.* 1963. American title: *A short history of eighteenth-century England.* New York, 1963.

191 Harvey, Arnold D. *Britain in the early nineteenth century.* New York, 1978. Covers period 1800–12.

192 Jarrett, Derek. *Britain 1688–1815.* 1968.

193 Lecky, William Edward Hartpole. *A history of England in the eighteenth century.* 1878–90, 8 vols. Classic.

194 Marshall, Dorothy. *Eighteenth-century England.* 1962; 2nd edn, 1974. To *c.* 1782.

195 Mathieson, William Law. *England in transition, 1789–1832: a study of movements.* 1920. Still a valuable and suggestive interpretation.

196 Owen, John Beresford. *The eighteenth century, 1714–1815.* 1975. Primarily political narrative and description.

197 Plumb, John Harold. *England in the eighteenth century.* 1950.

198 —— *The first four Georges.* 1953; rev. edn, 1975. With excellent illustrations.

199 Robertson, Sir Charles Grant. *England under the Hanoverians.* 15th edn, 1948. Old standard advanced textbook, progressively updated in appendices.

200 Stanhope, Philip Henry Stanhope, 5th Earl. *History of England from the peace of Utrecht to the peace of Versailles, 1713–83.* 1836–54, 7 vols; 3rd edn, 1853–4, 7 vols.

201 Thomson, David. *England in the nineteenth century, 1815–1914.* 1950.
202 Trevelyan, George Macaulay. *British history in the nineteenth century and after, 1782–1919.* 1922; 2nd edn, 1937.
203 Turberville, Arthur Stanley. *English men and manners in the eighteenth century: an illustrated narrative.* 1926; 2nd edn, rev. 1929; reprinted with corrections, 1957.
204 —— (ed.). *Johnson's England: an account of the life and manners of his age.* Oxford, 1933, 2 vols. Excellent essays by various hands on most aspects of mid-eighteenth-century life and civilization.
205 Watson, John Steven. *The reign of George III, 1760–1815.* Oxford, 1960.
206 Webb, Robert Kiefer. *Modern England from the eighteenth century to the present.* New York, 1968; 2nd edn, New York, 1980. Excellent textbook with useful critical bibliographies.
207 White, Reginald James. *The age of George III.* 1968.
208 —— *From Peterloo to the Crystal Palace.* 1972.
209 —— *Waterloo to Peterloo.* 1957.
210 Wiener, Joel H. (ed.). *Great Britain: the lion at home: a documentary history of domestic policy, 1689–1975.* Ann Arbor, Mich., 1974, 4 vols. Of the 444 documents in this collection, many are previously unpublished or uncollected; more than one hundred concern the years 1760–1837.
211 Woodward, Sir Ernest Llewellyn. *The age of reform, 1815–1870.* Oxford, 1938; 2nd edn, 1962.

IV. CONSTITUTIONAL, LEGAL AND ADMINISTRATIVE HISTORY

For military administration, see also (1738), (1744), (1749), (1784), (1791) and (1831).

1. Printed sources

212 Blackstone, Sir William. *Commentaries on the laws of England.* Oxford, 1765–9, 4 vols.; 9th edn [with last changes by the author], Oxford, 1783, 4 vols. Later editions with continuations by various hands. An edition of selections, Gareth Jones (ed.). *The sovereignty of the law.* 1973. Facsimile of the 1765–9 edn, Chicago, 1979.
213 Bramwell, George. *Analytical table of the private statutes [1727–1812].* 1813, 2 vols. Continued by Thomas Vardon. *Index to the local and personal and private acts: 1798–1839.* 1840.
214 Burn, Richard. *The justice of the peace and parish officer, upon a plan entirely new, and comprehending all the law to the present time.* 1755. Alphabetical digest covering every branch of civil, criminal and public law with which JPs might be concerned. It reached a 29th edition by 1845 with repeated enlargements.
215 Costin, William Conrad and John Steven Watson (eds.). *The law and working of the constitution: documents 1660–1914.* 1952, 2 vols.
216 *The English reports.* [Full reprint, 1120–1865.] 1900–32, 178 vols.
217 Hanham, Harold John (ed.). *The nineteenth-century constitution. 1815–1914.* Cambridge, 1969. Documents, with commentary.
218 Hatsell, John. *Precedents of proceedings in the House of Commons.* 1781, 4 vols.; new edn, 1818, 4 vols. Standard contemporary work; the new edition has additions by Speaker Abbott.
219 House of Lords Record Office. *Leaders and whips in the House of Lords, 1873–1964* (HLRO Memoranda 31), 1964; *The financial administration and records of the Parliament Office, 1824–1868 (ibid.* 37), 1967; *A list of representative peers for Scotland, 1707–1963, and for Ireland, 1800–1961 (ibid.* 39), 1968; *Officers of the House of Lords, 1485–1971 (ibid.* 45), 1971; *The origins of the office of chairman of committees in the House of Lords (ibid.* 52), 1974.
220 Howell, Thomas Bayly (ed.). *A complete collection of state trials and proceedings for high treason and other crimes and misdemeanors from the earliest period to ... 1783 ... and*

continued from ... *1783 to 1820 by Thomas Jones Howell.* 1816–28, 34 vols. Continued by Sir John MacDonell and John E. P. Wallis (eds.). *Reports of state trials, new ser., 1820–58.* 1888–98, 8 vols.

221 Jacob, Giles. *A new law dictionary: containing, the interpretation and definition of words and terms used in the law.* 1729; 11th edn, ed. and rev. Sir Thomas Edlyne Tomlins, 1797, 2 vols. 4th edn of this edition, ed. Thomas Colpitts Granger, 1835, 2 vols. Most important contemporary law dictionary.

222 Lambert, Sheila (ed.). *The House of Commons Sessional Papers of the eighteenth century.* Wilmington, Del., 1975–. 147 vols. Most complete edition, replacing earlier ones.

223 Oldfield, Thomas Hinton Burley. *The representative history of Great Britain and Ireland: being a history of the House of Commons, and of the counties, cities and boroughs of the United Kingdom.* 1816, 6 vols. Detailed contemporary electoral history of every constituency.

224 Pickering, Danby (ed.). *The statutes at large from Magna Carta to 1806.* Cambridge, 1762–1807, 46 vols. With indexes; best collection for this period; continued by (229).

225 Redington, Joseph and Richard Arthur Roberts (eds.). *Calendar of Home Office papers of the reign of George III, 1760–1775.* 1878–99, 4 vols.

226 Roseveare, Henry (ed.). *The Treasury, 1660–1870: the foundations of control.* 1973. Documents with introduction. See also (288).

227 *The royal kalendar: or, complete and annual register.* 1767–1814. Annual list of holders of political, public and court offices; in 1814 amalgamated with its rival, *The court and city register,* 1742–1814. Continued as *The royal kalendar or court and city register.* 1814–.

228 Sainty, John Christopher, et al. (comps.). *Office-holders in modern Britain: Admiralty officials, 1660–1870.* 1975. *Colonial Office officials, 1794–1870.* 1976. *Foreign Office officials, 1782–1870.* 1979. *Home Office officials, 1782–1870.* 1975. *Navy Board officials, 1660–1832.* 1978. *Officials of the Board of Trade, 1660–1870.* 1974. *Officials of the secretaries of state, 1660–1782.* 1973. *Treasury officials, 1660–1870.* 1972.

229 Tomlins, Sir Thomas Edlyne, et al. (eds.). *The statutes of the United Kingdom of Great Britain and Ireland. With notes, references and an index.* 1804–69, 29 vols. Best edition for the early nineteenth century; continues (224).

230 Williams, E. Neville. *The eighteenth-century constitution, 1688–1815.* Cambridge, 1960. Documents with commentary.

2. Surveys

231 Emden, Cecil Stuart. *The people and the constitution: being a history of the development of the people's influence in British government.* Oxford, 1933; 2nd edn, 1956. Important general essay.

232 Harding, Alan. *A social history of English law.* Harmondsworth, Middx, 1966.

233 Holdsworth, Sir William Searle. *A history of English law.* 7th edn, ed. Stanley B. Chrimes, et al., 1956–66, 16 vols. Vol. 10 is wholly on the eighteenth century.

234 Jenks, Edward. *A short history of English law.* 1912; 6th edn, 1949.

235 Jennings, Sir William Ivor. *Party politics.* Cambridge, 1960–2, 3 vols. Much historical material.

236 Keir, Sir David Lindsay. *The constitutional history of modern Britain since 1485.* 1938; 9th edn, 1969.

237 Maitland, Frederic William. *The constitutional history of England.* Cambridge, 1908. The last section of this classic discusses the eighteenth and nineteenth centuries.

238 Pike, Luke Owen. *A constitutional history of the House of Lords.* 1894.

239 Plucknett, Theodore Frank Thomas. *A concise history of the common law.* 5th edn, 1956. Best short history.

240 Smith, Goldwin Albert. *A constitutional and legal history of England.* New York, 1955. Good textbook.

241 Taswell-Langmead, Thomas Pitt. *English constitutional history from the Teutonic conquest to the present time.* 11th edn, ed. Theodore Frank Thomas Plucknett, 1960. Earlier editions are out of date.

242 Thomson, Mark Almeras. *A constitutional history of England, 1642–1801.* 1938.

3. Monographs

243 Baker, Norman. *Government and contractors: the British Treasury and war supplies, 1775–83.* 1971.

244 Basye, Arthur Herbert. *The Lords Commissioners of Trade and Plantations, commonly known as the Board of Trade, 1748–1782.* New Haven, Conn., 1925.

245 Binney, John Edward Douglas. *British public finance and administration, 1774–92.* Oxford, 1958.

246 Birks, Michael. *Gentlemen of the law.* 1960. History of solicitors. See also (286).

247 Boorstin, Daniel Joseph. *The mysterious science of the law: an essay on Blackstone's Commentaries.* Cambridge, Mass., 1941; reprinted Gloucester, Mass., 1973.

248 Bryson, William Hamilton. *The equity side of the Exchequer: its jurisdiction, administration, procedures, and records.* Cambridge, 1975.

249 Bush, Graham William Arthur. *Bristol and its municipal government, 1820–51.* (Bristol Record Society, 29.) 1976.

250 Carson, Edward. *The ancient and rightful customs: a history of the English customs service.* 1972. See also (264).

251 Clark, Dora Mae. *The rise of the British Treasury: colonial administration in the eighteenth century.* New Haven, Conn., 1960; reprinted, Hamden, Conn., 1969.

252 Clarke, John Joseph. *A history of local government of the United Kingdom.* 1955. See also (267), (291) and (304).

253 Clode, Charles Mathew. *The military forces of the Crown: their administration and government.* 1864, 2 vols. Indispensable, although seriously outdated.

254 Clokie, Hugh MacDowall and Joseph William Robinson. *Royal commissions of inquiry: the significance of investigations in British politics.* 1937. See also (262).

255 Cohen, Emmeline Waley. *The growth of the British civil service, 1780–1939.* 1941; reprinted, Hamden, Conn., 1965. See also (280).

256 Craig, Sir John Herbert McCutcheon. *A history of red tape: an account of the origin and development of the civil service.* 1955.

257 Duncan, G. I. O. *The High Court of Delegates.* Cambridge, 1971. From the mid-sixteenth century to its abolition in 1832.

258 Ellis, Kenneth. *The Post Office in the eighteenth century: a study in administrative history.* Oxford, 1958. See also (285).

259 Fergusson, Sir James. *The sixteen peers of Scotland: an account of the elections of the representative peers of Scotland, 1707–1959.* Oxford, 1960.

260 France, Reginald Sharpe. *The Lancashire sessions act, 1798.* Preston, Lancs., 1945. Detailed study of rivalries in local administration; one of the few studies of county government in this period.

261 Gardiner, Leslie. *The British Admiralty.* 1968. See also (360).

262 Gordon, Strathern and Thomas G. B. Cocks. *A people's conscience.* 1952. Parliamentary inquiries 1729–1838. See also (254).

263 Hanbury, Harold Greville. *The Vinerian Chair and legal education.* Oxford, 1968. Much on Blackstone, the first holder of the Chair.

264 Hoon, Elizabeth Evelynola (Mrs Robert Cawley). *The organization of the English customs system, 1696–1786.* New York, 1938; reprinted, with introduction by Rupert Charles Jarvis, Newton Abbot, Devon, 1968. See also (250).

265 Jones, Gareth Hywel. *History of the law of charity, 1532–1827.* 1969.

266 Keeton, George Williams and Georg Schwarzenberger (eds.). *Jeremy Bentham and the law: a symposium.* 1948. See also (339) and (350).

267 Keith-Lucas, Bryan. *The English local government franchise: a short history.* Oxford, 1952.

268 Kemp, Betty. *King and Commons, 1660–1832.* 1957. Changing constitutional relations between them.

269 Lambert, Sheila. *Bills and acts: legislative procedure in eighteenth-century England.* Cambridge, 1971. See also (298).

270 Laundy, Philip Alan Charles. *The office of Speaker.* 1964.

271 McCahill, Michael W. *Order and equipoise: the peerage and the House of Lords, 1783–1806.* 1978. Argues that the Lords were independent of the Crown and Ministry. See also (301).

272 MacDonagh, Oliver Ormond Gerard Michael. *A pattern of government growth, 1800–1860: the Passenger Acts and their enforcement.* 1961. Administration of Atlantic immigration as a study in government growth.

273 McDowell, Robert Brendan. *The Irish administration, 1801–1914.* 1964.

274 May, Sir Thomas Erskine, Baron Farnborough. *A treatise upon the law, privileges, proceedings and usages of Parliament.* 1844; 10th edn, much enlarged, 1893; 17th edn, 1964. Fundamental treatise on the subject.

275 Middleton, Charles Ronald. *The administration of British foreign policy, 1782–1846.* Durham, NC, 1977. See also (746).

276 Moir, Esther Aline Lowndes. *The justice of the peace.* Harmondsworth, Middx, 1969.

277 —— *Local government in Gloucestershire, 1775–1800: a study of the justices of the peace.* Bristol, 1969.

278 Muir, Ramsay and Edith May Platt. *A history of municipal government in Liverpool from the earliest times to the Municipal Reform Act of 1835.* 1906.

279 Nelson, Ronald Roy. *The Home Office, 1782–1801.* Durham, NC, 1969.

280 Parris, Henry Walter. *Constitutional bureaucracy: the development of British central administration since the eighteenth century.* 1969. See also (255) and (256).

281 Pool, Bernard. *Navy Board contracts, 1660–1832: contract administration under the Navy Board.* 1966.

282 Porritt, Edward and Annie Gertrude Porritt. *The unreformed House of Commons: parliamentary representation before 1832.* 1903–9, 2 vols. Classic.

283 Radzinowicz, Sir Leon. *A history of the English criminal law and its administration from 1750.* 1948–68, 4 vols. See also (294).

284 Redford, Arthur and Ina Stafford Russell. *The history of local government in Manchester.* 1939–40, 3 vols.

285 Robinson, Howard. *Britain's Post Office: a history of developments from the beginnings to the present day.* 1953. See also (258).

286 Robson, Robert. *The attorney in eighteenth-century England.* Cambridge, 1959. See also (246).

287 Roscoe, Edward Stanley. *A history of the English prize court.* 1924. See also (323).

288 Roseveare, Henry. *The Treasury: the evolution of a British institution.* 1969. See also (226).

289 Sheppard, Francis Henry Wollaston. *Local government in St Marylebone, 1688–1835: a study of the vestry and the Turnpike Trust.* 1958.

290 Simpson, Alfred William Brian. *An introduction to the history of the land law.* 1961. See also (1518).

291 Smellie, Kingsley Bryce Speakman. *A history of local government.* 1968. See also (252), (267) and (304).

292 Spector, Margaret Marion. *The American department of the British government, 1768–1782.* 1940; reprinted, New York, 1976. See also (306) and (310).

293 Squibb, George Drewry. *Doctor's Commons: a history of the College of Advocates and Doctors of Law.* Oxford, 1977.

294 Stephen, Sir James Fitzjames. *A history of the criminal law of England.* 1883, 3 vols. See also (283).

295 Stevens, Robert Bocking. *Law and politics: the House of Lords as a judicial body, 1800–1976.* Chapel Hill, NC, 1978.

296 Styles, Philip. *The development of county administration in the late XVIIIth and early XIXth centuries.* (Dugdale Society Occasional Publications, 4.) Oxford, 1934. Based on Warwickshire Quarter Sessions records.

297 Sutherland, Gillian Ray (ed.). *Studies in the growth of nineteenth-century government.* 1972. Several of the essays discuss conditions in various government departments before 1837.

298 Thomas, Peter David Garner. *The House of Commons in the eighteenth century.* Oxford, 1971. Fundamental on organization and procedure. See also (269), (270), (307), (308) and (430).

299 Thompson, Richard. *The Charity Commission and the age of reform.* 1979. One of the earliest of such bodies; sat from 1817–37.

300 Thomson, Mark Almeras. *The secretaries of state, 1681–1782.* Oxford, 1932; reprinted, 1968.

301 Turberville, Arthur Stanley. *The House of Lords in the age of reform, 1784–1837.* 1958. Written before 1945. See also (271).

302 —— *The House of Lords in the XVIIIth century.* Oxford, 1927.

303 Ward, William Reginald. *The English land tax in the eighteenth century.* Oxford, 1953. Principally concerned with the administration of the tax.

304 Webb, Sidney James and Beatrice Webb. *English local government from the Revolution to the Municipal Corporations Act.* 1906–29, 9 vols. Vol. 1: *The parish and the county*; Vols. 2 and 3: *The manor and the borough*; Vol. 4: *Statutory authorities for special purposes*; Vol. 5: *The king's highway*; Vol. 6: *Prisons*; Vols. 7–9: *The Poor Law.* Classic and fundamental.

305 Weston, Corinne Comstock. *English constitutional theory and the House of Lords, 1556–1832.* New York, 1965.

306 Wickwire, Franklin B. *British subministers and colonial America, 1763–1783.* Princeton, NJ, 1966. See also (292) and (310).

307 Williams, Orlo Cyprian. *The clerical organization of the House of Commons, 1661–1850.* Oxford, 1954. See also (298).

308 —— *The historical development of private bill procedure and standing orders in the House of Commons.* 1948–9, 2 vols.

309 Young, Douglas MacMurray. *The colonial office in the early nineteenth century.* 1961. Covers period 1794–1830.

4. Biographies

310 Bellot, Leland J. *William Knox: the life and thought of an eighteenth-century imperialist.* Austin, Texas, 1977. Under-secretary of state for America, 1770–82.

311 Campbell, John Campbell, Baron. *Lives of the Lord Chancellors.* 1845–7; 8th edn, 1880–1, 12 vols. More useful in this period than earlier.

312 Cockroft, Grace Amelia. *The public life of George Chalmers.* New York, 1939. Loyalist refugee who was chief clerk of the Board of Trade, 1786–1825.

313 Eeles, Henry Swanston. *Lord Chancellor Camden and his family.* 1934. Unsatisfactory, but the only biographies of first and second Earls Camden.

314 Foss, Edward. *Biographia juridica. A biographical dictionary of the judges of England … 1066–1870.* 1870.

315 Gore-Browne, Robert. *Chancellor Thurlow: the life and times of an XVIIIth century lawyer.* 1953.

316 Heward, Edmund. *Lord Mansfield.* Chichester, Sussex and London. 1979.

317 Kenyon, George Thomas. *The life of Lloyd, first Lord Kenyon, Lord Chief Justice of England.* 1873.

318 Lloyd, Christopher. *Mr Barrow of the Admiralty: a life of Sir John Barrow.* 1970. Secretary of the Admiralty, 1804–45.

319 Lovat-Fraser, James Alexander. *Erskine.* Cambridge, 1932. The most useful biography. See also (324).

320 Mackintosh, Robert James (ed.). *Memoirs of the life of … Sir James Mackintosh.* 1835; 2nd edn, 1836, 2 vols. Letters and journals of a law reformer.

321 Medd, Patrick. *Romilly: a life of Sir Samuel Romilly, lawyer and reformer.* 1968.

322 Oakes, Cecil George. *Sir Samuel Romilly, 1757–1818, 'The friend of freedom'.* 1935. Balanced study, with full bibliography.

323 Roscoe, Edward Stanley. *Lord Stowell: his life and the development of English prize law.* 1916. See also (287).

324 Stryker, Lloyd Paul. *For the defence: Thomas Erskine, the most enlightened liberal of his times, 1750–1823.* New York, 1947. See also (319).

325 Twiss, Horace. *The public and private life of Lord Chancellor Eldon, with selections from his correspondence.* 1844, 3 vols. Letters, 1762–1837. No modern biography.

5. Articles

326 Aspinall, Arthur. 'The Cabinet Council, 1783–1835', *Proceedings of the British Academy*, 68 (1952), 145–252.

327 Baker, Norman. 'Changing attitudes towards government in eighteenth-century Britain', in Anne Whiteman, et al. (eds.), *Statesmen, scholars and merchants.* Oxford, 1973, pp. 202–19.

328 Beckett, James Camlin. 'Anglo-Irish constitutional relations in the later eighteenth century', *Irish Historical Studies*, 14 (1964–5), 20–38.

329 Belchem, J. C. 'Henry Hunt and the evolution of the mass platform', *EHR*, 93 (1978), 739–73.

330   Best, Geoffrey Francis Andrew. 'The constitutional revolution, 1828–32', *Theology*, 62 (1959), 226–34.

331   Bowler, R. A. 'The American Revolution and British Army administrative reform', *Journal of the Society for Army Historical Research*, 58 (1980), 66–77.

332   Brockington, Colin Fraser. 'Public health at the Privy Council, 1831–34', *JHMed*, 16 (1961), 161–85.

333   Butterfield, Sir Herbert. 'Some reflections on the early years of George III's reign', *JBS*, 4, 2 (1964–5), 78–101. Neo-Whig. See also (609).

334   Cannon, John Ashton and W. A. Speck. 'Re-election on taking office, 1706–90', *BIHR*, 51 (1978), 206–9.

335   Christie, Ian Ralph. 'The cabinet during the Grenville administration, 1763–1765', *EHR*, 73 (1958), 86–92.

336   —— 'The cabinet in the reign of George III, to 1790', in his *Myth and reality in late eighteenth-century British politics and other papers*. 1970, pp. 55–108.

337   Crimmin, P. K. 'Admiralty relations with the Treasury, 1783–1806: the preparation of naval estimates and the beginnings of Treasury control', *Mariner's Mirror*, 53 (1967), 63–72.

338   —— 'The financial and clerical establishment of the Admiralty office, 1783–1806', *Mariner's Mirror*, 55 (1969), 299–309.

339   Cross, Rupert. 'Blackstone v. Bentham', *Law Quarterly Review*, 92 (1976), 516–27.

340   Dinwiddy, John Rowland. 'The use of the Crown's power of deportation under the Aliens Act, 1793–1826', *BIHR*, 41 (1968), 193–211.

341   Duman, Daniel. 'A social and occupational analysis of the English judiciary: 1770–1790 and 1855–1875', *American Journal of Legal History*, 17 (1973), 353–64.

342   —— 'Pathway to professionalism: the English bar in the eighteenth and nineteenth centuries', *Journal of Social History*, 13 (1980), 615–28.

343   Fraser, Peter. 'Public petitioning and Parliament before 1832', *History* NS, 46 (1961), 195–211.

344   Gee, Olive. 'The British war office in the later years of the American War of Independence', *JMH*, 26 (1954), 123–36.

345   Guy, Alan J. 'Regimental agency in the British standing army, 1715–1793: a school of Georgian military administration', *Bulletin of the John Rylands Library*, 62 (1979–80), 423–53; 63 (1980–1), 31–57.

346   Hanbury, Harold Greville. 'Blackstone as a judge', *American Journal of Legal History*, 3 (1959), 1–27.

347   Henriques, Ursula Ruth Quixano. 'Jeremy Bentham and the machinery of social reform', in Harry Hearder and Henry Royston Loyn (eds.). *British government and administration: studies presented to S. B. Chrimes*. Cardiff, 1974, pp. 169–86.

348   Heward, Edmund. 'Lord Mansfield's notebooks', *Law Quarterly Review*, 92 (1976), 438–55.

349   Hill, Brian W. 'Executive monarchy and the challenge of parties, 1689–1832: two concepts of government and two historiographical interpretations', *HJ*, 13 (1970), 379–401.

350   Holdsworth, Sir William Searle. 'Bentham's place in English legal history', *California Law Review*, 28 (1940), 568–86.

351   —— 'The House of Lords, 1689–1783', *Law Quarterly Review*, 5 (1929), 307–42, 432–58.

352   —— 'The movement for reform in the law, 1793–1832', *Law Quarterly Review*, 56 (1940), 33–48, 208–28, 340–53.

353   Kahn-Freund, Otto. 'Blackstone's neglected child: the contract of employment', *Law Quarterly Review*, 93 (1977), 508–28.

354   Leigh, L. H. 'Law reform and the law of treason and sedition', *Public Law* (1977), 128–48.

355   Lucas, Paul. 'Blackstone and the reform of the legal profession', *EHR*, 77 (1962), 456–89.

356   —— 'A collective biography of students and barristers of Lincoln's Inn, 1680–1804: a study in the "aristocratic resurgence" of the eighteenth century', *JMH*, 46 (1974), 227–61.

357   McCracken, J. L. 'The Irish Viceroyalty, 1760–73', in Henry Alfred Cronne, et al. (eds.), *Essays in British and Irish history in honour of James Eadie Todd*. 1949, pp. 152–68.

358 MacLeod, Roy M. 'Statesmen undisguised', *AHR*, 78 (1973), 1386–405. Excellent discussion of the debate between Parris and MacDonagh over state intervention.

359 Marshall, Dorothy. 'The role of the Justice of the Peace in social administration', in Harry Hearder and Henry Royston Loyn (eds.), *British government and administration: studies presented to S. B. Chrimes.* Cardiff, 1974, pp. 155–68.

360 Murray, Sir Oswyn Alexander Ruthven. 'The Admiralty', *Mariner's Mirror*, 23 (1937), 13–35, 129–47, 316–31; 24 (1938), 101–4, 204–25, 329–52, 458–78; 25 (1939), 89–111, 216–28, 328–38. See also (261).

361 Parris, Henry Walter. 'The origins of the permanent civil service, 1780–1830', *Public Administration*, 46 (1968), 143–66.

362 Phillips, I. Lloyd. 'Lord Barham and the Admiralty, 1805–6', *Mariner's Mirror*, 64 (1978), 217–33.

363 Sainty, John Christopher. 'The evolution of the parliamentary and financial secretaryships of the Treasury', *EHR*, 91 (1976), 566–84.

364 —— 'The origin of the leadership of the House of Lords', *BIHR*, 47 (1974), 53–73.

365 —— 'The secretariat of the chief governors of Ireland, 1690–1800', *Proceedings of the Royal Irish Academy*, 77 (1977), 1–33.

366 Sutherland, Dame Lucy Stuart. 'Edmund Burke and the relations between members of Parliament and their constituents', *Studies in Burke and His Times*, 10 (1968–9), 1005–21.

367 Swinfen, D. B. 'Henry Brougham and the Judicial Committee of the Privy Council', *Law Quarterly Review*, 90 (1974), 396–411.

368 Torrance, J. R. 'Sir George Harrison and the growth of bureaucracy in the early nineteenth century', *EHR*, 83 (1968), 52–88.

369 Ward, William Reginald. 'The administration of the window and assessed taxes, 1696–1798', *EHR*, 67 (1952), 522–42; reprinted separately, Chichester, Sussex, 1963.

370 —— 'The Office for Taxes, 1665–1798', *BIHR*, 25 (1952), 204–12.

371 ——'Some eighteenth-century civil servants: the English revenue commissioners, 1754–98', *EHR*, 70 (1955), 25–54.

372 Welby, Glynne. 'Rulers of the countryside: the justices of the peace in Nottinghamshire, 1775–1800', *Transactions of the Thoroton Society*, 78 (1974), 75–87.

373 Wickwire, Franklin B. 'Admiralty secretaries and the British civil service', *HLQ*, 28 (1964–5), 235–54.

374 —— 'King's friends, civil servants, or politicians?', *AHR*, 71 (1965–6), 18–42.

375 Willis, Richard E. 'Cabinet politics and executive policy-making procedures, 1794–1801', *Albion*, 7 (1975), 1–23.

V.   POLITICAL HISTORY

For specialized bibliographies, catalogues and lists, see (64), (76), (84), (103), (123), (156) and (167). For political thought, see Section XIV. For further studies of radicalism and popular disorders, see (912), (935), (945), (953), (955), (991), (993), (995), (1006), (1007), (1026), (1038), (1045) and (1097).

1.   Printed sources

376 Anson, Sir William Reynell (ed.). *Autobiography and political correspondence of Augustus Henry, third Duke of Grafton.* 1898. Letters cover period 1761–1800.

377 Aspinall, Arthur (ed.). *The correspondence of George, Prince of Wales, 1770–1812.* 1963–71, 8 vols. Continued in (379). For biography, see (551).

378 —— *The later correspondence of George III.* Cambridge, 1962–70, 5 vols. Letters of 1784–1810; most of those printed elsewhere are omitted. For earlier correspondence, see (390) and (405); additional letters are in (388) and (413); for biographies, see (521) and (526).

379 —— *The letters of King George IV, 1812–1830.* Cambridge, 1938, 3 vols. For earlier correspondence, see (377); for biography, see (551).

380 Bourne, Kenneth (ed.). *The letters of the third Viscount Palmerston to Laurence and*

Elizabeth Sulivan, 1804–1863. (Camden Society 4th ser., 73.) 1979. Previously unpublished letters, nearly all before 1837, with much new information on his early life. For biographies, see (524), (577) and (583).

381 Buckingham and Chandos, Richard Plantagenet Temple Nugent Brydges Chandos Grenville, 2nd Duke of (ed.). *Memoirs of the court and cabinets of George the third ... to ... William IV and Victoria.* 1853–61, 10 vols. Correspondence of the Grenville family from 1782. For earlier family correspondence, see (414).

382 Burke, Edmund. *Works.* 1808–13, 12 vols., and many subsequent editions. A new critical edition of Burke's *Works and Speeches*, general ed. Paul Langford, is just beginning. The most comprehensive volume of selections is *Burke's Politics*, ed. Ross John Swartz Hoffman and Paul Levack, New York, 1949. Of the many editions of the *Reflections on the Revolution in France*, one of the best is that edited by Conor Cruise O'Brien, Harmondsworth, Middx, 1969; the most accurate text is William Burton Todd's edition, New York, 1959. For Burke bibliography, see (59); for his correspondence, see (386); for biographies, see (533) and (560); for his thought, see (2303), (2304), (2306), (2313), (2330), (2368), (2379), (2382), (2406), (2425), (2480), (2481), (2493) and (2501).

383 Cavendish, Sir Henry (comp.). *Sir Henry Cavendish's debates of the House of Commons, during the thirteenth Parliament ... commonly called the unreported Parliament ... (1768–1771).* 1841–3, 2 vols. Other debates, from Cavendish's notes, are given in appendices.

384 Cobban, Alfred Bert Carter (ed.). *The debate on the French Revolution, 1789–1800.* 1950; 2nd edn, 1960. Representative selection of sources.

385 Cobbett, William and Thomas Curson Hansard (eds.). *Cobbett's parliamentary history of England to 1803.* 1806–20, 36 vols. *Cobbett's parliamentary debates.* 1803–20, 41 vols. *Parliamentary debates* NS. 1820–30, 25 vols. *Parliamentary debates* 3rd ser. 1830–91, 356 vols. *General index to the first and second series*, 1803–30, comp. Sir John Philippart. 1832–3, 2 vols. See also (383). For guides to other reports, see (64), (167) and (603).

386 Copeland, Thomas Wellsted, et al. (eds.). *Correspondence of Edmund Burke.* Cambridge and Chicago, Ill., 1958–78, 10 vols. All of Burke's surviving letters and a selection of those he received. For other Burke references, see (382).

387 Davies, Kenneth Gordon (ed.). *Documents of the American Revolution, 1770–1783 (Colonial Office Series).* Shannon, 1972–81, 21 vols. Calendars and transcripts.

388 Dobrée, Bonamy (ed.). *The Letters of King George III.* 1935. Contains letters not published elsewhere.

389 Foner, Philip S. (ed.). *The complete writings of Thomas Paine.* New York, 1945. Not quite complete. For biographies, see (518) and (534); for his ideas, see (2323), (2474) and (2502).

390 Fortescue, Sir John William (ed.). *The correspondence of King George the third from 1760 to December 1783.* 1927–8, 6 vols. For corrections to Vol. 1, see (405). Continued in (378).

391 Ginter, Donald Eugene (ed.). *Whig organization in the general election of 1790: selections from the Blair Adam papers.* Berkeley, Calif., 1967. Selections from William Adam's papers with a long introduction on the development of party.

392 Grey, Henry George Grey, 3rd Earl (ed.). *The correspondence of ... Earl Grey and ... William IV ... Nov. 1830 to June 1832.* 1867, 2 vols.

393 Gunn, John A. W. (ed.). *Factions no more. Attitudes to party in government and opposition in eighteenth-century England.* 1972. Selections, many from less well-known writers.

394 Hardy, Thomas. *Memoir of Thomas Hardy, founder of and secretary to the London Corresponding Society. Written by himself.* 1832. Reprinted in David Vincent (ed.), *Testaments of radicalism: memoirs of working-class politicians, 1790–1885.* 1977, pp. 25–102.

395 Holland, Henry Richard Vassall Fox, 3rd Baron. *Memoirs of the Whig party during my time.* Ed. Henry Edward Fox, 4th Baron Holland. 1852–4, 2 vols. *Further memoirs of the Whig party, 1807–1821.* Ed. Lord Stavordale. 1905. Principal source for Whig politics *c.* 1790–1820. See also (399).

396 Ilchester, Giles Stephen Holland Fox-Strangways, Earl of (ed.). *The journal of Elizabeth, Lady Holland (1791–1811).* 1908, 2 vols. See also (559).

397 Jennings, Louis John (ed.). *The Croker papers: the correspondence and diaries of ... John Wilson Croker ... secretary to the Admiralty from 1809 to 1830;* 1884, 2 vols.

Correspondence from period 1809–57; a 'new and abridged' edition, ed. Bernard Pool, as *The Croker papers: 1808–1857*. 1967.

398 Jucker, Ninetta (ed.). *The Jenkinson papers, 1760–1766*. 1949.

399 Kriegel, Abraham D. (ed.). *The Holland House diaries 1831–1840: the diary of Henry Richard Vassall Fox, third Lord Holland, with extracts from the diary of Dr John Allen*. 1977. See also (395).

400 Laprade, William Thomas (ed.). *The parliamentary papers of John Robinson, 1774–1784*. (Camden Society 3rd ser., 33.) 1922.

401 Lewis, Wilmarth Sheldon, et al. (eds.). *The Yale edition of Horace Walpole's correspondence*. New Haven, Conn., 1936–. Now complete except for the comprehensive index. For Walpole's memoirs, see (419); for biographies, see (1005) and (1037).

402 Maxwell, Sir Herbert Eustace (ed.). *The Creevey papers: a selection from the correspondence and diaries of ... Thomas Creevey MP*. 1903, 2 vols.; 2nd edn, 1904, 2 vols. Covers 1802–38.

403 Melville, Lewis (pseud. of Lewis Saul Benjamin) (ed.). *The Windham papers: the life and correspondence of ... William Windham, 1750–1810*. 1913, 2 vols.

404 Minto, Emma Eleanor Elizabeth Elliot-Murray-Kynynmond, Countess of (ed.). *Life and letters of Sir Gilbert Elliot, first Earl of Minto, from 1751 to 1808*. 1874, 3 vols.

405 Namier, Sir Lewis Bernstein. *Additions and corrections to Sir John Fortescue's edition of the correspondence of King George the third (Vol. 1)*. Manchester, 1937.

406 O'Connell, Maurice Richard (ed.). *The correspondence of Daniel O'Connell*. Dublin, 1972–. Vol. 1, *1792–1814*; Vol. 2, *1815–1823*; Vol. 3, *1824–1828*.

407 Parker, Charles Stuart (ed.). *Sir Robert Peel ... from his private correspondence*. 1891–9, 3 vols. Basic but incomplete collection; covers 1788–1818 and 1822–7. For Peel's biography, see (548).

408 Price, Cecil (ed.). *The letters of Richard Brinsley Sheridan*. Oxford, 1966, 3 vols. For biography, see (580).

409 Rowe, David John (ed.). *London radicalism 1830–1843: a selection from the papers of Francis Place*. 1970.

410 Russell, Francis Albert Rollo (ed.). *Early correspondence of Lord John Russell, 1805–1840*. 1913, 2 vols. For biography, see (575).

411 Russell, Lord John (ed.). *The correspondence of John, fourth Duke of Bedford*. 1842–6, 3 vols. Correspondence covers 1742–70.

412 —— *Memorials and correspondence of Charles James Fox*. 1853–7, 4 vols. Contains most of Fox's important letters 1764–1806. For biography, see (538).

413 Sedgwick, Romney (ed.). *Letters from George III to Lord Bute, 1756–1766*. 1939. Long, important introduction.

414 Smith, William James (ed.). *The Grenville papers: being the correspondence of Richard Grenville, Earl Temple, KG, and the Right Hon. George Grenville, their friends and contemporaries*. 1852–3, 4 vols. Letters for years 1742–77 and George Grenville's diary for 1763–6. See also (418).

415 Strachey, Giles Lytton and Roger Thomas Baldwin Fulford (eds.). *The Greville memoirs, 1814–60*. 1938, 8 vols.

416 Taylor, William Stanhope and John Henry Pringle (eds.). *Correspondence of William Pitt, Earl of Chatham*. 1838–40, 4 vols. For biographies, see (520), (529), (572) and (594).

417 Thomas, Peter David Garner (ed.). 'Parliamentary diaries of Nathaniel Ryder, 1764–7', *Camden Miscellany*, 23 (1969). (Camden Society 4th ser., 7.) 229–351.

418 Tomlinson, John R. G. (ed.). *Additional Grenville papers, 1763–1765*. Manchester, 1962.

419 Walpole, Horace. *Memoirs of the reign of King George III*. Ed. G. F. Russell Baker. 1894, 4 vols. Covers years 1760–71; a new edition is being prepared. For Walpole's correspondence, see (401); for biographies, see (1005) and (1037).

420 Wellington, Gerald Wellesley, 7th Duke of (ed.). *Wellington and his friends: letters of the first Duke of Wellington to the Rt Hon. Charles and Mrs Arbuthnot, the Earl and Countess of Wilton, Princess Lieven, and Miss Burdett-Coutts*. 1965. Previously unpublished letters; for the main collection of Wellington's correspondence, see (1746); for biography, see (561).

421 Wilberforce, Anna Maria (ed.). *Private papers of William Wilberforce*. 1897; reprinted,

New York, 1968. Letters from Pitt and other documents. For biographies, see (546) and (573).

422 Wilberforce, Robert Isaac and Samuel Wilberforce (eds.). *The correspondence of William Wilberforce.* 1840, 2 vols.

423 Wraxall, Sir Nathaniel William. *The historical and the posthumous memoirs of Sir Nathaniel William Wraxall, 1772–1784.* Ed. Henry Benjamin Wheatley. 1884, 5 vols. Valuable source of political gossip.

2. Surveys

424 Cannon, John Ashton. *Parliamentary reform, 1640–1832.* Cambridge, 1973.

425 Davis, Henry William Carless. *The age of Grey and Peel.* Oxford, 1929; reprinted, Oxford, 1964.

426 Feiling, Sir Keith Grahame. *The second Tory Party, 1714–1832.* 1938; reprinted, 1951.

427 Gipson, Lawrence Henry. *The British empire before the American Revolution.* New York, 1936–70, 15 vols; rev. edn, New York, 1958–70.

428 Harlow, Vincent Todd. *The founding of the second British Empire.* 1952–64, 2 vols.

429 McDowell, Robert Brendan. *Ireland in the age of imperialism and revolution, 1760–1801.* Oxford, 1979. Major study; see also (470).

430 Namier, Sir Lewis Bernstein and John Brooke. *The history of Parliament: the House of Commons, 1754–1790.* 1964, 3 vols. Brooke's introduction was published separately as *The House of Commons, 1754–1790.* Oxford, 1968.

431 Pares, Richard. *King George III and the politicians.* Oxford, 1953.

432 —— *Limited monarchy in Great Britain in the eighteenth century.* (Historical Association, London. General Series, 35.) 1957. Brief but excellent.

433 Smith, Robert Arthur. *Eighteenth-century English politics: patrons and place hunters.* New York, 1972.

3. Monographs

434 Aspinall, Arthur. *Politics and the press, c. 1780–1850.* 1949.

435 Barnes, Donald Grove. *George III and William Pitt: a new interpretation based upon a study of their unpublished correspondence.* Stanford, Calif., 1938.

436 Black, Eugene Charlton. *The Association: British extraparliamentary political organization, 1769–1793.* Cambridge, Mass., 1963.

437 Bolton, Geoffrey Curgenven. *The passing of the Irish Act of Union: a study in parliamentary politics.* Oxford, 1966.

438 Brady, Alexander. *William Huskisson and liberal reform: an essay on the changes in economic policy in the twenties of the nineteenth century.* 1928; 2nd edn, 1967.

439 Brewer, John. *Party ideology and popular politics at the accession of George III.* Cambridge, 1976.

440 Brock, Michael G. *The great Reform Act.* 1973. Important reassessment. See also (444).

441 Brock, William Ranulf. *Lord Liverpool and liberal toryism, 1820 to 1827.* Cambridge, 1941; reprinted, Hamden, Conn., 1967. Good brief study.

442 Brooke, John. *The Chatham administration, 1766–1768.* 1956.

443 Brown, Phillip Anthony. *The French revolution in English history.* 1918; reprinted, New York, 1965.

444 Butler, James Ramsay Montagu. *The passing of the great Reform Bill.* 1914; reprinted, 1964. Standard; see also (440).

445 Butterfield, Sir Herbert. *George III and the historians.* 1957. Historiographical study with sharp criticism of the Namierian school.

446 —— *George III, Lord North, and the people, 1779–80.* 1949.

447 Cannon, John Ashton. *The Fox–North Coalition: crisis of the constitution, 1782–4.* 1969.

448 Christie, Ian Ralph. *Crisis of Empire: Great Britain and the American colonies 1754–1783.* 1966.

449 —— *The end of North's ministry, 1780–1782.* 1958.

450 —— *Myth and reality in late-eighteenth-century British politics, and other papers.* 1970. Seventeen essays, five printed for the first time, most of them important for the period 1760–90.

451 —— *Wilkes, Wyvill and reform: the parliamentary reform movement in British politics, 1760–1785.* 1962.

452 Christie, Ian Ralph and Benjamin Woods Labaree. *Empire or independence 1760–1776: a British–American dialogue on the coming of the American Revolution.* New York, 1976.

453 Clark, George Sidney Roberts Kitson. *Peel and the Conservative Party: a study in party politics, 1832–1841.* 1929; 2nd edn, Hamden, Conn., 1964.

454 Cookson, John Ernest. *Lord Liverpool's administration: the crucial years, 1815–1822.* Edinburgh, 1975.

455 Davis, Richard W. *Political change and continuity, 1760–1885: a Buckinghamshire study.* Newton Abbot, Devon, 1972.

456 Derry, John Wesley. *English politics and the American Revolution.* 1976.

457 —— *The Regency crisis and the Whigs, 1788–9.* 1963.

458 Dickerson, Oliver Morton. *The Navigation Acts and the American Revolution.* Philadelphia, Pa, 1951.

459 Donoughue, Bernard. *British politics and the American Revolution: the path to war 1773–1775.* 1964.

460 Flick, Carlos T. *The Birmingham Political Union and the movements for reform in Britain, 1830–1839.* 1978.

461 Foord, Archibald S. *His Majesty's Opposition, 1714–1830.* Oxford, 1964.

462 Gash, Norman. *Politics in the age of Peel: a study in the technique of parliamentary representation, 1830–1850.* 1953; 2nd edn, 1977.

463 —— *Reaction and reconstruction in English politics, 1832–1852.* Oxford, 1965. Revises some of the judgments in (462).

464 George, Mary Dorothy. *English political caricature: a study of opinion and propaganda.* Oxford, 1960, 2 vols. See also (2082).

465 Goodwin, Albert. *The friends of liberty: the English democratic movement in the age of the French Revolution.* Cambridge, Mass., 1979.

466 Hall, Walter Phelps. *British radicalism, 1791–1797.* New York, 1912; reprinted, New York, 1976. Detailed study of pamphlet literature.

467 Hayter, Tony. *The army and the crowd in mid-Georgian England.* 1978. Use of the army in suppressing disorders 1750–80.

468 Hill, Richard Leslie. *Toryism and the people, 1832–1846.* 1929; new edn, 1975. Conservative attitudes to social problems.

469 Hilton, Boyd. *Corn, cash, commerce: the economic policies of the Tory governments, 1815–1830.* Oxford, 1978.

470 Johnston, Edith Mary. *Great Britain and Ireland, 1760–1800.* Edinburgh, 1963. See also (429).

471 Knollenberg, Bernard. *Origin of the American Revolution: 1759–1766.* New York, 1960. Emphasis on growing friction before the Stamp Act crisis.

472 Langford, Paul. *The first Rockingham administration, 1765–1766.* 1973.

473 McDowell, Robert Brendan. *Irish public opinion, 1750–1800.* 1944. *Public opinion and government policy in Ireland, 1801–1846.* 1952.

474 Machin, George Ian Thom. *The Catholic question in English politics, 1820 to 1830.* Oxford, 1964.

475 Mahoney, Thomas Henry Donald. *Edmund Burke and Ireland.* Cambridge, Mass., 1960.

476 Marlow, Joyce. *The Peterloo massacre.* 1969. See also (496) and (514).

477 —— *The Tolpuddle martyrs.* 1971.

478 Marshall, Léon Soutierre. *The development of public opinion in Manchester, 1780–1820.* Syracuse, NY, 1946. See also (497).

479 Marshall, Peter James. *The impeachment of Warren Hastings.* 1965.

480 Meikle, Henry William. *Scotland and the French Revolution.* Glasgow, 1912; reprinted, New York, 1969.

481 Mitchell, Austin Vernon. *The Whigs in opposition, 1815–1830.* Oxford, 1967.

482 Mitchell, Leslie George. *Charles James Fox and the disintegration of the Whig Party, 1782–1794.* 1971.

483 —— *Holland House.* 1980. Excellent on career of Lord Holland. See also (395) and (503).

484 Moore, David Cresap. *The politics of deference: a study of the mid-nineteenth-century English political system.* 1976. A restatement of his arguments in the controversy over the Whig objectives in 1832.

485 Morgan, Edmund Sears and Helen M. Morgan. *The Stamp Act crisis: prologue to revolution.* Durham, NC, 1953.
486 Namier, Sir Lewis Bernstein. *Crossroads of power.* 1962. Contains nearly all of Namier's shorter essays and lectures on the eighteenth century.
487 —— *England in the age of the American Revolution.* 1930; 2nd edn, 1961.
488 —— *The structure of politics at the accession of George III.* 1929, 2 vols; 2nd edn, 1957.
489 Nobbe, George. *The 'North Briton': a study in political propaganda.* New York, 1939.
490 Norris, John Mackenzie. *Shelburne and reform.* 1963.
491 O'Gorman, Frank. *The rise of party in England: the Rockingham Whigs, 1760–82.* 1975.
492 —— *The Whig Party and the French Revolution.* 1967.
493 Pares, Richard. *The historian's business and other essays.* Oxford, 1961. Reprints of most of his important articles.
494 Prothero, Iorwerth J. *Artisans and politics in early nineteenth-century London: John Gast and his times.* Folkestone, Kent, 1978. Much on London radicalism in general.
495 Rea, Robert Right. *The English press in politics, 1760–1774.* Lincoln, Nebr., 1963. See also (2420) and (2421).
496 Read, Donald. *Peterloo: the 'massacre' and its background.* Manchester, 1958. See also (476) and (514).
497 —— *Press and people, 1790–1850: opinion in three English cities.* 1961. Investigates Leeds, Manchester and Sheffield. See also (478).
498 Ritcheson, Charles Ray. *British politics and the American Revolution.* Norman, Okla., 1954.
499 Roberts, Michael. *The Whig Party, 1807–1812.* 1939; reprinted, New York, 1965.
500 Royle, Edward. *Radical politics, 1790–1900: religion and unbelief.* Harlow, Essex, 1971.
501 Rudé, George Frederick Elliot. *Wilkes and liberty: a social study of 1763 to 1774.* Oxford, 1962.
502 Sack, James J. *The Grenvillites, 1801–29: party politics and factionalism in the age of Pitt and Liverpool.* Urbana, Ill., 1979.
503 Sanders, Lloyd Charles. *The Holland House circle.* New York, 1969. See also (483).
504 Senior, Hereward. *Orangeism in Ireland and Britain, 1795–1836.* 1966.
505 Sosin, Jack. *Agents and merchants: British colonial policy and the origins of the American Revolution, 1763–1775.* Lincoln, Nebr., 1965.
506 —— *Whitehall and the wilderness: the Middle West in British colonial policy, 1760–1775.* Lincoln, Nebr., 1961.
507 Sutherland, Dame Lucy Stuart. *The City of London and the opposition to government, 1768–1774: a study in the rise of metropolitan radicalism.* 1959; reprinted in John Stevenson (ed.), *London in the age of reform.* Oxford, 1977, pp. 30–54. See also (680).
508 —— *The East India Company in eighteenth-century politics.* Oxford, 1952. See also (1250).
509 Thomas, Peter David Garner. *British politics and the Stamp Act crisis: the first phase of the American Revolution, 1763–1767.* Oxford, 1975.
510 Thomis, Malcolm Ian. *Politics and society in Nottingham, 1785–1835.* Oxford, 1969.
511 Thomis, Malcolm Ian and Peter Holt. *Threats of revolution in Britain, 1789–1848.* 1977.
512 Thornton, Archibald Paton. *The habit of authority: paternalism in British history.* Toronto, 1966.
513 Veitch, George Stead. *The genesis of parliamentary reform.* 1913; reprinted, with an introduction by Ian Ralph Christie, Hamden, Conn., 1965.
514 Walmsley, Robert. *Peterloo: the case reopened.* Manchester, 1969. See also (476) and (496).
515 Wardroper, John. *Kings, lords, and wicked libellers: satire and protest, 1760–1837.* 1973.
516 Winstanley, Denys Arthur. *Lord Chatham and the Whig opposition.* Cambridge, 1912; reprinted, 1966.
517 —— *Personal and party government ... 1760–1766.* Cambridge, 1910.

4. Biographies

518 Aldridge, Alfred Owen. *Man of reason: the life of Thomas Paine.* Philadelphia, 1959. See also (534). For Paine's writings, see (389); for his ideas, see (2323), (2474) and (2502).
519 Aspinall, Arthur. *Lord Brougham and the Whig Party.* Manchester, 1927; reprinted, Hamden, Conn., 1972. See also (566).

520 Ayling, Stanley Edward. *The elder Pitt, Earl of Chatham.* 1976. See also (529), (572) and (594); for correspondence, see (416).

521 —— *George the Third.* 1972. See also (526); for correspondence, see (378), (388), (390), (405) and (413); for the king's illness, see (1585) and (1604).

522 Bargar, B. D. *Lord Dartmouth and the American Revolution.* Columbia, SC, 1965.

523 Bartlett, Christopher John. *Castlereagh.* 1966. See also (537), (552) and (555); for his correspondence, see (699); for his foreign policy, see (797).

524 Bell, Herbert Clifford Francis. *Lord Palmerston.* 1936, 2 vols; reprinted, Hamden, Conn., 1966. Best older study. See also (577) and (583); for his correspondence, see (380); for his foreign policy, see (798).

525 Bleackley, Horace. *Life of John Wilkes.* 1917. Indispensable for full and careful use of contemporary printed material. See also (531) and (574).

526 Brooke, John. *King George III.* 1972. Best biography. See also (521). For correspondence, see (378), (388), (390), (405) and (413); for the king's illness, see (1585) and (1604).

527 Brown, Garland Saxon. *The American secretary: the colonial policy of Lord George Germain, 1775–1778.* Ann Arbor, Mich., 1963. Sympathetic; compare (591).

528 Brown, Peter Douglas. *The Chathamites: a study in the relationship between personalities and ideas in the second half of the eighteenth century.* 1967.

529 —— *William Pitt, Earl of Chatham, the Great Commoner.* 1978. See also (520), (572) and (594); for his correspondence, see (416).

530 Cecil, Lord Edward Christian David Gascoyne. *The young Melbourne, and the story of his marriage with Caroline Lamb.* 1939. *Lord M., or the later life of Lord Melbourne.* 1954. See also (600).

531 Chenevix Trench, Charles Pocklington. *Portrait of a patriot: a biography of John Wilkes.* Edinburgh, 1962. See also (525) and (574).

532 Cole, George Douglas Howard. *Life of William Cobbett.* 1924; 3rd edn, 1947. Classic life. See also (570) and (579).

533 Cone, Carl B. *Burke and the nature of politics.* Lexington, Ky, 1975–80, 2 vols. Most comprehensive life. See also (560). For other Burke references, see (382).

534 Conway, Moncure Daniel. *The life of Thomas Paine.* New York, 1892; new edn by Hypatia Bradlaugh Bonner, 1909. Standard. See also (518).

535 Cooper, Leonard. *Radical Jack: the life of John George Lambton, first Earl of Durham ... (1792–1840).* 1959.

536 Davis, Richard W. *Dissent in politics, 1780–1830: the political life of William Smith, MP.* 1971.

537 Derry, John Wesley. *Castlereagh.* 1976. See also (523), (552) and (555); for his correspondence, see (699); for his foreign policy, see (797).

538 —— *Charles James Fox.* 1972. Best life. For Fox's correspondence, see (412).

539 Dixon, Peter. *George Canning: politician and statesman.* 1976. See also (553) and (562); for his foreign policy, see (792).

540 Edwardes, Michael. *Warren Hastings, king of the nabobs.* 1976. See also (542).

541 Ehrman, John Patrick William. *The younger Pitt: the years of acclaim.* 1969. Definitive; comprehensive bibliography to 1792. See also (557), (576), (578) and (586).

542 Feiling, Sir Keith Grahame. *Warren Hastings.* 1954; reprinted, Hamden, Conn., 1967. See also (540).

543 Fitzmaurice, Lord Edmond. *Life of William, Earl of Shelburne, afterwards first Marquess of Lansdowne.* 2nd edn, rev., 1912, 2 vols. Letters cover 1761–94.

544 Fulford, Roger Thomas Baldwin. *Samuel Whitbread, 1764–1815: a study in opposition.* 1967.

545 Furber, Holden. *Henry Dundas, first Viscount Melville, 1742–1811, political manager of Scotland, statesman, and administrator of British India.* 1931. See also (564).

546 Furneaux, Robin S. *William Wilberforce.* 1974. See also (573). For correspondence, see (421) and (422).

547 Garrett, Robert. *Robert Clive.* 1976. See also (584).

548 Gash, Norman. *Mr Secretary Peel: the life of Robert Peel to 1830.* 1961. *Sir Robert Peel: the life of Sir Robert Peel after 1830.* 1972. Definitive; Gash's *Peel*, 1976, is a briefer version. For Peel's papers, see (407).

549 Gray, Denis. *Spencer Perceval: the evangelical prime minister.* Manchester, 1963.

550 Hedley, Olwen. *Queen Charlotte.* 1975.

551 Hibbert, Christopher. *George IV, Prince of Wales, 1762–1811.* 1972. *George IV, regent and king, 1811–1830.* 1973. For his correspondence, see (377) and (379).

552 Hinde, Wendy. *Castlereagh.* 1981. See also (523), (537) and (555); for his correspondence, see (699); for his foreign policy, see (797).

553 —— *George Canning.* 1973. See also (539) and (562); for his foreign policy, see (792).

554 Hoffman, Ross John Swartz. *The Marquis: a study of Lord Rockingham, 1730–1782.* Fordham, NY, 1973.

555 Hyde, Harford Montgomery. *The rise of Castlereagh.* 1933. Good account to 1801; see also (523), (537) and (552); for his correspondence, see (699); for his foreign policy, see (797).

556 Ilchester, Giles Stephen Holland Fox-Strangways, Earl of. *Henry Fox, first Lord Holland, his family and relations.* 1920, 2 vols.

557 Jarrett, Derek. *Pitt the younger.* 1974. See also (541), (576), (578) and (586).

558 Kemp, Betty. *Sir Francis Dashwood: an eighteenth-century independent.* 1967.

559 Keppel, Sonia. *The sovereign lady: a life of Elizabeth Vassall, third Lady Holland, with her family.* 1974. See also (396).

560 Kramnick, Isaac. *The rage of Edmund Burke: portrait of an ambivalent conservative.* New York, 1977. Psychobiography; hostile, and dubious at many points. See also (533).

561 Longford, Elizabeth (Harman) Pakenham, Countess of. *Wellington: the years of the sword.* 1969. *Wellington: pillar of state.* 1972. Best life. For correspondence, see (420) and (1746). For his military career, see Section XI.

562 Marshall, Dorothy. *The rise of George Canning.* 1938. To 1806. See also (539) and (553).

563 Martelli, George. *Jemmy Twitcher: a life of the fourth Earl of Sandwich, 1718–1792.* 1962. Attempt at rehabilitation. See also (703).

564 Matheson, Cyril. *The life of Henry Dundas, first Viscount Melville.* 1933. See also (545).

565 Namier, Sir Lewis Bernstein and John Brooke. *Charles Townshend.* 1964.

566 New, Chester William. *The life of Henry Brougham to 1830.* Oxford, 1961. See also (519).

567 Newman, Aubrey Norris. *The Stanhopes of Chevening: a family biography.* 1969. Model study. See also (585).

568 Olson, Alison Gilbert. *The radical duke: career and correspondence of Charles Lennox, third Duke of Richmond.* 1961. Includes many political letters.

569 Osborne, John Walter. *John Cartwright.* Cambridge, 1972.

570 —— *William Cobbett: his thought and his times.* New Brunswick, NJ, 1966. See also (532) and (579).

571 Patterson, Melville Watson. *Sir Francis Burdett and his times (1770–1844).* 1931, 2 vols.

572 Plumb, John Harold. *Chatham.* 1953. Best short biography. See also (520), (529) and (594); for his correspondence, see (416).

573 Pollock, John Charles. *Wilberforce.* 1977. See also (546); for his correspondence, see (421) and (422).

574 Postgate, Raymond William. *That devil Wilkes.* 1930. One of the better biographies. See also (525) and (531).

575 Prest, John Michael. *Lord John Russell.* Columbia, SC, 1972. Good but partisan. For his correspondence, see (410).

576 Reilly, Robin. *William Pitt the younger.* 1978. See also (541), (557), (578) and (586).

577 Ridley, Jasper Godwin. *Lord Palmerston.* 1970. See also (524) and (583); for his correspondence, see (380); for his foreign policy, see (798).

578 Rose, John Holland. *Life of William Pitt.* 1923. One volume edition of his *William Pitt and the national revival.* 1911; and *William Pitt and the great war.* 1911. Still useful. See also (541), (557), (576) and (586).

579 Sambrook, James. *William Cobbett.* 1973. See also (532) and (570).

580 Sichel, Walter Sydney. *Sheridan, from new and original material, including a manuscript diary by Georgiana, Duchess of Devonshire.* 1909, 2 vols. Important older life. For his correspondence, see (408).

581 Smith, Charles Daniel. *The early career of Lord North, the prime minister.* 1979. See also (588) and (592).

582 Smith, Ernest Anthony. *Whig principles and party politics: Earl Fitzwilliam and the Whig Party, 1748–1833.* Manchester, 1975.

583 Southgate, Donald George. '*The most English minister': the policies and politics of Palmerston.* 1966. See also (524) and (577); for his correspondence, see (380); for his foreign policy, see (798).

584 Spear, Thomas George Percival. *Master of Bengal: Clive and his India.* 1975. See also (547).

585 Stanhope, Ghita and George Peabody Gooch. *The life of Charles, third Earl Stanhope.* 1914. Includes letters, 1780–1815, of a radical peer. See also (567).

586 Stanhope, Philip Henry Stanhope, 5th Earl. *Life of the Right Honourable William Pitt.* 1861–2, 4 vols; new edn, 1879, 3 vols. Includes much correspondence not printed elsewhere and still of value as a biography. See also (541), (557), (576) and (578).

587 Stephens, Alexander. *Memoirs of John Horne Tooke.* 1813, 2 vols; reprinted, New York, 1968. Includes letters 1766–1812. See also (595).

588 Thomas, Peter David Garner. *Lord North.* 1976. Sympathetic; the best biography. See also (581) and (592).

589 Trevelyan, George Macaulay. *Lord Grey of the Reform Bill, being the life of Charles, second Earl Grey.* 1920; 2nd edn, 1929; reprinted, 1952. Standard.

590 Turberville, Arthur Stanley. *A history of Welbeck Abbey and its owners, 1539–1879.* 1938–9, 2 vols. Most of the second volume is a biography of the third Duke of Portland.

591 Valentine, Alan Chester. *Lord George Germain.* Oxford, 1962. See also (527).

592 —— *Lord North.* Norman, Okla., 1967, 2 vols. Wide-ranging but many inaccuracies of detail. See also (581) and (588).

593 Ward, John Trevor. *Sir James Graham.* 1967.

594 Williams, Basil. *The life of William Pitt, Earl of Chatham.* 1913, 2 vols; reprinted, New York, 1966, 2 vols. Standard. See also (520), (529) and (572); for his correspondence, see (416).

595 Yarborough, Minnie Clare. *John Horne Tooke.* New York, 1926. See also (587).

596 Yonge, Charles Duke. *The life and administration of Robert Banks, second Earl of Liverpool ... compiled from original documents.* 1868, 3 vols. Limited selection of letters; there has been no modern biography.

597 Yorke, Philip Chesney. *The life and correspondence of Philip Yorke, Earl of Hardwicke, lord high chancellor of Great Britain.* Cambridge, 1913, 3 vols; reprinted, New York, 1977, 3 vols. To 1764, but important for the beginning of George III's reign.

598 Ziegler, Philip. *Addington: a life of Henry Addington, first Viscount Sidmouth.* 1965.

599 —— *King William IV.* 1973.

600 —— *Melbourne: a biography of William Lamb, second Viscount Melbourne.* 1976. See also (530).

5. Articles

601 Aspinall, Arthur. 'Canning's ministry', *EHR*, 42 (1927), 201–26.

602 —— 'English party organization in the early nineteenth century', *EHR*, 41 (1926), 389–411.

603 —— 'The reporting and publishing of the House of Commons debates, 1771–1834', in Richard Pares and Alan John Percival Taylor (eds.), *Essays presented to Sir Lewis Namier.* 1956, pp. 227–57. See also (64), (167) and (682).

604 Bradfield, B. T. 'Sir Richard Vyvyan and the country gentlemen, 1830–1834', *EHR*, 83 (1968), 729–43.

605 Briggs, Asa. 'The background of the parliamentary reform movement in three English cities (1830–2)', *Cambridge Historical Journal*, 10 (1952), 293–317. Manchester, Birmingham and Leeds.

606 —— 'Middle-class consciousness in English politics, 1780–1846', *PP*, 9 (1956), 65–74.

607 —— 'Thomas Attwood and the economic background of the Birmingham Political Union', *Cambridge Historical Journal*, 9 (1947–9), 190–216.

608 Butterfield, Sir Herbert. 'Charles James Fox and the Whig opposition in 1792', *Cambridge Historical Journal*, 9 (1947–9), 293–330.

609 —— 'George III and the constitution', *History* NS, 43 (1958), 14–33. Neo-Whig. See also (333).

610 Christie, Ian Ralph. 'Was there a "New Toryism" in the earlier part of George III's reign?', *JBS*, 5, 1 (1965), 60–76. Concludes that there was not.

611 Close, David. 'The formation of a two-party alignment in the House of Commons between 1832 and 1841', *EHR*, 84 (1969), 257–77.

612 Collins, H. 'The London Corresponding Society', in John Saville (ed.), *Democracy and the labour movement: essays in honour of Dina Torr*. 1954, pp. 103–34.

613 Davis, Richard W. 'Deference and aristocracy in the time of the Great Reform Act', *AHR*, 81 (1976), 532–9.

614 —— 'The strategy of "Dissent" in the repeal campaign, 1820–1828', *JMH*, 38 (1966), 374–93.

615 —— 'Toryism to Tamworth: the triumph of reform, 1827–1835', *Albion*, 12 (1980), 132–46.

616 Dinwiddy, John Rowland. 'Charles James Fox and the people', *History* NS, 55 (1970), 342–59.

617 —— 'Sir Francis Burdett and Burdettite radicalism', *History* NS, 65 (1980), 17–31.

618 Ditchfield, G. M. 'The parliamentary struggle over the repeal of the Test and Corporation Acts, 1787–1790', *EHR*, 89 (1974), 551–77.

619 —— 'The Scottish campaign against the Test Act, 1790–1791', *HJ*, 23 (1980), 37–61. See also (2030).

620 Donnelly, F. K. and J. L. Baxter. 'Sheffield and the English revolutionary tradition, 1791–1820', *International Review of Social History*, 20 (1975), 398–423. Debate on the subject with John Rowland Dinwiddy in *PP*, 64 (1974), 113–23.

621 Elliott, Marianne. 'The "Despard Conspiracy" reconsidered', *PP*, 75 (1977), 46–61.

622 Emsley, Clive. 'The Home Office and its sources of information and investigation, 1791–1801', *EHR*, 94 (1979), 532–61.

623 —— 'The London "Insurrection" of December 1792: fact, fiction or fantasy?', *JBS*, 17, 2 (1978), 66–86.

624 Finlayson, Geoffrey Beauchamp Alistair Mowbray. 'The politics of municipal reform, 1835', *EHR*, 81 (1966), 673–92.

625 Flick, Carlos T. 'The fall of Wellington's government', *JMH*, 37 (1965), 62–71.

626 Foord, Archibald S. 'The waning of "the influence of the Crown"', *EHR*, 62 (1947), 484–507.

627 Fryer, W. R. 'King George III: his political character and conduct, 1760–1784: a new Whig interpretation', *Renaissance and Modern Studies*, 6 (1962), 68–101.

628 —— 'The study of British politics between the Revolution and the Reform Act', *Renaissance and Modern Studies*, 1 (1957), 91–114. Neo-Whig.

629 Gash, Norman. 'English reform and French revolution in the general election of 1830', in Richard Pares and Alan John Percival Taylor (eds.), *Essays presented to Sir Lewis Namier*. 1956, pp. 258–88.

630 George, Mary Dorothy. 'Fox's martyrs: the general election of 1784', *TRHS* 4th ser., 21 (1939), 133–68. See also (646).

631 Ginter, Donald Eugene. 'The financing of the Whig party organization, 1783–1793', *AHR*, 71 (1965–6), 421–40.

632 —— 'The Loyalist Association movement of 1792–93 and British public opinion', *HJ*, 9 (1966), 179–90. Questions significance of the movement; critical of interpretation in (436) and (658).

633 Gross, Itzac. 'The abolition of negro slavery and British parliamentary politics, 1832–3', *HJ*, 23 (1980), 63–85.

634 Gunn, John A. W. 'Influence, parties, and the constitution: changing attitudes, 1783–1832', *HJ*, 17 (1974), 301–28.

635 Haas, James M. 'The pursuit of political success in eighteenth-century England: Sandwich, 1740–71', *BIHR*, 43 (1970), 56–77.

636 Harvey, Arnold D. 'The ministry of all the talents: the Whigs in office, February 1806 to March 1807', *HJ*, 15 (1972), 619–48.

637 —— 'The third party in British politics, 1818–21', *BIHR*, 51 (1978), 146–59.

638 Hill, Brian W. 'Fox and Burke: the Whig party and the question of principles, 1784–1789', *EHR*, 89 (1974), 1–24.

639 Hone, J. Ann. 'Radicalism in London, 1796–1802: convergence and continuity', in John Stevenson (ed.), *London in the age of reform*. Oxford, 1977, pp. 79–101.

640 Jarrett, Derek. 'The regency crisis of 1765', *EHR*, 85 (1970), 282–315.

641 Johnson, D. T. 'Charles James Fox: from government to opposition, 1771–1774', *EHR*, 89 (1974), 750–84.

642 Jupp, Peter James. 'Earl Temple's resignation and the question of a dissolution in December 1783', *HJ*, 15 (1972), 309–13. See also (645).

643 Keir, Sir David Lindsay. 'Economical reform, 1779–1787', *Law Quarterly Review*, 30 (1934), 368–85.

644 Kelly, Paul. 'British and Irish politics in 1785', *EHR*, 90 (1975), 536–63.

645 —— 'The Pitt–Temple administration: 19–22 December 1783', *HJ*, 17 (1974), 157–61. See also (642).

646 —— 'Radicalism and public opinion in the general election of 1784', *BIHR*, 45 (1972), 73–88. See also (630).

647 Kemp, Betty. 'Crewe's Act, 1782', *EHR*, 68 (1953), 258–63.

648 Kriegel, Abraham D. 'The Irish policy of Lord Grey's government', *EHR*, 86 (1971), 22–45.

649 —— 'The politics of the Whigs in opposition, 1834–1835', *JBS*, 7, 2 (1968), 65–91.

650 Langford, Paul. 'London and the American Revolution', in John Stevenson (ed.), *London in the age of reform*. Oxford, 1977, pp. 55–78.

651 Large, David. 'The decline of "the Party of the Crown" and the rise of parties in the House of Lords, 1783–1837', *EHR*, 78 (1963), 669–95.

652 Lawson, Philip. 'George Grenville and America: the years of opposition, 1765 to 1770', *W&MQ* 3rd ser., 37 (1980), 561–76.

653 Lowe, William Curtis. 'Bishops and Scottish representative peers in the House of Lords, 1760–1775', *JBS*, 18, 1 (1978), 86–106.

654 McDowell, Robert Brendan. 'The Fitzwilliam episode', *Irish Historical Studies*, 15 (1966–7), 115–30.

655 Machin, George Ian Thom. 'Resistance to repeal of the Test and Corporation Acts, 1828', *HJ*, 22 (1979), 115–39.

656 Miller, Naomi Churgin. 'John Cartwright and radical parliamentary reform, 1808–1819', *EHR*, 83 (1968), 705–28.

657 Milton-Smith, John. 'Earl Grey's cabinet and the objects of parliamentary reform', *HJ*, 15 (1972), 55–74.

658 Mitchell, Austin Vernon. 'The Association Movement of 1792–3', *HJ*, 4 (1961), 56–77. See also (436) and (632).

659 Moore, David Cresap. 'The other face of reform', *Victorian Studies*, 5 (1961–2), 7–34. The ultra-Tory supporters of reform.

660 Newbould, I. D. C. 'William IV and the dismissal of the Whigs, 1834', *Canadian Journal of History*, 11 (1976), 311–30.

661 Norris, John Mackenzie. 'Samuel Garbett and the early development of industrial lobbying in Great Britain', *EcHR* 2nd ser., 10 (1957–8), 450–60. See also (671).

662 O'Brien, George Augustine Thomas. 'The Irish free trade agitation of 1779', *EHR*, 38 (1923), 564–81; 39 (1924) 95–109.

663 Parssinen, T. M. 'Association, convention, and anti-parliament in British radical politics, 1771–1848', *EHR*, 88 (1973), 504–33.

664 —— 'The revolutionary party in London, 1816–20', *BIHR*, 45 (1972), 266–82.

665 Phillips, John A. 'Popular politics in unreformed England', *JMH*, 52 (1980), 599–625.

666 —— 'The structure of electoral politics in unreformed England', *JBS*, 19 (Fall 1979), 76–100.

667 Phillips, Neville Crompton. 'Edmund Burke and the county movement, 1779–1780', *EHR*, 76 (1961), 254–78.

668 Prochaska, Franklyn K. 'English state trials in the 1790s: a case study', *JBS*, 13, 1 (1973), 63–82.

669 Reitan, E. A. 'The civil list in eighteenth-century British politics: parliamentary supremacy versus the independence of the Crown', *HJ*, 9 (1966), 318–37.

670 —— 'The civil list, 1761–77: problems of finance and administration', *BIHR*, 47 (1974), 186–201.

671 Robinson, Eric. 'Matthew Boulton and the art of parliamentary lobbying', *HJ*, 7 (1964), 209–29. See also (661).

672 Rogers, Nicholas. 'Aristocratic clientage, trade and independency: popular politics in pre-radical Westminster', *PP*, 61 (1973), 70–106.

673 Rowe, David John. 'London radicalism in the era of the great Reform Bill', in John Stevenson (ed.), *London in the age of reform*. Oxford, 1977, pp. 149–76.

674 Schweizer, Karl W. 'Lord Bute and William Pitt's resignation in 1761', *Canadian Journal of History*, 8 (1973), 111–25.

675 Seaman, Allan W. L. 'Reform politics at Sheffield, 1791–1797', *Transactions of the Hunter Archaeological Society*, 7 (1957), 215–28.

676 Searby, Peter. 'Paternalism, disturbance and parliamentary reform: society and politics in Coventry, 1819–32', *International Review of Social History*, 22 (1977), 198–225.

677 Smith, Ernest Anthony. 'The election agent in English politics, 1734–1832', *EHR*, 84 (1969), 12–35.

678 Spring, David. 'Lord Chandos and the farmers, 1818–1846', *HLQ*, 33 (1969–70), 257–81. Leader of the protectionists.

679 Stevenson, John. 'The Queen Caroline affair', in John Stevenson (ed.), *London in the age of reform*. Oxford, 1977, pp. 117–48.

680 Sutherland, Dame Lucy Stuart. 'The City of London in eighteenth-century politics', in Richard Pares and Alan John Percival Taylor (eds.), *Essays presented to Sir Lewis Namier*. 1956, pp. 49–74. See also (507).

681 —— 'Edmund Burke and the first Rockingham ministry', *EHR*, 47 (1932), 46–72.

682 Thomas, Peter David Garner. 'The beginning of parliamentary reporting in newspapers, 1768–1774', *EHR*, 74 (1959), 623–36. See also (64), (167) and (603).

683 —— 'Charles Townshend and American taxation in 1767', *EHR*, 83 (1968), 33–51. A comment on this by Derek H. Watson, *ibid.* 84 (1969), 561–5.

684 Thomas, W. E. S. 'Whigs and radicals in Westminster: the election of 1819', *Guildhall Miscellany*, 3 (1970), 174–217.

685 Turberville, Arthur Stanley. 'Leeds and parliamentary reform, 1820–32', *Thoresby Society Miscellany*, 41 (1957), 1–89.

686 Walker, Franklin A. 'The Grenville–Fox "junction" and the problem of peace', *Canadian Journal of History*, 12 (1977–8), 51–63.

687 Watson, Derek H. 'The rise of the opposition at Wildman's Club', *BIHR*, 44 (1971), 55–77. The origins of the Rockinghams in the early 1760s.

688 Western, John Randle. 'The Volunteer Movement as an anti-revolutionary force, 1793–1801', *EHR*, 71 (1956), 603–14.

689 Willis, Richard E. 'Fox, Grenville, and the recovery of opposition, 1801–1804', *JBS*, 11, 2 (1972), 24–43.

690 —— '"An handful of violent people": the nature of the Foxite opposition, 1794–1801', *Albion*, 8 (1976), 236–54.

691 Wooley, S. F. 'The personnel of the parliament of 1833', *EHR*, 53 (1938), 240–62.

VI. FOREIGN RELATIONS

For specialized bibliography, see (166).

1. Printed sources

692 Auckland, Robert John Eden, 3rd Baron (ed.). *The journal and correspondence of William, Lord of Auckland*. 1861–2, 4 vols.

693 Bindoff, Stanley Thomas, et al. (comps.). *British diplomatic representatives, 1789–1852*. (Camden Society 3rd ser., 50.) 1934. See also (698). Gives dates of missions and where their despatches can be found.

694 Browning, Oscar (ed.). *Despatches from Paris, 1784–1790, selected and edited from the Foreign Office correspondence*. 1909–10, 2 vols. *The despatches of Earl Gower, English ambassador at Paris, from June 1790 to August 1792*. Cambridge, 1885.

695 Chance, James Frederick and Leopold George Wickham Legge (eds.). *British diplomatic instructions, 1689–1789*. (Camden Society 3rd ser., 32, 35, 36, 38, 39, 43, 49.) 1922–34, 7 vols. Covers France (4 vols.); Sweden (2 vols.); and Denmark (1 vol.).

696 Collyer, Adelaide D'Arcy (ed.). *The despatches and correspondence of John, second Earl of Buckinghamshire, ambassador to the court of Catherine II of Russia, 1762–1765*. (Camden Society 3rd ser., 2, 3.) 1900–2, 2 vols.

697 Doniol, Henri (ed.). *Histoire de la participation de la France à l'établissement des Etats-Unis d'Amérique: correspondence diplomatique et documents.* Paris, 1886–92, 5 vols. Supplement to Vol. 5, 1899, brought work down to the conclusion of the peace treaties in 1783. Fundamental collection of documents from the French side.

698 Horn, David Bayne (comp.). *British diplomatic representatives, 1689–1789.* (Camden Society 3rd ser., 46.) 1932. See also (693).

699 Londonderry, Charles William Vane-Stewart, 3rd Marquess of (ed.). *Memoirs and correspondence of Viscount Castlereagh, second Marquess of Londonderry.* 1850–53, 12 vols. Good collection but not complete, omitting most family correspondence. For biographies of Castlereagh, see (523), (537), (552) and (555); for his foreign policy, see (797).

700 Malmesbury, James Howard Harris, 3rd Earl of (ed.). *Diaries and correspondence of James Harris, first Earl of Malmesbury: containing an account of his missions at the courts of Madrid, Frederick the Great, Catherine the Second, and the Hague, and his special missions to Berlin, Brunswick, and the French Republic.* 1844, 4 vols.; reprinted, New York, 1970, 4 vols.

701 Mayo, Bernard (ed.). *Instructions to the British ministers to the United States, 1791–1812.* Washington, DC, 1941.

702 Pallain, Georges (ed.). *La Mission de Talleyrand à Londres en 1792: correspondence inédite de Talleyrand avec le département des affaires étrangères.* Paris, 1889. *Correspondence diplomatique de Talleyrand: ambassade de Talleyrand à Londres, 1830–34.* Paris, 1891.

703 Spencer, Frank (ed.). *The fourth Earl of Sandwich: diplomatic correspondence, 1763–1765.* Manchester, 1961.

704 Temperley, Harold William Vazeille and Dame Lillian Margery Penson (eds.). *Foundations of British foreign policy: from Pitt (1792) to Salisbury (1902).* 1938; reprinted, 1966. Important collection of representative documents.

705 Vaucher, Paul (ed.). *Recueil des instructions données aux ambassadeurs et ministres de France depuis les traités de Westphalie jusqu' à la Révolution Française ... .* Vol. XXV–2. *Angleterre* (Vol. 3). Paris, 1965. Documents, 1698–1791.

706 Webster, Sir Charles Kingsley (ed.). *Britain and the independence of Latin America, 1812–1830: select documents from the Foreign Office archives.* 1938, 2 vols. Important collection.

707 —— *British diplomacy, 1813–1815: select documents dealing with the reconstruction of Europe.* 1921.

2. Surveys

708 Hayes, Paul M. *The nineteenth century, 1814–80.* 1975.

709 Horn, David Bayne. *Great Britain and Europe in the eighteenth century.* Oxford, 1967. Standard, with good bibliographies.

710 Langford, Paul. *The eighteenth century, 1688–1815.* 1976.

711 Renouvin, Pierre (ed.). *Histoire des relations internationales.* Paris, 1953–8, 12 vols. The standard French account. Vol. 3 by Gaston Zeller, Vol. 4 by André Fugier and Vol. 5 by Pierre Renouvin are concerned with parts of this period.

712 Seton-Watson, Robert William. *Britain in Europe 1789–1914: a survey of foreign policy.* Cambridge, 1937; reprinted, Cambridge, 1955. Excellent survey.

713 Ward, Sir Adolphus William and George Peabody Gooch (eds.). *The Cambridge history of British foreign policy, 1783–1919.* Cambridge, 1922–3, 3 vols.; reprinted, 1970. Vol. 1, 1783–1815; Vol. 2, 1815–1866.

3. Monographs

714 Allen, Harry Cranbrook. *Great Britain and the United States: a history of Anglo-American relations (1783–1952).* 1954; reprinted, Hamden, Conn., 1969. Standard survey; an enlarged version of Part 1 was published as *The Anglo-American relationship since 1783.* 1960. For Anglo-American relations, see also (718), (725), (769), (777), (778), (786) and (802).

715 Anderson, Matthew Smith. *Britain's discovery of Russia, 1553–1815.* 1958. Half of the book is concerned with the period 1791–1815. See also (739).

716 —— *The Eastern Question, 1774–1923: a study in international relations.* 1966. Standard survey.

717 Bemis, Samuel Flagg. *The diplomacy of the American Revolution*. New York, 1935; new edn, 1957. Older standard. See also (794).

718 —— *Jay's treaty: a study in commerce and diplomacy*. New York, 1924; 2nd edn, New Haven, Conn., 1965. Exhaustive, but weighted to the American side. See also (714), (725), (769), (777), (778), (786) and (802).

719 Bethell, Leslie. *The abolition of the Brazilian slave trade: Britain, Brazil and the slave trade question, 1807–1869*. Cambridge, 1970. See also (737).

720 Beverina, Juan. *Las invasiones inglesas al Rio de la Plata (1806–7)*. Buenos Aires, 1939, 2 vols. See also (736) and (749).

721 Bindoff, Stanley Thomas. *The Scheldt question to 1839*. 1945.

722 Brebner, John Bartlet. *North Atlantic triangle: the interplay of Canada, the United States and Great Britain*. New Haven, Conn. and Toronto, 1945.

723 Buckland, Charles Stephen Buckland. *Metternich and the British government from 1809 to 1813*. 1932.

724 Buist, Marten G. *At spes non fracta: Hope and Co., 1770–1817, merchant bankers and diplomats at work*. The Hague, 1974. Anglo-Dutch banking house.

725 Burt, Alfred Leroy. *The United States, Great Britain, and British North America from the Revolution to the establishment of peace after the war of 1812*. New Haven, Conn., 1940. Emphasizes Canadian issues. See also (714), (718), (769), (777) and (778).

726 Cammann, Schuyler. *Trade through the Himalayas: the early British attempts to open Tibet*. Princeton, NJ, 1951.

727 Charles-Roux, François. *L'Angleterre, l'Isthme de Suez, et l'Egypte au xviii⁰ siècle*. Paris, 1922. See also (734) and (757).

728 Clapham, Sir John Harold. *The causes of the war of 1792*. Cambridge, 1899; reprinted, 1969.

729 Cobban, Alfred Bert Carter. *Ambassadors and secret agents: the diplomacy of the first Earl of Malmesbury at the Hague*. 1954.

730 Conn, Stetson. *Gibraltar in British diplomacy in the eighteenth century*. New Haven, Conn., 1942.

731 Coquelle, P. *Napoleon and England, 1803–1813*. Trans. Gordon D. Knox. 1904.

732 Crawley, Charles William. *The question of Greek independence: a study of British policy in the Near East, 1821–1833*. Cambridge, 1930; reprinted, 1973. Standard. See also (783).

733 Deschamps, Jules Albert. *Les Iles Britanniques et la Révolution Française, 1789–1803*. Brussels, 1949.

734 Douin, Georges and E. C. Fawtier Jones. *L'Angleterre et l'Egypte: la politique mameluke, 1801–7*. Cairo, 1929–30, 2 vols. Primarily a collection of documents from the British Foreign and War Offices. See also (727) and (757).

735 Ehrman, John Patrick William. *The British government and commercial negotiations with Europe, 1783–1793*. Cambridge, 1962.

736 Ferns, Henry Stanley. *Britain and Argentina in the nineteenth century*. Oxford, 1960; reprinted, New York, 1977. See also (720).

737 Freitas, Caio de. *George Canning e o Brasil: influência da diplomacia inglêsa na formaçâo brasileira*. São Paulo, 1958, 2 vols. See also (719).

738 Gillard, David. *The struggle for Asia, 1828–1914: a study of British and Russian imperialism*. 1977. See also (747).

739 Gleason, John Howes. *The genesis of Russophobia in Great Britain: a study of the interaction of policy and opinion*. Cambridge, Mass., 1950. See also (715).

740 Goldmann, Karl. *Die preussische–britischen Beziehungen in den Jahren 1812–1815*. Würzburg, 1934.

741 Greenberg, Michael. *British trade and the opening of China, 1800–42*. Cambridge, 1951. Based on the papers of Jardine, Matheson and Co. See also (773).

742 Haight, Mabel Violet (Jackson). *European powers and south-east Africa: a study of international relations on the south-east coast of Africa, 1796–1856*. New York, 1942; reprinted, 1967. Anglo–Portuguese–French relations.

743 Hatze, Margrit. *Die diplomatisch-politischen Beziehungen zwischen England und der Schweiz im Zeitalter der Restauration*. Basle, 1949.

744 Heckscher, Elie Filip. *The continental system: an economic interpretation*. Oxford, 1922.

745 Helleiner, Karl Ferdinand. *The imperial loans: a study in financial and diplomatic history*. Oxford, 1965. British loans to Austria in 1795.

746   Horn, David Bayne. *The British diplomatic service, 1689–1789.* Oxford, 1961. See also (275).

747   Ingram, Edward. *The beginning of the great game in Asia, 1828–1834.* Oxford, 1979. See also (738).

748   Jarrett, Derek. *The begetters of revolution: England's involvement with France, 1759–1789.* 1973. Cultural, intellectual and financial relations.

749   Kaufmann, William Weed. *British policy and the independence of Latin America, 1804–28.* New Haven, Conn., 1951; reprinted, Hamden, Conn., 1967. Standard. See also (720) and (736).

750   Kent, Heinz Sigfrid Kaplowitz. *War and trade in northern seas: Anglo-Scandinavian economic relations in the mid-eighteenth century.* Cambridge, 1973.

751   Kissinger, Henry Alfred. *A world restored: Metternich, Castlereagh, and the problems of peace, 1812–22.* Boston, Mass., 1957. See also (767) and (796).

752   Lodge, Sir Richard. *Great Britain and Prussia in the eighteenth century.* Oxford, 1923; reprinted, New York, 1972.

753   Lührs, Wilhelm. *Die freie Hansestadt Bremen und England in der Zeit des Deutschen Bundes, 1815–1867.* Bremen, 1958. Economic relations.

754   Madariaga, Isabel de. *Britain, Russia and the armed neutrality of 1780.* 1962.

755   Mardal, Magnus. *Norge, Sverige og den engelske tretasttoll 1817–1850.* Oslo, 1957. English–Scandinavian commercial relations.

756   Marks, Harry Julian. *The first contest for Singapore, 1819–1824.* The Hague, 1959. See also (789).

757   Marlowe, John. *A history of modern Egypt and Anglo-Egyptian relations, 1800–1953.* 1954; reprinted, Hamden, Conn., 1965. See also (727) and (734).

758   —— *Perfidious Albion: the origins of Anglo-French rivalry in the Levant.* 1971. Covers period 1763–1841.

759   Marshall, Peter James. *Problems of empire: Britain and India, 1757–1813.* 1968. Documents with a long, comprehensive introduction.

760   Meier, Markus. *Die diplomatische Vertretung Englands in der Schweiz im 18. Jahrhundert (1689–1789).* Basle, 1952.

761   Metcalf, Michael F. *Russia, England and Swedish party politics 1762–1766: the interplay between great power diplomacy and domestic politics during Sweden's Age of Liberty.* Stockholm, 1977. See also (779).

762   Miller, Daniel A. *Sir Joseph Yorke and Anglo-Dutch relations, 1774–1780.* The Hague, 1970.

763   Misra, G. S. *British foreign policy and Indian affairs, 1783–1815.* Bombay, 1963.

764   Mitchell, Harvey. *The underground war against revolutionary France: the missions of William Wickham 1794–1800.* Oxford, 1965.

765   Monk, Winston Francis. *Britain in the Western Mediterranean.* 1953.

766   Morris, Richard B. *The peacemakers: the great powers and American independence.* New York, 1965.

767   Nicolson, Sir Harold George. *The Congress of Vienna: a study in allied unity, 1815–1818.* 1946. See also (751) and (796).

768   Nightingale, Pamela. *Trade and empire in western India, 1784–1806.* Cambridge, 1970.

769   Perkins, Bradford. *The first rapprochement: England and the United States, 1795–1805.* Philadelphia, Pa, 1955. *Prologue to war: England and the United States, 1805–1812.* Berkeley, Calif., 1961. *Castlereagh and Adams: England and the United States, 1812–1823.* Berkeley, Calif., 1964. See also (714), (718), (725), (777), (778), (786) and (802).

770   Pirenne, Jacques-Henri. *La Sainte Alliance: organisation européenne de la paix mondiale.* Neuchâtel, 1946–9, 2 vols. Emphasizes Anglo-Russian rivalry, 1815–1818.

771   Platt, Desmond Christopher St Martin. *Finance, trade, and politics in British foreign policy, 1815–1914.* Oxford, 1968.

772   —— *Latin America and British trade, 1806–1914.* 1972.

773   Pritchard, Earl Hampton. *The crucial years of early Anglo-Chinese relations, 1750–1800.* Pullman, Wash., 1937; reprinted, New York, 1970. See also (741).

774   Ramsey, John Fraser. *Anglo-French relations, 1763–1770: a study of Choiseul's foreign policy.* Berkeley, Calif., 1939.

775   Rashed, Zenab Esmat. *The peace of Paris, 1763.* Liverpool, 1951. Thorough; based on British and French archives.

776 Renier, Gustaaf Johannes. *Great Britain and the establishment of the Kingdom of the Netherlands, 1813–1815: a study in British foreign policy.* 1930.

777 Rippy, James Fred. *Rivalry of the United States and Great Britain over Latin America (1808–30).* Baltimore, Md, 1929. See also (823).

778 Ritcheson, Charles Ray. *Aftermath of revolution: British policy toward the United States, 1783–1795.* Dallas, Texas, 1969. See also (714), (718), (725) and (769).

779 Roberts, Michael. *British diplomacy and Swedish party politics, 1756–1763.* Minneapolis, Minn., 1980. See also (761).

780 —— *Splendid isolation, 1763–1780.* (The Stenton Lecture for 1969.) Reading, Berks., 1970. Excellent brief account.

781 Rosselli, John. *Lord William Bentinck and the British occupation of Sicily, 1811–1814.* Cambridge, 1956.

782 Rosselli, Nello. *Inghilterra e regno di Sardegna dal 1815 al 1847.* Turin, 1954.

783 St Clair, William Linn. *That Greece might still be free: the Philhellenes in the War of Independence.* 1972. See also (732).

784 Sherwig, John Martin. *Guineas and gunpowder: British foreign aid in the wars with France, 1793–1815.* Cambridge, Mass., 1969.

785 Shupp, Paul Frederick. *The European powers and the Near Eastern question, 1806–1807.* New York, 1931.

786 Soulsby, Hugh Graham. *The right of search and the slave trade in Anglo-American relations, 1814–1862.* Baltimore, Md, 1933.

787 Stoker, John Teasdale. *William Pitt et la Révolution Française (1789–1793).* Paris, 1935. Based on British and French diplomatic archives.

788 Swain, James Edgar. *The struggle for the control of the Mediterranean prior to 1848: a study in Anglo-French relations.* Boston, Mass., 1933; reprinted, New York, 1973.

789 Tarling, Nicholas. *Anglo-Dutch rivalry in the Malay world, 1780–1824.* Cambridge, 1962. See also (756).

790 Taylor, Alan John Percival. *The trouble-makers: dissent over foreign policy, 1792–1939.* 1957. Much on the opposition to the French Revolutionary and Napoleonic Wars.

791 Temperley, Harold William Vazeille. *England and the Near East: the Crimea.* 1936. Largely concerned with years before 1837.

792 —— *The foreign policy of Canning, 1822–1827: England, the neo-Holy Alliance and the New World.* 1925; reprinted with introduction by Sir Herbert Butterfield, Hamden, Conn., 1966. For biographies of Canning, see (539), (553) and (562).

793 Trulsson, Sven G. *British and Swedish policies and strategies in the Baltic after the Peace of Tilsit in 1807: a study of decision-making.* Lund, 1976.

794 Van Alstyne, Richard William. *Empire and independence: the international history of the American Revolution.* New York, 1965. See also (717).

795 Villa-Urrutia, Wenceslao Ramírez de Villa-Urrutia, Marquis de. *Relaciones entre España é Inglaterra durante la guerra de la independencia: apuntes par la historia diplomática de España de 1808 à 1814.* Madrid, 1911–14, 3 vols.

796 Webster, Sir Charles Kingsley. *The Congress of Vienna, 1814–15.* 1919; reprinted, 1950. Standard. See also (751) and (767).

797 —— *The foreign policy of Castlereagh.* Vol. 1: *1812–1815: Britain and the reconstruction of Europe.* 1931; reprinted, 1950. Vol. 2: *1815–1822: Britain and the European alliances.* 1925; 2nd edn, 1934; reprinted, 1947. For Castlereagh's correspondence, see (699); for biographies, see (523), (537), (552) and (555).

798 —— *The foreign policy of Palmerston, 1830–41: Britain, the liberal movement, and the Eastern Question.* 1951, 2 vols. For biographies of Palmerston, see (524), (577) and (583); for his correspondence, see (380).

799 Weisser, Henry. *British working-class movements and Europe, 1815–48.* Manchester, 1975.

4. Biographies

800 Balfour, Frances. *The life of George, fourth Earl of Aberdeen.* 1923, 2 vols.

801 Lacour-Gayet, Georges. *Talleyrand, 1754–1838.* Paris, 1928–34, 4 vols; reprinted, Paris, 1946–7, 3 vols. Useful for several episodes in British diplomacy.

802 Lester, Malcolm. *Anthony Merry redivivus: a reappraisal of the British minister to the United States, 1803–6.* Charlottesville, Va, 1978.

803 Minto, Emma Eleanor Elizabeth Elliot-Murray-Kynynmond, Countess of. *A memoir of the Right Honourable Hugh Elliot*. Edinburgh, 1868. Includes letters 1762–1811, many of them concerning his diplomatic missions.

804 Robbins, Helen Henrietta (Macartney). *Our first ambassador to China: an account of the life of George, Earl of Macartney*. 1908. Includes letters 1764–1802.

805 Srbik, Heinrich, Ritter von. *Metternich: der Staatsman und der Mensch*. Munich, 1925–6, 2 vols; reprinted, Munich, 1954–7, 2 vols. Standard.

5. Articles

806 Anderson, Matthew Smith. 'Eighteenth-century theories of the balance of power', in Ragnhild Hatton and Matthew Smith Anderson (eds.), *Studies in diplomatic history: essays in memory of David Bayne Horn*. 1970, pp. 183–99.

807 —— 'Great Britain and the Barbary States in the eighteenth century', *BIHR*, 29 (1956), 87–107.

808 —— 'Great Britain and the Russo-Turkish War of 1768–74', *EHR*, 69 (1954), 39–58.

809 Blanning, T. C. W. '"That horrid electorate" or "Ma patrie germanique"? George III, Hanover, and the Fürstenbund of 1785', *HJ*, 20 (1977), 311–44.

810 Bolton, Geoffrey Curgenven and B. E. Kennedy. 'William Eden and the Treaty of Mauritius, 1786–7', *HJ*, 16 (1973), 681–96.

811 Brown, Vera Lee. 'Anglo-Spanish relations in America in the closing years of the colonial era', *Hispanic–American Historical Review*, 5 (1922), 325–483.

812 Bullen, Roger. 'Party politics and foreign policy: Whigs, Tories and Iberian affairs, 1830–6', *BIHR*, 51 (1978), 37–59.

813 Carrillo, Elisa A. 'The Corsican Kingdom of George III', *JMH*, 34 (1962), 254–74.

814 Cobban, Alfred Bert Carter. 'The beginnings of the Channel Isles correspondence, 1789–1794', *EHR*, 77 (1962), 38–52. Relations with the French royalists.

815 —— 'British secret service in France, 1784–1792', *EHR*, 69 (1954), 226–61.

816 Donaghay, Marie. 'The Maréchal de Castries and the Anglo-French commercial negotiations of 1786–1787', *HJ*, 22 (1979), 295–312. See also (822).

817 Dorn, Walter L. 'Frederick the Great and Lord Bute', *JMH*, 1 (1929), 529–60. See also (840) and (842).

818 Evans, Howard V. 'The Nootka Sound controversy in Anglo-French diplomacy – 1790', *JMH*, 46 (1974), 609–40. Based on newly discovered documents.

819 —— 'William Pitt, William Miles and the French Revolution', *BIHR*, 43 (1970), 190–213.

820 Feldbaek, Ole. 'The Anglo-Russian rapprochement of 1801: a prelude to the Peace of Amiens', *Scandinavian Journal of History*, 3 (1978), 205–27.

821 Goebel, Dorothy Burne. 'British trade to the Spanish colonies, 1796–1823', *AHR*, 43 (1937–8), 288–320.

822 Henderson, William Otto. 'The Anglo-French Commercial Treaty of 1786', *EcHR* 2nd ser., 10 (1957–8), 104–12. See also (816).

823 Humphreys, Robert Arthur. 'Anglo-American rivalries and Spanish-American emancipation', *TRHS* 5th ser., 16 (1966), 131–56. See also (777).

824 Huttenback, Robert A. 'The French threat to India and British relations with Sind, 1799–1809', *EHR*, 76 (1961), 590–99.

825 Ingram, Edward. 'An aspiring buffer state: Anglo-Persian relations in the Third Coalition, 1804–1807', *HJ*, 16 (1973), 509–33.

826 —— 'From trade to empire in the Near East': I: 'The end of the spectre of the overland trade, 1775–1801'; II: 'The repercussions of the incident at Nakhilu in 1803'; III: 'The uses of the residency at Baghdad, 1794–1804', *Middle Eastern Studies*, 14 (1978), 3–21, 182–204, 278–306.

827 —— 'A preview of the Great Game in Asia': I: 'The British occupation of Perim and Aden in 1799'; II: 'The proposal of an alliance with Afghanistan, 1798–1800'; III: 'The origins of the British expedition to Egypt in 1801'; IV: 'British agents in the Near East in the War of the Second Coalition, 1798–1801', *Middle Eastern Studies*, 9 (1973), 3–18, 157–74, 296–314; 10 (1974), 15–35.

828 —— 'The rules of the game: a commentary on the defence of British India, 1798–1829', *Journal of Imperial and Commonwealth History*, 3 (1975), 257–79.

829 Jupp, Peter James. 'The aims and achievements of Lord Grenville', in John Bossy

and Peter James Jupp (eds.), *Essays presented to Michael Roberts*. Belfast, 1976, pp. 93–103.

830 Lynch, John. 'British policy and Spanish America, 1783–1808', *Journal of Latin American Studies*, 1 (1969), 1–30.

831 Mackay, David L. 'Direction and purpose in British imperial policy, 1783–1801', *HJ*, 17 (1974), 487–501.

832 Macmillan, David Sterling. 'Russo-British trade relations under Alexander I', *Canadian–American Slavic Studies*, 9 (1975), 437–48.

833 Marshall, Peter James. 'British expansion in India in the eighteenth century: a historical revision', *History* NS, 60 (1975), 28–43.

834 Mooney, Gary. 'British diplomatic relations with the Holy See, 1793–1830', *Recusant History*, 14 (1978), 193–210.

835 Reddaway, William Fiddian. 'Great Britain and Poland, 1762–72', *Cambridge Historical Journal*, 4 (1932–4), 223–62.

836 —— 'Macartney in Russia, 1765–67', *Cambridge Historical Journal*, 3 (1929–31), 260–94.

837 Roberts, Michael. 'Great Britain, Denmark and Russia, 1763–1770', in Ragnhild Hatton and Matthew Smith Anderson (eds.), *Studies in diplomatic history: essays in memory of David Bayne Horn*. 1970, pp. 236–67.

838 —— 'Macartney in Russia', *EHR*, Supplement 7, 1974.

839 Rodkey, Frederick Stanley. 'Lord Palmerston and the rejuvenation of Turkey, 1830–41', *JMH*, 1 (1929), 570–93; 2 (1930), 193–225.

840 Schweizer, Karl W. 'Lord Bute, Newcastle, Prussia and the Hague overtures: a re-examination', *Albion*, 9 (1977), 72–97. See also (817) and (842).

841 Scott, H. M. 'Great Britain, Poland, and the Russian alliance, 1763–1767', *HJ*, 19 (1976), 53–74.

842 Spencer, Frank. 'The Anglo-Prussian breach of 1762: an historical revision', *History* NS, 41 (1956), 100–12. See also (817) and (840).

843 Tracy, Nicholas. 'The administration of the Duke of Grafton and the French invasion of Corsica', *ECS*, 8 (1974–5), 169–82.

844 —— 'The Falkland Islands crisis of 1770: use of naval force', *EHR*, 90 (1975), 40–75.

845 —— 'The gunboat diplomacy of the government of George Grenville, 1764–1765: the Honduras, Turks Island and Gambian incidents', *HJ*, 17 (1974), 711–31.

846 —— 'Parry of a threat to India, 1768–1774', *Mariner's Mirror*, 59 (1973), 35–48.

847 Wright, Harold Richard Charles. 'The Anglo-Dutch dispute in the East, 1814–1824', *EcHR* 2nd ser., 3 (1950–1), 229–39.

VII. SOCIAL HISTORY

For specialized bibliographies, lists and catalogues, see (7), (14), (18), (20), (25), (27), (29), (33), (39), (41), (98), (100), (115), (131) and (138). Studies of rural society are listed in Section IX, those concentrating on the social impact of religion in Section XII. For the legal profession, see also (286), (341), (342) and (356); and for the scientific and medical professions, see (1574), (1575), (1609), (1618), (1635), (1693), (1710) and (1732).

1. Printed sources

848 Anstey, Roger T. and P. E. H. Hair (eds.). *Liverpool, the African slave trade and abolition*. Liverpool, 1976. Documents.

849 Aspinall, Arthur (ed.). *The early English trade unions*. 1949. Important collection of documents from the Home Office papers for 1792–1825.

850 Checkland, Sydney George and E. O. A. Checkland (eds.). *The Poor Law Report of 1834*. Harmondsworth, Middx, 1974.

851 Coats, Alfred William (ed.). *Poverty in the Victorian age*. Farnborough, Hants., 1973, 4 vols. Reprints of articles on the subject from the reviews from the beginning of the nineteenth century.

852 Colquhoun, Patrick. *A treatise on the police of the metropolis, explaining the various crimes and*

misdemeanors which at present are felt as a pressure upon the community; and suggesting remedies for their prevention. 1796; 6th edn, corr. and enlarged, 1800; 7th edn, 1806. Classic study.

853 Donnan, Elizabeth (ed.). *Documents illustrative of the history of the slave trade to America.* Washington, DC, 1930–5, 4 vols.; reissued, New York, 1965.

854 Eden, Sir Frederick Morton. *Observations on friendly societies, for the maintenance of the industrious classes during sickness, infirmity, old age and other exigencies.* 1801. Describes their working in the 1790s, earlier than the general studies of them.

855 —— *The state of the poor.* 1797; abridged edn by A. G. L. Rogers, 1929; facsimile of the 1797 edn, 1966. Important source on social conditions.

856 Field, John (ed.). *Correspondence of John Howard the philanthropist, not before published.* 1855.

857 Glass, David Victor (ed.). *The development of population statistics: a collective reprint of materials concerning the history of census taking and vital registration in England and Wales.* Farnborough, Hants., 1973.

858 ——(ed.). *The population controversy: a collective reprint of material concerning the eighteenth-century controversy on the trend of population in England and Wales.* Farnborough, Hants., 1973.

859 Heath, James (ed.). *Eighteenth-century penal theory.* 1963. Extracts from the works of penal reformers.

860 Kay, James Phillips, afterwards Kay-Shuttleworth. *The moral and physical condition of the working classes employed in the cotton manufacture in Manchester.* 1832; 2nd edn, enlarged, 1832; reprinted, Manchester, 1969. Important contemporary account by a Benthamite reformer.

861 Meyer, J. P. and André Jourdan (eds.). [*Alexis de Tocqueville's*] *Journeys to England and Ireland.* Trans. George Lawrence and K. F. Meyer. 1958. Trips of 1833 and 1835.

862 Pottle, Frederick A., et al. (eds.). *The Yale edition of the private papers of James Boswell.* New York, 1950–. Twelve volumes of the 'trade edition' so far published, beginning with the *London Journal 1762–1763* and extending to 1785; each contains a selection of the best material for the period covered. The 'research' edition is less advanced, but three volumes of Boswell's correspondence have so far been published.

863 Ratcliffe, Barrie M. and William Henry Chaloner (eds. and trans.). *A French sociologist looks at Britain: Gustave d'Eichthal and British society in 1828.* Manchester, 1977. Notes on England by a Comtian.

864 Rose, Michael E. (ed.). *The English Poor Law, 1780–1930.* Newton Abbot, Devon, 1971. Documents.

865 Salmon, David (ed.). *The practical parts of Lancaster's 'Improvement' and Bell's 'Experiment'.* Cambridge, 1932.

866 Silver, Harold (ed.). *Robert Owen on education: selections edited with an introduction and notes.* 1969. Contains most of *A new view of society.*

867 Spencer, Alfred (ed.). *Memoirs of William Hickey, 1749–1809.* 1913–25, 4 vols; a condensed edn by Peter Quennell as *The prodigal rake.* 1960.

868 Thale, Mary (ed.). *Autobiography of Francis Place, 1771–1854.* Cambridge, 1972. Mostly concerned with his early life; important for working-class conditions in late eighteenth century London.

869 Thomis, Malcolm Ian (ed.). *Luddism in Nottinghamshire.* (Thoroton Society Record Series, 26.) 1972. Documents from the Home Office Papers.

870 Walvin, James (ed.). *The black presence: a documentary history of the negro in England, 1555–1860.* 1971.

871 Ward, John Towers (ed.). *The age of change, 1770–1870: documents in social history.* 1975.

See also (401), Horace Walpole's correspondence, for another major source for social history.

2. Surveys

872 Arkell, Vincent Thomas John. *Britain transformed: the development of British society since the mid-eighteenth century.* Harmondsworth, Middx, 1973.

873 Beer, Max. *A history of British socialism.* 1919–20, 2 vols.; 2nd edn, 1940; reprinted, 1953, 2 vols.

874 Burnett, John. *A history of the cost of living*. Harmondsworth, Middx, 1969. Good general social and economic history of England.

875 Clarke, John. *Price of progress: Cobbett's England 1780–1835*. St Albans, Herts., 1977. General social history.

876 Cole, George Douglas Howard. *A short history of the British working class movement*. 1925–7, 3 vols; new edn, 1948, 1 vol.

877 Emsley, Clive. *British society and the French wars, 1793–1815*. 1979.

878 George, Mary Dorothy. *England in transition*. 1931; reprinted, Harmondsworth, Middx, 1953.

879 —— *Hogarth to Cruikshank: social change in graphic satire*. 1967. Splendid illustrations with excellent narrative.

880 Laslett, Peter. *The world we have lost*. 2nd edn, 1971. Introduction to one of the new approaches to social history.

881 Marshall, Dorothy. *English people in the eighteenth century*. 1956.

882 Osborne, John Walter. *The silent revolution: the industrial revolution as a source of cultural change*. New York, 1970.

883 Perkin, Harold James. *The origins of modern English society, 1780–1880*. 1969. Best 'modern' social history.

884 Quinlan, Maurice James. *Victorian prelude: a history of English manners, 1700–1830*. New York, 1941; reprinted, 1965.

885 Taylor, Arthur John (ed.). *The standard of living in Britain in the industrial revolution*. 1975. Reprinted essays by various scholars with a long, helpful introduction.

886 Thomis, Malcolm Ian. *Responses to industrialization: the British experience 1780–1850*. Newton Abbot, Devon, 1976. Vigorous restatement of the 'optimistic' interpretation in reply to the new 'pessimists'.

887 Williams, Raymond. *The long revolution*. 1961. The development of mass culture.

888 Wrigley, Edward Anthony (ed.). *Nineteenth-century society: essays in the use of quantitative methods for the study of social data*. Cambridge, 1972. Most useful guide to the newer methodologies.

3. Monographs

889 Alexander, David. *Retailing in England during the industrial revolution*. 1970.

890 Altick, Richard Daniel. *The English common reader: a social history of the mass reading public, 1800–1900*. Chicago, Ill., 1957.

891 —— *The shows of London*. 1978. Popular exhibitions and the like.

892 Anstey, Roger T. *The Atlantic slave trade and British abolition, 1760–1810*. 1975.

893 Armytage, Walter Harry Green. *Four hundred years of English education*. Cambridge, 1964; 2nd edn, Cambridge, 1970. Best survey.

894 Barker, Theodore Cardwell and John Raymond Harris. *A Merseyside town in the industrial revolution: St Helens 1750–1900*. Liverpool, 1954; reprinted, with corrections, 1959.

895 Barker, Theodore Cardwell, et al. (eds.). *Our changing fare: two hundred years of British food habits*. 1966. See also (899) and (915).

896 Bell, Colin John and Rose Bell. *City fathers: the early history of town planning in Britain*. 1969.

897 Brundage, Anthony. *The making of the new Poor Law: the politics of inquiry, enactment and implementation, 1832–39*. New Brunswick, NJ, 1978.

898 Buer, Mabel Craven. *Health, wealth, and population in the early days of the industrial revolution*. 1926. Study of public health.

899 Burnett, John. *Plenty and want: a social history of diet in England from 1815 to the present day*. 1966; rev. edn, 1979. See also (895) and (915).

900 —— *A social history of housing, 1815–1970*. Newton Abbot, Devon, 1978. Ordinary housing for the working and middle classes.

901 Chalkin, C. W. *The provincial towns of Georgian England: a study of the building process, 1740–1820*. Montreal, 1974.

902 Chambers, Jonathan David. *Nottinghamshire in the eighteenth century: a study of life and labour under the squirarchy*. 1932; 2nd edn, 1966.

903 Chandler, George. *Liverpool*. 1957. Best recent history; full bibliography.

904 Collier, Francis. *The family economy of the working classes in the cotton industry, 1784–1833*. Manchester, 1964.

905 Connell, Kenneth Hugh. *The population of Ireland, 1750–1845.* Oxford, 1950. Frequently criticized on specific points, but the most useful general account.

906 Cowherd, Raymond Gibson. *The humanitarians and the ten hour movement in England.* Boston, Mass., 1956.

907 —— *Political economists and the English Poor Laws: a historical study of the influence of classical economics on the formation of social welfare policy.* Athens, Ohio, 1977. Period 1785–1834.

908 Cunnington, Cecil Willett and Phillis Cunnington. *Handbook of English costume in the eighteenth century.* 1957. *Handbook of English costume in the nineteenth century.* 1959; 3rd edn, 1970. Most useful books on the subject.

909 Curtin, Philip D. *The Atlantic slave trade: a census.* Madison, Wis., 1969.

910 Curtis, Stanley James. *History of education in Great Britain.* 1948; 7th edn, 1967. Standard, with useful bibliographies.

911 Darton, Frederick Joseph Harvey. *Children's books in England: five centuries of social life.* Cambridge, 1932; 2nd edn, Cambridge, 1958.

912 Darvall, Frank Ongley. *Popular disturbances and public order in Regency England: being an account of the Luddite and other disorders in England during ... 1811–1817, and of the attitude and activity of the authorities.* 1934; reprinted, 1969.

913 Davis, David Brion. *The problem of slavery in the age of revolution, 1770–1823.* Ithaca, NY, 1975.

914 Drescher, Seymour. *Econoside: British slavery in the era of abolition.* Pittsburg, Pa, 1977. Vigorous reassertion of older view that the principal motive for abolition was humanitarian.

915 Drummond, Sir Jack Cecil and Anne Wilbraham. *The Englishman's food: a history of five centuries of English diet.* 1939; reprinted, 1958. Best general history; see also (895) and (899) for more recent periods.

916 Dyos, Harold James (ed.). *The study of urban history.* 1968. Useful introduction to modern approaches to the subject.

917 Emmison, Frederick George. *The relief of the poor at Eaton Socon, 1706–1834.* (Bedfordshire Historical Records Society, 15.) Apsley Guise, Beds., 1933. Model local study.

918 Endelman, Todd M. *The Jews of Georgian England, 1714–1830: tradition and change in a liberal society.* Philadelphia, Pa, 1979. See also (1973).

919 Flinn, Michael Walter. *British population growth 1700–1850.* 1970. Best brief general treatment.

920 Foster, John. *Class struggle and the industrial revolution: early industrial capitalism in three English towns.* With foreword by Eric John Ernest Hobsbawm. 1974. Study of Oldham, South Shields and Northampton; Marxist. Important criticism by Gareth Stedman Jones in *New Left Review*, 90 (1975), 35–69, reprinted in *Languages of class.* Cambridge, 1983, pp. 25–75; and by Albert Edward Musson in *Social History*, 1 (1976), 335–56, with a reply by Foster, *ibid.*, pp. 357–66. See also (1058) and (1099).

921 Garnett, Ronald George. *Co-operation and the Owenite socialist communities in Britain, 1825–45.* Manchester, 1972.

922 George, Mary Dorothy. *London life in the XVIIIth century.* 1925; 2nd edn, 1930; reprinted, New York, 1964.

923 Gill, Conrad, et al. *History of Birmingham.* 1952–74, 3 vols. Vol. 1: *Manor and borough to 1865* is by Gill.

924 Glass, David Victor. *Numbering the people: the eighteenth-century population controversy and the development of census and vital statistics in Britain.* Farnborough, Hants., 1973.

925 Glass, David Victor and David Edward Charles Eversley (eds.). *Population in history: essays in historical demography.* 1965. Collection of important essays by various hands, ten of them concerned with England in this period.

926 Hammond, John Lawrence LeBreton and Lucy Barbara Hammond. *The skilled labourer, 1760–1830.* 1919; reprinted, New York, 1967.

927 —— *The town labourer: the new civilization, 1760–1832.* 1917; the text of the 1925 edition reprinted with an introduction and substantial bibliography by John C. Lovell, 1978. Compare (1010).

928 —— *The village labourer, 1760–1832: a study in the government of England before the Reform Bill.* 1911; 4th edn, 1927; reprinted with an introduction and substantial

bibliography by Gordon Edmund Mingay, 1948, 2 vols.; another reprint, New York, 1967.

929 Hampson, Ethel Mary. *The treatment of poverty in Cambridgeshire, 1597–1834.* Cambridge, 1934. Model county study.

930 Hay, Douglas, et al. *Albion's fatal tree: crime and society in eighteenth-century England.* 1975.

931 Hecht, Joseph Jean. *The domestic servant class in eighteenth-century England.* 1956.

932 Henriques, Ursula Ruth Quixano. *Before the welfare state: social administration in early industrial Britain.* 1979.

933 Hindle, G. B. *Provision for the relief of the poor in Manchester, 1754–1826.* Manchester, 1975.

934 Hobsbawm, Eric John Ernest. *Labouring men: studies in the history of labour.* 1964. Collected essays, principally on working classes and the 'standard of living' controversy.

935 Hobsbawm, Eric John Ernest and George Frederick Elliot Rudé. *Captain Swing.* 1969; new edn, 1973. Agrarian disturbances of 1830.

936 Hollingsworth, Thomas Henry. *The demography of the British peerage.* (Supplement to *Population Studies,* 18.) 1964.

937 Hughes, Edward. *North country life in the eighteenth century.* 1952–65, 2 vols.

938 Hurt, John S. *Education in evolution: church, state, society and popular education, 1800–1870.* 1971.

939 Ignatieff, Michael. *A just measure of pain: penitentiaries in the industrial revolution 1750–1850.* New York, 1978.

940 Inglis, Brian. *Poverty and the industrial revolution.* 1971. American title: *Men of conscience;* most comprehensive study, but based upon published material only.

941 Jackson, Gordon. *Hull in the eighteenth century: a study in economic and social history.* 1971.

942 Johnson, Stanley Currie. *A history of emigration from the United Kingdom to North America, 1763–1912.* 1913.

943 Johnson, William Branch. *The English prison hulks.* 1957; rev. edn, Chichester, Sussex, 1976.

944 Johnston, Hugh James Morton. *British emigration policy, 1815–1830: 'Shovelling out the paupers'.* Oxford, 1972.

945 Jones, David John Victor. *Before Rebecca: popular protests in Wales, 1793–1835.* 1973.

946 Jones, J. P. *Gambling yesterday and today: a complete history.* Newton Abbot, Devon, 1973.

947 Jones, Kathleen. *Lunacy, law and conscience, 1744–1845: the social history of the care of the insane.* 1955.

948 Jones, Louis Clark. *The clubs of the Georgian rakes.* New York, 1942. Not always reliable, but the most comprehensive account.

949 Jones, Mary Gwladys. *The charity school movement: a study of eighteenth-century puritanism in action.* Cambridge, 1938; reprinted, Hamden, Conn., 1964.

950 Laqueur, Thomas W. *Religion and respectability: Sunday schools and working-class culture 1780–1850.* New Haven, Conn., 1976.

951 Laslett, Peter. *Family life and illicit love in earlier generations: eassays in historical sociology.* Cambridge, 1977. Mainly a statistical study of the incidence of bastardy.

952 —— (ed.). *Household and family in past time: comparative studies in the size and structure of the domestic group over the last three centuries in England, France ....* Cambridge, 1972.

953 Logue, Kenneth J. *Popular disturbances in Scotland 1780–1815.* Edinburgh, 1979.

954 Longrigg, Robert. *The English squire and his sport.* 1977.

955 Maccoby, Simon. *English radicalism.* 1935–61, 6 vols. Vol. 1: *1763–1785: the origins;* Vol. 2: *1786–1832: from Paine to Cobbett.*

956 McCord, Norman. *North-east England: an economic and social history.* 1979.

957 McGrath, Patrick (ed.). *Bristol in the eighteenth century.* Newton Abbot, Devon, 1972. Reprint of eight pamphlets previously published by the Bristol Branch of the Historical Association.

958 Mack, Edward Clarence. *Public schools and British opinion, 1780–1860: the relationship between contemporary ideas and the evaluation of an English institution.* New York, 1941.

959 McKeown, Thomas. *The modern rise of population.* 1976. General, with emphasis on England; stress on improvements in nutrition and health from the eighteenth century.

960 McLachlan, Herbert. *English education under the Test Acts: being the history of the nonconformist academies, 1662–1820.* Manchester, 1931.

961 Malcolmson, Robert William. *Popular recreations in English society, 1700–1850.* Cambridge, 1973. Excellent social history.

962 Malmgreen, G. *Neither bread nor roses: utopian feminism and the English working-class, 1800–50.* Brighton, Sussex, 1978.

963 Marshall, Dorothy. *The English poor in the eighteenth century: a study in social and administrative history.* 1926; reprinted, New York, 1969.

964 Maxwell, Constantia Elizabeth. *Dublin under the Georges 1714–1830.* 1947; rev. edn, 1956.

965 Mead, William Edward. *The grand tour in the eighteenth century.* Boston, Mass. and New York, 1914.

966 Merewether, Henry Alworth and Archibald John Stephens. *The history of the boroughs and municipal corporations of the United Kingdom from the earliest to the present time.* 1835, 3 vols.; new edn, ed. Geoffrey Haward Martin, Brighton, Sussex, 1973. Much miscellaneous information on the towns.

967 Mingay, Gordon Edmund. *The gentry: the rise and fall of a ruling class.* 1976. Excellent general account.

968 Moir, Esther Aline Lowndes. *The discovery of Britain: the English tourists, 1540 to 1840.* 1964. Useful bibliography of tours.

969 Money, John. *Experience and identity: Birmingham and the West Midlands, 1760–1800.* Manchester, 1977.

970 Morris, R. J. *Class and class-consciousness in the industrial revolution.* 1979. Brief but well-balanced between the extremes of the debate on the subject, for which see (920), (1058) and (1099).

971 Musson, Albert Edward. *British trade unions, 1800–75.* 1972. Collected articles.

972 Nicolson, C. *Strangers to England: immigration to England, 1100–1952.* 1974.

973 Norton, Mary Beth. *The British–Americans: the loyalist exiles in England 1774–1789.* 1974.

974 O'Dea, William Thomas. *The social history of lighting.* 1958.

975 Olsen, Donald James. *The growth of Victorian London.* 1976. From c. 1800; emphasis on the social and cultural aspects.

976 —— *Town planning in London: the eighteenth and nineteenth centuries.* New Haven, Conn., 1964. Principally concerns the Bedford and Foundling Hospital estates.

977 Onslow, R. *The heath and the turf: a history of Newmarket.* 1971.

978 Owen, David Edward. *English philanthropy, 1660–1960.* Cambridge, Mass., 1964.

979 Pinchbeck, Ivy. *Women workers and the industrial revolution, 1750–1850.* 1930; reprinted, 1977.

980 Pinchbeck, Ivy and Margaret Hewitt. *Children in English society.* 1969–73, 2 vols.

981 Plumb, John Harold. *The commercialization of leisure in eighteenth-century England.* Reading, Berks., 1973. A lecture.

982 Pons, Jacques. *L'Education en Angleterre entre 1750 et 1800: aperçu sur l'influence pédagogique de J. J. Rousseau en Angleterre.* Paris, 1919.

983 Porteus, John Douglas. *Canal ports: the urban achievement of the canal age.* 1977.

984 Poynter, Frederick Noël Lawrence (ed.). *The evolution of hospitals in Britain.* 1961. Contains a useful bibliography of hospitals compiled by E. Gaskell.

985 Rasmussen, Steen Eiler. *London, the unique city.* 1934; rev. edn, 1937; condensed edn, Harmondsworth, Middx, 1960. Classic account of the building of London.

986 Redford, Arthur. *Labour migration in England, 1800–50.* 1926; 2nd edn, rev. by William Henry Chaloner, 1964; 3rd edn, rev. by Chaloner, 1976.

987 Reith, Charles. *The police idea: its history and evolution in England in the eighteenth century and after.* 1938. *British police and the democratic ideal.* Oxford, 1943. Covers period 1829–40.

988 Ribton-Turner, Charles James. *A history of vagrants and vagrancy, and beggars and begging.* 1887; reprinted, 1972. Classic.

989 Robson, Lloyd L. *The convict settlers of Australia: an inquiry into the origins and character of the convicts transported to New South Wales and Van Diemen's Land, 1787–1852.* Carleton, Victoria, 1965. Study of the English backgrounds of a five per cent sample of the convicts.

990 Rodgers, Betsey (Aiken-Sneath). *Cloak of charity: studies in eighteenth-century philanthropy.* 1950.

991 Rudé, George Frederick Elliot. *The crowd in history: a study in popular disturbances in France and England 1730–1848*. 1964.

992 —— *Hanoverian London 1714–1808*. 1971. Best recent study of the city for this period. Continued in (996).

993 —— *Paris and London in the eighteenth century: studies in popular protest*. 1970. Collected essays, including most of his studies of English 'mobs'.

994 Salaman, Redcliffe Nathan. *The history and social influence of the potato*. Cambridge, 1949.

995 Shelton, Walter J. *English hunger and industrial disorders; a study of social conflict during the first decade of George III's reign*. 1973.

996 Sheppard, Francis Henry Wollaston. *London, 1808–1870: the infernal wen*. 1971. Companion volume to (992).

997 Shyllon, Folarin O. *Black people in Britain, 1555–1833*. 1977.

998 —— *Black slaves in Britain*. Oxford, 1974. Impassioned but closely reasoned criticism of Mansfield's decision in the Somerset Case and its significance. Compare (1109).

999 Silver, Harold. *The concept of popular education: a study of ideas and social movements in the early nineteenth century*. 1965. Extensive use of the Robert Owen papers.

1000 Simmons, Jack. *Leicester past and present*. 1974, 2 vols. Vol. 1 to 1860.

1001 Simon, Brian. *Studies in the history of education, 1780–1870*. 1960. Good study of the growth of elementary and middle-class education.

1002 Simpson, M. A. and T. H. Lloyd (eds.). *Middle-class housing in Britain*. Newton Abbot, Devon, 1977. Essays 1750–1914.

1003 Smelser, Neil Joseph. *Social change in the industrial revolution: an application of theory to the Lancashire cotton industry, 1770–1840*. 1959. Pioneering study.

1004 Smith, Joe William Ashley. *The birth of modern education: the contribution of the dissenting academies 1660–1800*. 1954.

1005 Smith, Warren Hunting (ed.). *Horace Walpole: writer, politician and connoisseur*. New Haven, Conn., 1967. Essays on many sides of Walpole's interests and activities.

1006 Stevenson, John. *Popular disturbances in England, 1700–1870*. 1979.

1007 Stevenson, John and Roland Quinault (eds.). *Popular protest and public order: six studies in British history, 1790–1920*. 1974.

1008 Stone, Lawrence Joseph. *The family, sex and marriage in England, 1500–1800*. 1977. See also (1018).

1009 Thomis, Malcolm Ian. *The Luddites: machine-breaking in Regency England*. Newton Abbot, Devon, 1970. Refuting interpretation in (1011).

1010 —— *The town labourer and the industrial revolution*. 1974. Vigorous dissent from (927).

1011 Thompson, Edward Palmer. *The making of the English working class*. 1963; new edn, Harmondsworth, Middx, 1968. For criticism see (1057).

1012 Thompson, Francis Michael Longstreth. *Hampstead: building a borough 1650–1964*. 1974. Outstanding local study.

1013 Thompson, William Harry. *History of Manchester to 1852*. Manchester, 1967. Only recent general history of the city.

1014 Tobias, John Jacob. *Crime and police in England 1700–1900*. 1979.

1015 Tranter, N. L. *Population since the industrial revolution: the case of England and Wales*. 1973. Good, comprehensive account from 1690s to 1930s.

1016 Trease, Geoffrey. *The grand tour*. 1967.

1017 Trudgill, Eric. *Madonnas and magdalens: the origins and development of Victorian sexual attitudes*. New York, 1976. Goes back to mid-eighteenth century.

1018 Trumbach, Randolph. *The rise of the egalitarian family: aristocratic kinship and domestic relations in eighteenth-century England*. New York, 1978. Independently reaches conclusions similar to those of (1008).

1019 Turner, Barry. *Equality for some: the story of girls' education*. 1974.

1020 Walton, Mary. *Sheffield: its story and its achievements*. 3rd edn, Sheffield, 1952. Best general history.

1021 Walvin, James. *Black and white: the negro and English society, 1555–1945*. 1973.

1022 Wells, Roger A. E. *Dearth and distress in Yorkshire, 1793–1802*. (Bothwick Papers, 52.) York, 1977.

1023 White, Cynthia L. *Women's magazines 1693–1968*. 1970.

1024 Whiting, John Roger Scott. *Prison reform in Gloucestershire, 1776–1820: a study of the work of Sir George Onesiphorus Paul, Bart*. 1975. Important local study.

1025 Williams, Eric. *Capitalism and slavery*. Chapel Hill, NC, 1944. Classic statement of the thesis that slavery was abolished only when and because it had ceased to be profitable.

1026 Williams, Gwyn Alfred. *Artisans and sans-culottes: popular movements in France and Britain during the French Revolution.* 1968.

1027 Wrigley, Edward Anthony, et al. (eds.). *An introduction to English historical demography: from the sixteenth to the nineteenth century.* 1966. Also important for methodology.

1028 Wroth, Warwick. *The London pleasure gardens of the eighteenth century.* 1896; reprinted, Hamden, Conn., 1979.

1029 Wroughton, John (ed.). *Bath in the age of reform (1830–1841).* Bath, 1972. Essays by various hands.

4. Biographies

1030 Bamford, Thomas William. *Thomas Arnold.* 1960.

1031 Checkland, Sydney George. *The Gladstones, a family biography 1764–1851.* Cambridge, 1971.

1032 Griggs, Earl Leslie. *Thomas Clarkson, the friend of slaves.* 1936.

1033 Highfill, Philip H., Jr, et al. (comps.). *A biographical dictionary of actors, actresses, musicians, dancers, managers, and other stage personnel in London 1660–1800.* Carbondale, Ill., 1973–. Six volumes so far published to the end of 'G'.

1034 Howard, Derek C. *John Howard: prison reformer.* New York, 1958. See also (1044) and (1077).

1035 Hutchins, John Harold. *Jonas Hanway, 1712–1786.* New York, 1940.

1036 Kent, John Henry Somerset. *Elizabeth Fry.* 1962.

1037 Ketton-Cremer, Robert Wyndham. *Horace Walpole: a biography.* 1940; 3rd edn, 1964. See also (1005); for Walpole's correspondence, see (401); for his memoirs, see (419).

1038 Knight, Freda. *The strange case of Thomas Walker: ten years in the life of a Manchester radical.* 1957.

1039 Oman, Carola Mary Anima. *David Garrick.* 1958.

1040 Pankhurst, Richard Keir Pethick. *William Thompson, 1775–1833: Britain's pioneer socialist, feminist, and co-operator.* 1954.

1041 Pottle, Frederick A. *James Boswell: the earlier years, 1740–1769.* New York, 1972.

1042 Rodgers, Betsey (Aiken-Sneath). *Georgian chronicle: Mrs Barbauld and her family.* 1958. Includes appendix of letters 1779–1850.

1043 Shyllon, Folarin O. *James Ramsay: the unknown abolitionist.* Edinburgh, 1977.

1044 Southwood, Martin. *John Howard, prison reformer: an account of his life and travels.* 1958. See also (1034) and (1077).

1045 Wallas, Graham. *The life of Francis Place, 1771–1854.* 1918; 5th edn, 1951. See also (1102).

5. Articles

1046 Armstrong, W. A. 'La Population de l'Angleterre et du Pays de Galles (1789–1815)', *Annales de Démographie Historique (Etudes et Chronique)*, [2] (1965), 135–89. Very substantial article.

1047 Ashton, Thomas Southcliffe. 'Changes in standards of comfort in eighteenth-century England', *Proceedings of the British Academy*, 41 (1955), 171–87.

1048 —— 'The standard of life of the workers in England, 1790–1835', *JEcH*, Supplement 9 (1949); reprinted in Arthur John Taylor (ed.), *The standard of living in Britain in the industrial revolution.* 1975, pp. 36–57.

1049 Beattie, J. M. 'The criminality of women in eighteenth-century England', *Journal of Social History*, 8 (1975), 80–116.

1050 —— 'The pattern of crime in England 1660–1800', *PP*, 62 (1974), 47–95.

1051 Blaug, Mark. 'The Poor Law Report re-examined', *JEcH*, 24 (1964), 229–45. Defence of the Old Poor Law.

1052 Briggs, Asa. 'The language of "class" in early nineteenth-century England', in Asa Briggs and John Saville (eds.), *Essays in labour history.* 1960, pp. 43–73.

1053 —— 'The language of "mass" and "masses" in nineteenth-century England', in David E. Martin and David Rubenstein (eds.), *Ideology and the labour movement: essays presented to John Saville.* 1979, pp. 62–83.

1054 Crafts, N. F. R. 'Eighteenth-century local population studies in the context of aggregate estimates for England and Wales', *Local Population Studies*, 13 (Autumn 1974), 19–29.

1055 Cullen, M. J. 'The making of the Civil Registration Act of 1836', *Journal of Ecclesiastical History*, 25 (1974), 39–59. Registration of vital statistics.

1056 Daunton, M. J. 'Towns and economic growth in eighteenth-century England', in Philip Abrams and Edward Anthony Wrigley (eds.), *Towns in society: essays in economic history and historical sociology*. Cambridge, 1978, pp. 245–77.

1057 Donnelly, F. K. 'Ideology and early English working-class history: Edward Thompson and his critics', *Social History*, 2 (1976), 219–38. See (1011).

1058 Gadian, D. S. 'Class consciousness in Oldham and other north-west industrial towns 1830–1850', *HJ*, 21 (1978), 161–72. Very critical of (920); stresses 'class cooperation' rather than 'class war'. See also (920) and (1099).

1059 Gash, Norman. 'After Waterloo: British society and the legacy of the Napoleonic wars', *TRHS* 5th ser., 28 (1978), 145–57.

1060 Gilboy, Elizabeth Waterman. 'The cost of living and real wages in eighteenth-century England', *Review of Economic Statistics*, 18 (1936), 134–43; reprinted in Arthur John Taylor (ed.), *The standard of living in Britain in the industrial revolution*. 1975, pp. 1–20.

1061 Habakkuk, Sir John. 'England', in Albert Goodwin (ed), *The European nobility in the eighteenth century*. 1953, pp. 1–21. Excellent brief introduction to the landed classes.

1062 —— 'Marriage settlements in the eighteenth century', *TRHS* 4th ser., 32 (1950), 15–30.

1063 Hartwell, Ronald Maxwell. 'The rising standard of living in England, 1800–1850', *EcHR* 2nd ser., 13 (1960–1), 397–416; reprinted in Arthur John Taylor (ed.), *The standard of living in Britain in the industrial revolution*. 1975, pp. 93–123.

1064 —— 'The standard of living controversy: a summary', in Ronald Maxwell Hartwell (ed.), *The industrial revolution*. Oxford, 1970, pp.167–79.

1065 Henriques, Ursula Ruth Quixano. 'The rise and decline of the separate system of prison discipline', *PP*, 54 (1972), 61–93.

1066 Hobsbawm, Eric John Ernest. 'The British standard of living, 1790–1850', *EcHR* 2nd ser., 10 (1957–8), 46–68; reprinted in Arthur John Taylor (ed.), *The standard of living in Britain in the industrial revolution*. 1975, pp. 58–92. See also Hobsbawm's additional comments, *ibid*. pp. 179–88.

1067 Hobsbawm, Eric John Ernest and Ronald Maxwell Hartwell. 'The standard of living during the industrial revolution: a discussion', *EcHR* 2nd ser., 16 (1963–4), 119–46.

1068 Hughes, Edward. 'The professions in the eighteenth century', *Durham University Journal*, 44 (1952); reprinted in Daniel A. Baugh, *Aristocratic government and society in eighteenth-century England*. New York, 1975, pp. 184–200. Comprehensive survey.

1069 Jones, Eric Lionel. 'The fashion manipulators: consumer tastes and British industries, 1660–1800', in Lewis P. Cain and Paul J. Uselding (eds.), *Business enterprise and economic change*. Kent, Ohio, 1973, pp. 198–220.

1070 Kerr, Barbara M. 'Irish seasonal migration to Great Britain, 1800–38', *Irish Historical Studies*, 3 (1942–3), 365–80.

1071 Kirby, Chester. 'The English game law system', *AHR*, 38 (1932–3), 240–62.

1072 Laqueur, Thomas W. 'Literacy and social mobility in the industrial revolution in England', *PP*, 64 (1974), 96–112. With reply by Michael Sanderson.

1073 —— 'Working-class demand and the growth of English elementary education, 1750–1850', in Lawrence Stone (ed.), *Schooling and society: studies in the history of education*. Baltimore, Md, 1976, pp. 192–205.

1074 Law, C. M. 'Local censuses in the 18th century', *Population Studies*, 23 (1969), 87–100.

1075 McKendrick, Neil. 'Home demand and economic growth: a new view of the role of women and children in the industrial revolution', in Neil McKendrick (ed.), *Historical perspectives*. 1974, pp. 152–210.

1076 Mills, Dennis R. 'The quality of life in Melbourne, Cambridgeshire, in the period 1800–1850', *International Review of Social History*, 23 (1978), 382–404. Good local study.

1077 Morgan, Rod. 'Divine philanthropy: John Howard reconsidered', *History* NS, 62 (1977), 388–410. Critical of Howard. See also (1034) and (1044).

1078   Neale, R. S. 'The standard of living, 1780–1844: a regional and class study', *EcHR* 2nd ser., 19 (1966), 590–606; reprinted in Arthur John Taylor (ed.), *The standard of living in Britain in the industrial revolution*. 1975, pp. 154–77.

1079   Outhwaite, R. B. 'Age at marriage in England from the late seventeenth to the nineteenth century', *TRHS* 5th ser., 23 (1973), 55–70.

1080   Peirce, David. 'Crime and society in London 1700–1900: a bibliographical survey', *Harvard Library Bulletin*, 20 (1972), 430–43.

1081   Perkin, Harold J. 'The recruitment of elites in British society since 1800', *Journal of Social History*, 12 (1977–8), 222–34.

1082   —— 'The social causes of the British industrial revolution', *TRHS* 5th ser., 18 (1968), 123–43.

1083   Plumb, John Harold. 'The new world of children in eighteenth-century England', *PP*, 67 (1975), 64–95.

1084   Pollard, Sidney. 'The factory village in the industrial revolution', *EHR*, 79 (1964), 513–31.

1085   Razzell, P. E. 'Population growth and economic change in eighteenth- and early nineteenth-century England and Ireland', in Eric Lionel Jones and Gordon Edmund Mingay (eds.), *Land, labour and population in the industrial revolution*. 1967, pp. 260–81.

1086   Reid, Douglas A. 'The decline of St Monday, 1766–1876', *PP*, 71 (1976), 76–101.

1087   Richards, Eric. 'An anatomy of the Sutherland fortune: income, consumption, investments and returns, 1780–1880', *BusH*, 21 (1979), 45–78.

1088   —— 'Women in the British economy since about 1700: an interpretation', *History* NS, 59 (1974), 337–57.

1089   Richards, Paul. 'The state and early industrial capitalism: the case of the handloom weavers', *PP*, 83 (1979), 91–115.

1090   Rowe, David John. 'Francis Place and the historian', *HJ*, 16 (1973), 45–63.

1091   Sanderson, Michael. 'Literacy and social mobility in the industrial revolution in England', *PP*, 56 (1972), 75–104.

1092   Schofield, R. S. 'Dimensions of illiteracy, 1750–1850', *ExEcH* 2nd ser., 10 (1972–3), 437–54.

1093   Schwarz, L. D. 'Income distribution and social structure in London in the late eighteenth century', *EcHR* 2nd ser., 32 (1979), 250–9. Uses information from analysis of early income tax returns to question literary evidence.

1094   Sheridan, Richard B. 'The commercial and financial organization of the British slave trade, 1750–1807', *EcHR* 2nd ser., 11 (1958–9), 247–63. London's part in financing the trade.

1095   Sherwin, Oscar. 'An eighteenth-century Beveridge planner', *AHR*, 52 (1946–7), 281–90. Patrick Colquhoun.

1096   Stern, Walter Marcel. 'The bread crisis in Britain, 1795–96', *Economica* NS, 31 (1964), 168–87.

1097   Stevenson, John. 'Social control and the prevention of riots in England, 1789–1829', in A. P. Donajgrodzki (ed.), *Social control in nineteenth-century Britain*. 1977, pp. 27–50.

1098   Supple, Barry Emmanuel. 'Legislation and virtue: an essay on working-class self-help and the state in the early nineteenth century', in Neil McKendrick (ed.), *Historical perspectives*. 1974, pp. 211–54.

1099   Sykes, R. A. 'Some aspects of working-class consciousness in Oldham, 1830–1842', *HJ*, 23 (1980), 167–70. Attempting to strike a balance between (920) and (1058).

1100   Thomas, David. 'The social origins of marriage partners of the British peerage in the eighteenth and nineteenth centuries', *Population Studies*, 26 (1972), 99–111. Shows that pursuit of heiresses declined rapidly throughout the eighteenth century.

1101   Thomas, Robert Paul and Richard Nelson Bean. 'The fishers of men: the profits of the slave trade', *JEcH*, 34 (1974), 885–914.

1102   Thomas, W. E. S. 'Francis Place and working-class history', *HJ*, 5 (1962), 61–79. See also (1045).

1103   Thompson, Edward Palmer. 'Eighteenth-century English society: class struggle without class?', *Social History*, 3 (1978), 133–65.

1104   —— 'The moral economy of the English crowd in the eighteenth century', *PP*, 50 (1971), 76–136.

1105 —— 'Patrician society: plebeian culture', *Journal of Social History*, 7 (1974), 383–405.

1106 —— 'Time, work-discipline and industrial capitalism', *PP*, 38 (1967), 56–97; reprinted in Michael Walter Flinn and Thomas Christopher Smout (eds.), *Essays in social history*. Oxford, 1968, pp. 37–77.

1107 Tucker, Graham Shardalow Lee. 'The Old Poor Law revisited', *ExEcH* NS, 12 (1975), 233–52.

1108 Tucker, Rufus S. 'Real wages of artisans in London, 1729–1935', *Journal of the American Statistical Association*, 31 (1936), 79–84; reprinted in Arthur John Taylor (ed.), *The standard of living in Britain in the industrial revolution*. 1975, pp. 21–35.

1109 Wiecek, William M. '*Somerset*: Lord Mansfield and the legitimacy of slavery in the Anglo-American world', *University of Chicago Law Review*, 42 (1974), 86–146. See also (998).

1110 Williams, Dale Edward. 'Midland hunger riots in 1766', *Midland History*, 3 (1976), 256–97.

1111 Williams, James Eccles. 'The British standard of living, 1750–1850', *EcHR* 2nd ser., 19 (1966), 581–9.

1112 Wrigley, Edward Anthony. 'Births and baptisms: the use of Anglican baptism registers as a source of information about the numbers of births in England before the beginning of civil registration', *Population Studies*, 31 (1977), 281–312.

1113 —— 'The process of modernization and the industrial revolution in England', *Journal of Interdisciplinary History*, 3 (1972–3), 225–59.

VIII.   ECONOMIC HISTORY

For specialized bibliographies, lists and catalogues, see (7), (11), (20), (22), (139), (141) and (164). Studies of economic thought are listed in Section XIV, those dealing with technological innovation in Section X, and most of those discussing foreign economic and commercial relations in Section VI.

1. Printed sources

1114 Anderson, Bruce Louis and P. L. Cottrell (eds.). *Money and banking in England: the development of the banking system, 1694–1914*. Newton Abbot, Devon, 1974. Sources.

1115 Chalmers, George. *An estimate of the comparative strength of Britain during the present and four preceding reigns; and of the losses of her trade from every war since the Revolution*. 1782; new edn, corr., 1794; other edns, 1802, 1804, 1810. Important contemporary statistical compilation.

1116 Clapp, Brian W. (ed.). *Documents in English economic history*. Vol. 2: *England since 1760*. 1976. Small but representative selection of primary sources.

1117 Colquhoun, Patrick. *Treatise on the wealth, power and resources of the British Empire in every quarter of the globe*. 1814; 2nd edn, with additions, 1815. Includes a pioneering attempt to measure national income. For criticism, see (1365).

1118 Elsas, Madeleine (ed.). *Iron in the making: Dowlais Iron Company letters, 1782–1860*. Cardiff, 1960.

1119 Finer, Ann and George Savage (eds.). *The selected letters of Josiah Wedgwood*. 1965. For biography, see (1644).

1120 Galloway, Robert Lindsay (comp.). *Annals of coal mining and the coal trade*. 1898–1904, 2 vols.; reprinted, Newton Abbot, Devon, 1971. Major collection of material.

1121 Henderson, William Otto (ed.). *Industrial Britain under the Regency: the diaries of Escher, Bodmer, May and de Gallois, 1814–18*. 1968. Accounts by Europeans who came to England to study the industrialization there.

1122 McAdam, John Loudon. *Remarks on the present system of roadmaking*. Bristol, 1816; 8th edn, rev., with an appendix and report from the Select Committee of the House of Commons, June 1823, with extracts from the evidence, 1824.

1123 Macpherson, David. *Annals of commerce, manufactures, fisheries and navigation*. 1805, 4 vols. Contemporary compilation of economic statistics.

1124 Marshall, John. *A digest of all the accounts relating to the populations, revenues, financial operations ... etc. of the United Kingdom of Great Britain.* 1833; reprinted, Farnborough, Hants., 1969. Useful contemporary financial compilation.

1125 Minchinton, Walter Edward (ed.). *The trade of Bristol in the eighteenth century.* (Bristol Record Society, 20.) 1957. Documents.

1126 Sinclair, Sir John. *The history of the public revenue of the British Empire.* 3rd edn, 1803–4, 3 vols. Mostly concerned with the younger Pitt's fiscal reforms.

1127 Tooke, Thomas and William Newmarch. *A history of prices and of the state of the circulation from 1793 [to the present time].* 1838–57, 6 vols.; new edn with introduction by T. E. Gregory, 1928, six vols. in four. Basic contemporary compilation of prices. See also (1166) and (1263).

1128 Ure, Andrew. *The philosophy of manufactures.* 1835; 3rd edn, 1861. Well-known defence of industrialization and of the factory system.

2. Surveys

1129 Ashton, Thomas Southcliffe. *An economic history of England: the 18th century.* 1955.

1130 —— *The industrial revolution, 1760–1830.* 1948; reprinted, New York, 1964.

1131 Chambers, Jonathan David. *The workshop of the world: British economic history from 1820 to 1880.* 1961.

1132 Checkland, Sydney George. *The rise of industrial society in England, 1815–1885.* 1964. Good bibliography and a good survey.

1133 Cipolla, Carlo M. (ed.). *The Fontana economic history of Europe.* Vol. 3: *The industrial revolution.* 1973. Vol. 4 (2 parts): *The emergence of industrial society.* 1973. European-wide coverage *c.* 1700–1914 by various hands.

1134 Clapham, Sir John Harold. *An economic history of modern Britain.* Vol. 1: *The early railway age, 1820–1850.* 1926; 2nd edn, 1930; reprinted with corrections, 1950.

1135 Court, William Henry Bassano. *A concise economic history of Britain, from 1750 to recent times.* Cambridge, 1954.

1136 Cullen, Louis Michael. *An economic history of Ireland since 1660.* 1972.

1137 Darby, Henry Clifford (ed.). *A new historical geography of England.* Cambridge, 1973. Important essays on this period.

1138 Deane, Phyllis. *The first industrial revolution.* Cambridge, 1965; 2nd edn, Cambridge, 1979.

1139 Flinn, Michael Walter. *Origins of the industrial revolution.* 1966. Excellent summary, with much historiographical discussion.

1140 Gregg, Pauline. *A social and economic history of Britain, 1760–1972.* 7th edn, revised, 1972. Useful textbook.

1141 Habakkuk, Sir John and Michael Postan (eds.). *The industrial revolution and after: incomes, population, and technological change.* (Cambridge economic history of Europe, Vol. 6.) Cambridge, 1965. One vol. in two parts. See also (1151).

1142 Hamilton, Henry. *An economic history of Scotland in the eighteenth century.* Oxford, 1963.

1143 Hartwell, Ronald Maxwell. *The industrial revolution and economic growth.* 1971. Hartwell's collected essays, six of them printed for the first time; includes his contributions to the 'standard of living' controversy. See (1063), (1064) and (1067).

1144 —— (ed.). *The causes of the industrial revolution in England.* 1967. Reprints of significant articles by various hands with an important introduction; reprinted in Hartwell's *The industrial revolution and economic growth.* 1971, pp. 158–84.

1145 —— (ed.). *The industrial revolution.* Oxford, 1970. Eight important essays by various hands.

1146 Hobsbawm, Eric John Ernest. *Industry and empire: an economic history of Britain since 1750.* 1968. Sophisticated Marxian interpretation. For Hobsbawm's collected shorter essays and other works, see (934), (935), (1066) and (1067).

1147 Lipson, Ephraim. *The economic history of England.* Vols. 1 and 2: *The age of mercantilism.* 1931; 6th edn, 1956; reprinted, 1961. Classic.

1148 Mantoux, Paul Joseph. *La Révolution industrielle au XVIIIe siècle.* Paris, 1906; trans. and rev. as *The industrial revolution in the eighteenth century* by Marjorie Vernon, 1928; reprinted, with an introduction by Thomas Southcliffe Ashton, 1961. Still one of the best general treatments, although out of date at some points.

1149 Mathias, Peter. *The first industrial nation: an economic history of Britain, 1700–1914.* 1969. Excellent general survey.

1150 —— *The transformation of England: essays in the economic and social history of England in the eighteenth century.* 1979. Collection of sixteen of his major articles.

1151 Mathias, Peter and Michael Postan (eds.). *The industrial economies: capital, labour and enterprise.* (Cambridge economic history of Europe, Vol. 7.) Cambridge, 1978. One vol. in two parts. See also (1141).

1152 Musson, Albert Edward. *The growth of British industry.* 1978. General economic history concentrating on industrial development.

1153 Pawson, Eric. *The early industrial revolution: Britain in the eighteenth century.* New York, 1979. From the point of view of an economic geographer.

1154 Toynbee, Arnold. *Lectures on the industrial revolution of the eighteenth century in England.* 1884; 2nd edn, 1887; reprinted, with an introduction by Thomas Southcliffe Ashton, Newton Abbot, Devon, 1969. Classic.

3. Monographs

1155 Acworth, Angus Whiteford. *Financial reconstruction in England, 1815–1822.* 1925. Taxation and the national debt.

1156 Albert, William. *The turnpike road system in England, 1663–1840.* Cambridge, 1972. See also (1248).

1157 Aldcroft, Derek Howard and Peter Fearon (eds.). *British economic fluctuations, 1790–1939.* 1972. Reprints of articles with a substantial introduction.

1158 Armytage, Frances. *The free port system in the British West Indies: a study in commercial policy, 1766–1822.* 1952.

1159 Ashton, Thomas Southcliffe. *Economic fluctuations in England, 1700–1800.* Oxford, 1959.

1160 —— *Iron and steel in the industrial revolution.* Manchester, 1924; 3rd edn, Manchester, 1963. To *c.* 1815; interpretation modified by (1219).

1161 Ashton, Thomas Southcliffe and Joseph Sykes. *The coal industry of the eighteenth century.* Manchester, 1929; 2nd edn, rev., Manchester, 1964. Still the best study of the subject.

1162 Ashton, Thomas Southcliffe and Richard Sidney Sayers (eds.). *Papers in English monetary history.* Oxford, 1953. Eight of the eleven papers concern developments before 1850.

1163 Bailey, De Witt and Douglas A. Nie. *English gunmakers: the Birmingham and provincial gun trade in the 18th and 19th centuries.* 1978.

1164 Barker, Theodore Cardwell and Christopher Ivor Savage. *An economic history of transport in Britain.* 3rd edn, rev., 1974. First published in 1959 by Savage alone.

1165 Baxter, Bertram. *Stone blocks and iron rails.* 1966. Includes a list of all railways before 1830. See also (1229).

1166 Beveridge, William Henry Beveridge, Baron, et al. (comps.). *Prices and wages in England from the twelfth to the nineteenth century.* Vol. 1: *Price tables: mercantile era.* 1939. See also (1127) and (1263).

1167 Bisschop, W. R. *The rise of the London money market, 1640–1826.* 1910; reprinted, with introduction by H. S. Foxwell, New York, 1968.

1168 Booker, John. *Essex and the industrial revolution.* (Essex Record Office Publications, 60.) Chelmsford, Essex, 1974. See also (1170).

1169 Bowden, Witt. *Industrial society in England towards the end of the eighteenth century.* New York, 1925; 2nd edn, 1965.

1170 Brown, A. F. J. *Essex at work, 1700–1815.* (Essex Record Office Publications, 49.) Chelmsford, Essex, 1969. See also (1168).

1171 Bythell, Duncan. *The handloom weavers: a study in the English cotton industry during the industrial revolution.* Cambridge, 1969.

1172 Campbell, Roy Hutcheson. *Carron Company.* Edinburgh, 1961. The great iron works.

1173 Carlson, Robert Eugene. *The Liverpool & Manchester railway project, 1821–1831.* New York, 1969.

1174 Carter, Alice Clare. *The English public debt in the eighteenth century.* (Historical Association, Helps for Students of History, 74.) 1968. Brief but helpful.

1175 Chaloner, William Henry. *People and industries.* 1963. Essays on the industrial revolution.

1176 Chambers, Jonathan David. *The Vale of Trent, 1670–1800: a regional study of economic change.* (Supplement No. 3 to the *EcHR.*) Cambridge, 1957.

1177 Chapman, Stanley David. *The cotton industry in the industrial revolution.* 1972.

1178 —— *The early factory masters: the transition to the factory system in the Midlands textile industry.* Newton Abbot, Devon, 1967.

1179 Chapman, Sir Sydney John. *The Lancashire cotton industry: a study in economic development.* Manchester, 1904; reprinted, Clifton, NJ, 1973. Important bibliography of all the earlier literature on cotton including summaries of parliamentary papers to 1837. Basic work.

1180 Checkland, Sydney George. *Scottish banking: a history, 1695–1973.* Glasgow, 1975.

1181 Clapham, Sir John Harold. *The Bank of England: a history.* Cambridge, 1944, 2 vols.

1182 Coleman, Donald Cuthbert. *The British paper industry, 1495–1860: a study in industrial growth.* Oxford, 1958. See also (1273).

1183 Court, William Henry Bassano. *The rise of the Midland industries, 1600–1838.* 1938; reprinted, 1953.

1184 Crouzet, François. *L'Economie britannique et le blocus continental, 1806–1813.* Paris, 1958, 2 vols.

1185 —— (ed.). *Capital formation in the industrial revolution.* 1972. Seven essays by various hands with a long, important introduction.

1186 Cullen, Louis Michael. *Anglo-Irish trade, 1660–1800.* Manchester, 1968.

1187 Davis, Ralph. *Aleppo and Devonshire Square: English traders in the Levant in the eighteenth century.* 1969.

1188 —— *The industrial revolution and British overseas trade.* Leicester, 1979. Important attempt to compute and tabulate real values of trade, 1784–1856. See also (1268), (1269), (1354) and (1371).

1189 —— *The rise of the English shipping industry in the seventeenth and eighteenth centuries.* 1962; 2nd edn, Newton Abbot, Devon, 1972.

1190 Deane, Phyllis and William Alan Cole. *British economic growth, 1688–1959: trends and structure.* Cambridge, 1962; 2nd edn, Cambridge 1967. Major study; fundamental on the subject.

1191 Devine, T. M. *The tobacco lords: a study of the tobacco merchants of Glasgow and their trading activities, c. 1740–90.* Edinburgh, 1975.

1192 Dickson, Peter George Muir. *The financial revolution in England: a study in the development of public credit, 1688–1756.* 1967. Essential background to later eighteenth century finance.

1193 —— *The Sun Insurance Office, 1710–1960: the history of two and a half centuries of British insurance.* 1960. One of the best studies of the development of insurance. See also (1276).

1194 Dodd, Arthur Herbert. *The industrial revolution in North Wales.* Cardiff, 1933; 2nd edn, Cardiff, 1951.

1195 Dubois, Armand Budington. *The British business company after the Bubble Act, 1720–1800.* New York, 1938; reprinted, New York, 1971.

1196 Dyos, Harold James and Derek Howard Aldcroft. *British transport: an economic survey from the seventeenth century to the twentieth.* Leicester, 1969. Excellent critical bibliography.

1197 Edwards, Michael M. *The growth of the British cotton trade, 1780–1815.* Manchester, 1967.

1198 Farnie, D. A. *The English cotton industry and the world market, 1815–1896.* Oxford, 1979.

1199 Feavearyear, Albert Edgar. *The pound sterling: a history of English money.* Oxford, 1931; 2nd edn, rev. by Edward Victor Morgan, Oxford, 1963.

1200 Fitton, Robert Sucksmith and Alfred Percy Wadsworth. *The Strutts and the Arkwrights, 1758–1830: a study of the early factory system.* Manchester, 1958.

1201 Francis, Alan David. *The wine trade.* 1972. Mostly on the trade with Portugal from the seventeenth to nineteenth centuries.

1202 Gale, Walter Keith Vernon. *The British iron and steel industry: a technical history.* New York, 1967.

1203 Galloway, Robert Lindsay. *A history of coal mining in Great Britain.* 1882; reprinted, New York, 1969. Classic.

1204 Galpin, William Freeman. *The grain supply of England during the Napoleonic period: a thesis.* New York, 1925; reprinted, New York, 1977.

1205 Gayer, Arthur David, Walt Whitman Rostow and Anna Jacobson Schwartz. *The growth and fluctuations of the British economy, 1790–1850: an historical, statistical, and theoretical study of Britain's economic development.* Oxford, 1953, 2 vols; reprinted, with a new introduction, New York, 1975, 2 vols.

1206 Gilboy, Elizabeth Waterman. *Wages in eighteenth-century England.* Cambridge, Mass., 1934; reprinted, New York, 1969.

1207 Griffin, Alan R. *Mining in the East Midlands, 1550–1947.* 1971.

1208 Hadfield, Ellis Charles Raymond. *British canals: an illustrated history.* 1950; 5th edn, Newton Abbot, Devon, 1974. Based on his ten volumes on canals in the various parts of England.

1209 —— *The canal age.* Newton Abbot, Devon, 1968.

1210 Hall, Frederick George. *The Bank of Ireland, 1783–1946.* 1949.

1211 Handover, Phyllis Margaret. *Printing in London from 1476 to modern times: competitive practice and technical invention in the trade of book and Bible printing, periodical production, jobbing, etc.* Cambridge, Mass., 1960. See also (1251).

1212 Harris, John Raymond. *Liverpool and Merseyside: essays in the economic and social history of the port and its hinterland.* 1969. See also (1220).

1213 Henderson, William Otto. *Britain and industrial Europe, 1750–1870: studies in British influence on the industrial revolution in Western Europe.* Liverpool, 1954; 3rd edn, Leicester, 1972.

1214 Hidy, Ralph Willard. *The House of Baring in American trade and finance: English merchant bankers at work, 1763–1861.* Cambridge, Mass., 1949. See also (1249).

1215 Higgins, J. P. P. and Sidney Pollard (eds.). *Aspects of capital investment in Great Britain 1750–1850: a preliminary survey.* 1971. Five papers read at a conference in 1969.

1216 Hoffman, Walther Gustav. *British industry, 1700–1950.* Trans. William Otto Henderson and William Henry Chaloner. Oxford, 1955. First published Jena, E. Germany, 1940. Attempt at a quantitative analysis of Britain's entire industrial product since 1750. For a critical commentary, see William Alan Cole in *EcHR* 2nd ser., 11 (1958–9), 309–15.

1217 Hope-Jones, Arthur. *Income tax in the Napoleonic wars.* Cambridge, 1939. Basic on the subject. See also (1267).

1218 Hunt, Bishop Carleton. *The development of the business corporation in England, 1800–1867.* Cambridge, Mass., 1936.

1219 Hyde, Charles K. *Technological change and the British iron industry, 1700–1870.* Princeton, NJ, 1977. Revises previous interpretations, including Ashton's (1160) at important points.

1220 Hyde, Francis Edwin. *Liverpool and the Mersey: an economic history of a port, 1700–1970.* Newton Abbot, Devon, 1971. See also (1212).

1221 Imlah, Albert Henry. *Economic elements in the Pax Britannica: studies in British and foreign trade in the nineteenth century.* Cambridge, Mass., 1958.

1222 Jackson, Gordon. *The British whaling trade.* 1978.

1223 Jenkins, D. T. *The West Riding wool textile industry, 1770–1835: a study of fixed capital formation.* Edington, Wilts., 1975.

1224 Jenkins, John Geraint (ed.). *The wool textile industry in Great Britain.* 1972. Much historical material, both technological and by region by many hands.

1225 Jevons, William Stanley. *Investigations in currency and finance.* 1884; new edn, abridged, 1909. Classical discussion of the history of prices since 1782; one of his articles on the subject is reprinted in Eleanora Mary Carus-Wilson (ed.), *Essays in economic history.* 1954–62, iii, pp. 1–28.

1226 John, Arthur Henry. *The industrial development of South Wales, 1750–1850.* Cardiff, 1950.

1227 Leader, Robert Eadon. *History of the Company of Cutlers in Hallamshire in the county of York.* Sheffield, 1905–6, 2 vols.

1228 Lewenhak, Sheila. *Steamships and shipbuilders in the industrial revolution.* 1978.

1229 Lewin, Henry Grote. *Early British railways: a short history of their origin and development, 1801–1844.* 1925. Standard. See also (1165).

1230 Lewis, Frank. *Essex and sugar: historic and other connections.* 1976. Seventeenth and eighteenth century developments in refining.

1231 Lewis, John Parry. *Building cycles and Britain's growth, incorporating material of the late Bernard Weber.* 1965.

1232 Little, Anthony J. *Deceleration in the eighteenth-century British economy.* 1976.

1233 Lord, John. *Capital and steam-power, 1750–1800.* 1923; 2nd edn, with introduction by

William Henry Chaloner, 1966. Best short account of Boulton and Watt enterprise.

1234 Macadam, John. *The Macadam road.* 1957.

1235 McGrath, Patrick. *The Merchant Venturers of Bristol.* Bristol, 1975. From its origins to the present.

1236 Mann, Julia de Lacy. *The cloth industry in the west of England from 1640 to 1880.* Oxford, 1971. Useful bibliography.

1237 Marshall, John Duncan. *Furness and the industrial revolution: an economic history of Furness (1711–1900) and of the town of Barrow (1757–1897).* Barrow-in-Furness, Cumbria, 1958.

1238 Marshall, Peter James. *East India fortunes: the British in Bengal in the eighteenth century.* Oxford, 1976. How the fortunes were made, with much information on trading in India and to the East and West.

1239 Mathias, Peter. *The brewing industry in England, 1700–1830.* Cambridge, 1959.

1240 Mee, Graham. *Aristocratic enterprise: the Fitzwilliam industrial undertakings, 1795–1857.* Glasgow, 1975.

1241 Minchinton, Walter Edward (ed.). *The growth of English overseas trade in the seventeenth and eighteenth centuries.* 1969. Reprinted articles.

1242 —— (ed.). *Industrial South Wales, 1750–1914: essays in Welsh economic history.* 1969. Reprinted papers by various hands on population, industry, banking and agriculture.

1243 Morgan, Edward Victor. *The theory and practice of central banking, 1797–1913.* Cambridge, 1943; reprinted, 1965. The Bank of England and the London money market.

1244 Morgan, Edward Victor and William Arthur Thomas. *The Stock Exchange: its history and functions.* 1962.

1245 O'Brien, Patrick Karl and Caglar Keyder. *Economic growth in Britain and France, 1780–1914: two paths to the twentieth century.* 1978. Important comparative study, revising many earlier views of the French 'lag'.

1246 Parkinson, Cyril Northcote. *Trade in the eastern seas, 1793–1813.* Cambridge, 1937.

1247 —— (ed.). *The trade winds: a study of British overseas trade during the French wars 1793–1815.* 1948. Contributions by eight authors, covering most aspects of trade.

1248 Pawson, Eric. *Transport and economy: the turnpike roads of eighteenth-century Britain.* 1977. From the point of view of an economic geographer; important reinterpretation. See also (1156).

1249 Perkins, Edwin J. *Financing Anglo-American trade: the house of Brown, 1800–80.* Cambridge, Mass., 1975. See also (1214).

1250 Philips, Cyril Henry. *The East India Company, 1784–1834.* Manchester, 1940; rev. edn, Manchester, 1961. Best study of the internal politics of the Company and its relations with the government; for the earlier part of George III's reign, see (508).

1251 Plant, Marjorie. *The English book trade: an economic history of the making and sale of books.* 1939; 3rd edn, 1974. See also (1211).

1252 Pollard, Sidney. *The genesis of modern management: a study of the industrial revolution in Great Britain.* 1965.

1253 Ponting, Kenneth George. *The woollen industry of south-west England: an industrial, economic and technical survey.* Bath, 1971.

1254 Pressnell, Leslie Sedden. *Country banking in the industrial revolution.* Oxford, 1956.

1255 Prest, John Michael. *The industrial revolution in Coventry.* 1960. To the 1860s.

1256 Raistrick, Arthur and Bernard Jennings. *A history of lead-mining in the Pennines.* 1965. See also (1282).

1257 Raybould, Trevor John. *The economic emergence of the Black Country: a study of the Dudley estate.* Newton Abbot, Devon, 1973.

1258 Redford, Arthur. *Manchester merchants and foreign trade.* Manchester, 1934–56, 2 vols. Vol. 1: *1794–1858.*

1259 Reed, M. C. *Investment in railways in Britain, 1820–44: a study in the development of the capital market.* 1975.

1260 Rich, Edwin Ernest, *The history of the Hudson's Bay Company, 1670–1870.* 1958–9, 2 vols. See also (1394).

1261 Richards, Eric. *The Leviathan of Wealth: the Sunderland fortune in the industrial revolution.* Foreword by Sydney George Checkland. 1973.

1262 Rimmer, William Gordon. *Marshalls of Leeds, flaxspinners, 1788–1886.* Cambridge, 1960. Most important book on the linen industry in England.

1263 Rogers, James Edwin Thorold. *A history of agriculture and prices in England from …* *(1239) to … (1793) : comp. entirely from original and contemporaneous records.* Oxford, 1866–1902, 7 vols. The basic compilation of prices. See also (1127) and (1166).

1264 Rolt, Lionel Thomas Caswell. *Navigable waterways.* 1969.

1265 Rostow, Walt Whitman. *The process of economic growth.* Oxford, 1953; 2nd edn, Oxford, 1960.

1266 Rowe, William John. *Cornwall in the age of the industrial revolution.* Liverpool, 1953.

1267 Sabine, Basil Ernest Vyvyan. *A history of income tax.* 1966. See also (1217).

1268 Schlote, Werner. *British overseas trade from 1700 to the 1930's.* Trans. William Henry Chaloner and William Otto Henderson. Oxford, 1952. First published Jena, E. Germany, 1939; mainly concerned with the statistical measurement of trade. See also (1188), (1269), (1354) and (1371).

1269 Schumpeter, Elizabeth (Boody). *English overseas trade statistics, 1697–1808.* Oxford, 1960. See also (1188), (1268), (1354) and (1371).

1270 Schuyler, Robert Livingston. *The fall of the old colonial system : a study in British free trade, 1770–1870.* New York, 1945; reprinted, Hamden, Conn., 1966.

1271 Semmel, Bernard. *The rise of free trade imperialism : classical political economy, the empire of free trade and imperialism, 1750–1850.* Cambridge, 1970.

1272 Shapiro, Seymour. *Capital and the cotton industry in the industrial revolution.* Ithaca, NY, 1967.

1273 Shorter, Alfred Henry. *Paper mills and paper makers in England, 1495–1800.* Hilversum, Holland, 1957. From the point of view of historical geography; complements (1182).

1274 Smith, Raymond. *Sea coal for London : history of the coal factors in the London market.* 1961.

1275 Stacey, Nicholas A. *English accountancy : a study in social and economic history, 1800–1954.* 1954. See also (1292).

1276 Supple, Barry Emmanuel. *The Royal Exchange Assurance : a history of British insurance 1720–1970.* Cambridge, 1970. See also (1193).

1277 Sweezy, Paul Marlor. *Monopoly and competition in the English coal trade 1550–1850.* Cambridge, Mass., 1938. Mostly concerned with years after 1770.

1278 Tolley, B. H. *Liverpool and the American cotton trade.* 1978.

1279 Trinder, Barry Stuart. *The industrial revolution in Shropshire.* Chichester, Sussex, 1973.

1280 —— (ed.). *'The most extraordinary district in the world' : Ironbridge and Coalbrookdale.* 1977.

1281 Tupling, George Henry. *The economic history of Rossendale.* Manchester, 1927. Significant local study.

1282 Turnbull, Leslie. *The history of lead mining in the north east of England.* Newcastle-upon-Tyne, 1975. See also (1256).

1283 Unwin, George, Arthur Hulme and George Taylor. *Samuel Oldknow and the Arkwrights : the industrial revolution at Stockport and Marple.* Manchester, 1924; 2nd edn, with preface by William Henry Chaloner, 1968.

1284 Wadsworth, Alfred Percy and Julia de Lacy Mann. *The cotton trade and industrial Lancashire 1600–1780.* Manchester, 1931; reprinted, New York, 1968.

1285 Ward, J. R. *The finance of canal building in eighteenth-century England.* 1974.

1286 Wells, Frederick Arthur. *The British hosiery and knitwear industry : its history and organization.* 1935; reprinted, Newton Abbot, Devon, 1972.

1287 Williams, Judith Blow. *British commercial policy and trade expansion, 1750–1850.* Oxford, 1972. With a bibliographical chapter by David M. Williams.

1288 Wilson, Sir Charles. *Anglo-Dutch commerce and finance in the eighteenth century.* Cambridge, 1941.

1289 Wilson, Richard George. *Gentlemen merchants : the merchant community in Leeds, 1700–1830.* Manchester, 1971.

1290 Wood, Alfred Cecil. *A history of the Levant Company.* 1935.

1291 Wright, Charles and Charles Ernest Fayle. *A history of Lloyd's from the founding of Lloyd's Coffee House to the present day.* 1928. Standard.

1292 Yamey, Basil Selig, et al. *Accounting in England and Scotland : 1543–1800 : double entry in exposition and practice.* 1963. See also (1275).

1293 Yogev, Gedalia. *Diamonds and coral : Anglo-Dutch Jews and eighteenth-century trade.* Leicester, 1978.

ECONOMIC HISTORY

4. Biographies

1294   Ashton, Thomas Southcliffe. *An eighteenth-century industrialist: Peter Stubs of Warrington, 1756–1806.* Manchester, 1939; 2nd edn, 1961.

1295   Cameron, Hector Charles. *Samuel Crompton.* 1951.

1296   Coleridge, Ernest Hartley. *The life of Thomas Coutts, banker.* 1920, 2 vols. Includes letters 1767–1821.

1297   Fry, Howard Tyrell. *Alexander Dalrymple (1737–1808) and the expansion of British trade.* 1970. Primarily trade with south-east Asia and the East Indies.

1298   Lloyd, Humphrey. *The Quaker Lloyds in the industrial revolution.* 1975. The iron industry.

1299   Mallet, Hugh. *Bridgewater, the canal Duke, 1736–1803.* Manchester, 1977. Revised edn of a biography first published in 1961.

1300   Rolt, Lionel Thomas Caswell. *George and Robert Stephenson: the railway revolution.* 1960; 2nd edn, 1962; reprinted, Westport, Conn., 1977.

1301   Willan, Thomas Stuart. *An eighteenth-century shopkeeper: Abraham Dent of Kirby Stephen.* Manchester, 1970. Dent (1729–1803) was also a brewer, hosier and dealer in bills.

5. Articles

1302   Anderson, Bruce Louis. 'Provincial aspects of the financial revolution of the eighteenth century', *BusH*, 11 (1969), 11–22.

1303   Anderson, J. L. 'A measure of the effect of British public finance, 1793–1815', *EcHR* 2nd ser., 27 (1974), 610–19. Impact of government finance on the economy.

1304   Aström, Sven-Eric. 'English timber imports from northern Europe in the eighteenth century', *Scandinavian Economic History Review*, 18 (1970), 12–32.

1305   Bairoch, Paul. 'Commerce internationale et genèse de la révolution industrielle anglaise', *Annales*, 28 (1973), 541–71. Emphasizing the much greater importance of home demand over export demand in stimulating economic growth. See also (1329).

1306   Cairncross, Alexander Kirkland and Bernard Weber. 'Fluctuations in building in Great Britain, 1785–1849', *EcHR* 2nd ser., 9 (1956–7), 283–97; reprinted in Eleanora Mary Carus-Wilson (ed.), *Essays in economic history.* 1954–62, iii, pp. 318–33. See also (1336).

1307   Chapman, Stanley David. 'British marketing enterprise: the changing roles of merchants, manufacturers, and financiers, 1700–1860', *BusHR*, 53 (1979), 205–34.

1308   —— 'Financial restraints on the growth of firms in the cotton industry, 1790–1850', *EcHR* 2nd ser., 32 (1979), 50–69.

1309   —— 'The international houses: the continental contribution to British commerce, 1800–1860', *JEurEcH*, 6 (1977), 5–48.

1310   —— 'The Peels in the early English cotton industry', *BusH*, 11 (1969), 61–89.

1311   Checkland, Sydney George. 'Finance for the West Indies, 1780–1815', *EcHR* 2nd ser., 10 (1957–8), 461–9.

1312   Church, Roy Anthony. 'Labour supply and innovation, 1800–1860: the boot and shoe industry', *BusH*, 12 (1970), 25–45. One of the few studies of this industry.

1313   Clapham, Sir John Harold. 'The last years of the Navigation Acts', *EHR*, 25 (1910), 480–501, 687–707; reprinted in Eleanora Mary Carus-Wilson (ed.), *Essays in economic history.* 1954–62, iii, pp. 144–78.

1314   —— 'The Spitalfields Acts, 1773–1824', *Economic Journal*, 26 (1916), 459–71.

1315   Cole, William Alan. 'Eighteenth-century economic growth revisited', *ExEcH* 2nd ser., 10 (1972–3), 327–48.

1316   —— 'Trends in eighteenth-century smuggling', *EcHR* 2nd ser., 10 (1957–8), 395–410. Attempt to measure quantitative importance of smuggling; for subsequent controversy see (1363).

1317   Cope, S. R. 'The stock exchange revisited: a new look at the market in securities in London in the eighteenth century', *Economica* NS, 45 (1978), 1–21.

1318   Crafts, N. F. R. 'English economic growth in the eighteenth century: a re-examination of Deane and Cole's estimates', *EcHR* 2nd ser., 29 (1976), 226–35. Econometric.

1319   —— 'Industrial revolution in England and France: some thoughts on the question,

"Why was England first?"', *EcHR* 2nd ser., 30 (1977), 429–41. Econometric.

1320 Crouzet, François. 'Angleterre et France au XVIII'siècle: essai d'analyse comparée de deux croissances économiques', *Annales*, 21 (1966), 254–91; trans. in Ronald Maxwell Hartwell (ed.), *The causes of the industrial revolution*. 1967, pp. 139–74.

1321 —— 'Bilan de l'économie Britannique pendant les guerres de la Révolution et de l'Empire', *Revue Historique*, 234 (1965), 71–110.

1322 Daunton, M. J. 'The Dowlais Iron Company in the iron industry, 1800–1850', *Welsh Historical Review*, 6 (1972–3), 16–48.

1323 Deane, Phyllis. 'The role of capital in the industrial revolution', *ExEcH* 2nd ser., 10 (1972–3), 349–64. Capital not such a restraint on growth in the eighteenth century as it is today.

1324 —— 'War and industrialization', in J. M. Winter (ed.), *War and economic development: essays in memory of David Joslin*. Cambridge, 1975, pp. 91–102. England in the American and Napoleonic Wars.

1325 Deane, Phyllis and Sir John Habakkuk. 'The take-off in Britain', in Walt Whitman Rostow (ed.), *The economics of take-off into sustained growth*. 1963, pp. 63–82.

1326 Derry, Thomas Kingston. 'The repeal of the apprenticeship clauses of the Statute of Apprentices', *EcHR* 1st ser., 3 (1931–2), 67–87. Repealed in 1814.

1327 Eagly, Robert V. and V. Kerry Smith. 'Domestic and international integration of the London money market, 1731–1789', *JEcH*, 36 (1976), 198–216. With a comment by Stephen B. Baxter.

1328 Ellis, Joyce. 'The decline and fall of the Tyneside salt industry, 1660–1790: a re-examination', *EcHR* 2nd ser., 33 (1980), 45–58.

1329 Eversley, David Edward Charles. 'The home market and economic growth in England, 1750–80', in Eric Lionel Jones and Gordon Edmund Mingay (eds.), *Land, labour and population in the industrial revolution*. 1967, pp. 206–59. Argues that the growth of the home market and home demand were more important than growth of export demand in encouraging growth. See also (1305).

1330 Fetter, Frank Whitson. 'Some pitfalls in the use of Bank of England credit statistics, 1794–1832', *Review of Economics and Statistics*, 49 (1967), 619–23. Argues that they have often been misunderstood by economists and economic historians.

1331 Flinn, Michael Walter. 'Trends in real wages, 1750–1850', *EcHR* 2nd ser., 27 (1974), 395–413. A reply by Terence Richard Gourvish and a further comment by Flinn, *ibid.* 29 (1976), 136–45. See also (1391).

1332 Fry, Howard Tyrell. 'British trade in southeast Asia in its eighteenth-century setting', *Asian and Pacific Quarterly of Cultural and Social Affairs*, 7 (1975–6), 20–32.

1333 Gatrell, V. A. C. 'Labour, power, and the size of firms in Lancashire cotton in the second quarter of the nineteenth century', *EcHR* 2nd ser., 30 (1977), 95–139. See also (1351).

1334 Gilboy, Elizabeth Waterman. 'Demand as a factor in the industrial revolution', in *Facts and factors in economic history: articles by former students of Edwin Francis Gay*. Cambridge, Mass., 1932, pp. 620–39; reprinted, 1967.

1335 Glover, Frederick J. 'The rise of the heavy woollen trade of the West Riding of Yorkshire in the nineteenth century', *BusH*, 4 (1961–2), 1–21.

1336 Habakkuk, Sir John. 'Fluctuations in house-building in Britain and the United States in the nineteenth century', *JEcH*, 22 (1962), 198–230; reprinted in Derek Howard Aldcroft and Peter Fearon (eds.), *British economic fluctuations 1790–1939*. 1972, pp. 236–67. See also (1306).

1337 Harper, Lawrence Averell. 'The effect of the Navigation Acts on the thirteen colonies', in Richard B. Morris (ed.), *The era of the American Revolution*. New York, 1959, pp. 3–39.

1338 —— 'Mercantilism and the American Revolution', *Canadian Historical Review*, 23 (1942), 1–15. For the controversy over the interpretation of the impact of the Navigation Acts developed in this and (1337), see (1353), (1385), (1386) and (1392).

1339 Harris, John Raymond. 'Skills, coal and British industry in the eighteenth century', *History* NS, 61 (1976), 167–82.

1340 Hartwell, Ronald Maxwell. 'The causes of the industrial revolution: an essay in methodology', *EcHR* 2nd ser., 18 (1965), 164–82; reprinted in Hartwell's *The industrial revolution and economic growth*. 1971, pp. 131–57.

1341 —— 'Interpretations of the industrial revolution in England: a methodological

51

inquiry', *JEcH*, 19 (1959), 229–49; reprinted in Hartwell's *The industrial revolution and economic growth*. 1971, pp. 81–105.

1342 Horsefield, J. K. 'British banking practices, 1750–1850: some legal sidelights', *Economica* NS, 19 (1952), 308–21.

1343 —— 'The cash ratio in English banks before 1800', *Journal of Political Economy*, 57 (1949), 70–4.

1344 Jarvis, Rupert Charles. 'Eighteenth-century London shipping', in Albert E. J. Hollaender and William Kellaway (eds.), *Studies in London history presented to Philip Edmund Jones*. 1969, pp. 403–25.

1345 —— 'Official trade and revenue statistics', *EcHR* 2nd ser., 17 (1964–5), 43–62. Explains how statistics were compiled *c.* 1660–1850 and how to interpret them.

1346 John, Arthur Henry. 'Insurance investment and the London money market of the 18th century', *Economica* NS, 20 (1953), 137–58.

1347 Jones, Stuart. 'The cotton industry and joint stock banking in Manchester, 1825–50', *BusH*, 20 (1978), 165–85.

1348 —— 'Government, currency and country banks in England, 1770–1797', *South African Journal of Economics*, 44 (1976), 252–73.

1349 Joslin, D. M. 'London private bankers, 1720–1785', *EcHR* 2nd ser., 7 (1954–5), 167–86; reprinted in Eleanora Mary Carus-Wilson (ed.), *Essays in economic history*. 1954–62, ii, pp. 340–59.

1350 Kellock, Katharine A. 'London merchants and the pre-1776 American debts', *Guildhall Studies in London History*, 1 (1974–5), 109–49.

1351 Lloyd-Jones, Roger and A. A. LeRoux. 'The size of firms in the cotton industry: Manchester 1815–41', *EcHR* 2nd ser., 33 (1980), 72–82. See also (1333).

1352 McCahill, Michael W. 'Peers, patronage, and the industrial revolution, 1760–1800', *JBS*, 16, 1 (1976), 84–107. Survey of the part played by the peers in economic change.

1353 McClelland, Peter D. 'The cost to America of British imperial policy', *American Economic Review*, 59 (1969), 370–81. Econometric attack on arguments in (1337), (1338) and (1386) that the Navigation Acts were not economically oppressive; for the subsequent controversy, see (1392).

1354 McCusker, John J. 'The current value of English exports, 1697 to 1800', *W&MQ* 3rd ser., 28 (1971), 607–28. Statistics. See also (1188), (1268), (1269) and (1371).

1355 McKendrick, Neil, 'Josiah Wedgwood: an eighteenth-century entrepreneur in salesmanship and marketing techniques', *EcHR* 2nd ser., 12 (1959–60), 408–33; reprinted in Eleanora Mary Carus-Wilson (ed.), *Essays in economic history*. 1954–62, iii, pp. 353–79.

1356 —— 'Josiah Wedgwood and cost accounting in the industrial revolution', *EcHR* 2nd ser., 23 (1970), 45–67.

1357 —— 'Josiah Wedgwood and factory discipline', *HJ*, 4 (1961), 30–55.

1358 —— 'Josiah Wedgwood and Thomas Bentley: an inventor–entrepreneur partnership in the industrial revolution', *TRHS* 5th ser., 14 (1964), 1–33.

1359 Mathias, Peter and Patrick Karl O'Brien. 'Taxation in Britain and France, 1715–1810: a comparison of the social and economic incidence of taxes collected for the central governments', *JEurEcH*, 5 (1976), 601–50. Emphasizes the growing burden of taxation in England to fund the national debt and hence the shifting of income from the poor to the rich. Criticized by D. N. McCloskey in *JEurEcH*, 7 (1978), 209–10, with a reply by Mathias and O'Brien, *ibid.* 211–13.

1360 Mokyr, Joel. 'Demand vs supply in the industrial revolution', *JEcH*, 37 (1977), 981–1008. Critical of the weight usually given to demand in discussing economic growth; largely econometric.

1361 Mui, Hoh-Cheung and Lorna H. Mui. 'The Commutation Act and the tea trade in Britain, 1784–1793', *EcHR* 2nd ser., 16 (1963–4), 234–53.

1362 —— 'Smuggling and the British tea trade before 1784', *AHR*, 74 (1968–9), 44–73.

1363 —— '"Trends in eighteenth-century smuggling" reconsidered', *EcHR* 2nd ser., 28 (1975), 28–43. Criticism of (1316); reply by Cole, *ibid.* pp. 44–9.

1364 Neal, Larry. 'Deane and Cole on industrialization and population change in the eighteenth century', *EcHR* 2nd ser., 24 (1971), 643–7. Reply by Cole, *ibid.* pp. 648–52.

1365 O'Brien, Patrick Karl. 'British incomes and property in the early nineteenth century', *EcHR* 2nd ser., 12 (1959–60), 255–67. Based on income tax returns; questions the literary evidence on the subject, especially Colquhoun's estimates in (1117).

1366 Phelps Brown, E. H. and Sheila V. Hopkins. 'Seven centuries of building wages', *Economica* NS, 22 (1955), 195–206; reprinted in Eleanora Mary Carus-Wilson (ed.), *Essays in economic history*. 1954–62, ii, pp. 168–78. One of the basic measures of wages.

1367 —— 'Seven centuries of the prices of consumables, compared with builder's wage-rates', *Economica* NS, 23 (1956), 296–314; reprinted in Eleanora Mary Carus-Wilson (ed.), *Essay in economic history*, 1954–62, ii, pp. 179–96. One of the basic measures of prices.

1368 Pollard, Sidney. 'Factory discipline in the industrial revolution', *EcHR* 2nd ser., 16 (1963–4), 254–71.

1369 —— 'A new estimate of British coal production, 1750–1850', *EcHR* 2nd ser., 33 (1980), 212–35. Composite statistics.

1370 Price, Jacob M. 'Joshua Johnson in London, 1771–1775: credit and commercial organization in the British–Chesapeake trade', in Anne Whiteman, et al. (eds.), *Statesmen, scholars and merchants*. Oxford, 1973, pp. 153–80. Study of one of the few North American merchants whose papers have survived. Price has subsequently edited *Joshua Johnson's letterbook, 1771–1774.* (London Record Society, 15.) 1979.

1371 —— 'New time series for Scotland's and Britain's trade with the thirteen colonies and states, 1740 to 1791', *W&MQ* 3rd ser., 32 (1975), 307–25. Collating trade totals for Scotland and England to obtain a general index of the value of the trade. See also (1188), (1268), (1269) and (1354).

1372 Richards, Richard David. 'The Exchequer bill in the history of English government finance', *Economic History*, 3 (1934–7), 193–211.

1373 —— 'The lottery in the history of English government finance', *Economic History*, 3 (1934–7), 57–76.

1374 Riden, Philip. 'The output of the British iron industry before 1870', *EcHR* 2nd ser., 30 (1977), 442–59. Composite statistics; much on this period.

1375 Roberts, R. O. 'Bank of England branch discounting, 1826–59', *Economica* NS, 25 (1958), 230–45. Significance of the Bank in regional economic life.

1376 Robinson, Eric. 'Eighteenth-century commerce and fashion: Matthew Boulton's marketing techniques', *EcHR* 2nd ser., 16 (1963–4), 39–60. His early activity in the 'toy' market.

1377 Shannon, Herbert Austin. 'Bricks: a trade index, 1785–1849', *Economica* NS, 1 (1934), 300–18; reprinted in Eleanora Mary Carus-Wilson (ed.), *Essays in economic history.* 1954–62, iii, pp. 188–201.

1378 Sheridan, Richard B. 'The wealth of Jamaica in the eighteenth century', *EcHR* 2nd ser., 18 (1965), 292-311. Its great contribution to the wealth of the Empire: but see (1387).

1379 —— 'The West India sugar crisis and British slave emancipation, 1830–1833', *JEcH*, 21 (1961), 539–51.

1380 Stern, Walter Marcel. 'United Kingdom public expenditure by votes of supply, 1793–1817', *Economica* NS, 17 (1950), 196–210.

1381 Sterns, Peter. 'British industry through the eyes of French industrialists (1820–1848)', *JMH*, 37 (1965), 50–61.

1382 Sutherland, Dame Lucy Stuart. 'Sir George Colebrooke's world corner in alum, 1771–73', *Economic History*, 3 (1934–7), 237–58.

1383 Tann, Jennifer. 'Marketing methods in the international steam engine market: the case of Boulton and Watt', *JEcH*, 38 (1978), 363–91.

1384 —— 'Richard Arkwright and technology', *History* NS, 58 (1973), 29–44.

1385 Thomas, Robert Paul. 'British imperial policy and the economic interpretation of the American Revolution', *JEcH*, 28 (1968), 436–40.

1386 —— 'A quantitative approach to the study of the effects of British imperial policy upon colonial welfare: some preliminary findings', *JEcH*, 25 (1965), 615–38. Essentially confirmed, quantitatively, the interpretation in (1337) and (1338) of the limited economic effects of enforcement of the Navigation Acts; began the controversy on this subject, for which see also (1353) and (1392).

1387 —— 'The sugar colonies of the old Empire: profit or loss for Great Britain?'. *EcHR* 2nd ser., 21 (1968), 30–45. Reply to (1378), arguing that the sugar colonies were not, on balance, profitable; further reply by Sheridan, *ibid.* pp. 46–61.

1388 Tucker, Rufus S. 'Real wages of artisans in London, 1729–1935', *Journal of the American Statistical Association*, 31 (1936), 73–84.

1389 Turnbull, G. L. 'Provincial road carrying in England in the eighteenth century', *Journal of Transport History*, 4 (1977–8), 17–39.

1390 Uselding, Paul J. 'Wage and consumption levels in England and on the continent in the 1830's', *JEurEcH*, 4 (1975), 501–13.

1391 Von Tunzelmann, G. N. 'Trends in real wages, 1750–1850, revisited', *EcHR* 2nd ser., 32 (1979), 33–49. Criticizing the interpretation in (1331).

1392 Walton, Gary M. 'The new economic history and the burdens of the Navigation Acts', *EcHR* 2nd ser., 24 (1971), 533–42. Reply to (1353) and defence of (1337), (1338) and (1386).

1393 Ward, J. R. 'The profitability of sugar planting in the British West Indies, 1650–1834', *EcHR* 2nd ser., 31 (1978), 197–213.

1394 Williams, Glyndwr. 'The Hudson's Bay Company and its critics in the eighteenth century', *TRHS* 5th ser., 20 (1970), 149–71. See also (1260).

1395 Wilson, Sir Charles. 'The entrepreneur in the industrial revolution in Britain', *History* NS, 42 (1957), 101–17.

1396 Wilson, Richard George. 'The supremacy of the Yorkshire cloth industry in the eighteenth century', in Negley Boyd Harte and Kenneth George Ponting (eds.), *Textile history and economic history*. Manchester, 1973, pp. 225–46.

1397 Wolff, Klaus H. 'Textile bleaching and the birth of the chemical industry', *BusHR*, 48 (1974), 143–63.

1398 Wrigley, Edward Anthony. 'The supply of raw materials in the industrial revolution', *EcHR* 2nd ser., 15 (1962–3), 1–16; reprinted in Ronald Maxwell Hartwell (ed.), *The causes of the industrial revolution*. 1967, pp. 97–120. The fundamental importance of the change from organic to inorganic materials, especially coal and steam power.

IX.   AGRICULTURAL HISTORY

For specialized bibliographies, lists and catalogues, see (3) and (89).

1. Printed sources

1399 Davis, Richard. *A general view of the agriculture of the county of Oxford* .... 1794. One of the earliest of many similar county reports prepared for the Board of Agriculture; they were much criticized by contemporaries: see (1402).

1400 Hughes, Anne. *The diary of a farmer's wife, 1796–1797*. Comp. by Suzanne Beedell. 1964.

1401 Johnson, William Branch (ed.). '*Memorandums for* ... ': *the diary between 1798 and 1810 of John Carrington, farmer, chief constable, tax assessor, surveyor of the highways, and overseer of the poor of Bramfield in Hertfordshire*. 1973. Johnson's *The Carrington diary, 1797–1810*, 1956, is based on this diary.

1402 Marshall, William. *A review of the reports to the Board of Agriculture*. 1808–18, 6 vols. Highly critical of the county by county reports commissioned by the Board.

1403 —— *The rural economy of Norfolk*. 1787, 2 vols. First of a series of similar accounts of Yorkshire (1788, 2 vols.; 2nd edn, 1796); Gloucestershire (1789; 2nd edn, 1796); the Midland counties (1790; 2nd edn, 1796); the West of England (1796; 2nd edn, 1805, 2 vols.) and the Southern counties (1798).

1404 Mingay, Gordon Edmund (ed.). *Arthur Young and his times*. 1975. Selections, arranged chronologically, with connecting narrative and an introduction.

1405 Palmer, Roy (comp.). *The painful plough: a portrait of the agricultural labourer in the nineteenth century from folksongs and ballads and contemporary accounts*. Cambridge, 1972.

1406 Whiting, Charles Edwin (ed.). *The accounts of the churchwardens, constables, overseers of the poor and overseers of the highways of the parish of Hooton Pagnell, 1767–1820*.

(Yorkshire Archaeological Society, Record Series, 97.) Leeds, 1938. One of the few published sets of such accounts.

1407 Young, Arthur. *The autobiography of Arthur Young with selections from his correspondence.* Ed. Matilda Barbara Betham-Edwards. 1898; reprinted, New York, 1967. Journal and letters, 1755–1820. See also (1404) and, for Young's biography, see (1464).

1408 —— *The farmer's calendar: containing the business necessary to be performed on various kinds of farms during every month of the year.* 1771; 21st edn, 1862. Title varies.

1409 —— *A six weeks tour through the southern counties of England and Wales.* 1768. *The farmer's tour through the east of England.* 1771, 4 vols. *A six months tour through the north of England.* 1771, 4 vols.

1410 —— (ed.). *Annals of agriculture and other useful arts.* 1784–1815, 46 vols. Largely written by Young.

2. Surveys

1411 Chambers, Jonathan David and Gordon Edmund Mingay. *The agricultural revolution, 1750–1880.* 1966. Best single book on the subject.

1412 Handley, James Edmund. *The agricultural revolution in Scotland.* Glasgow, 1963.

1413 Jones, Eric Lionel. *Agriculture and the industrial revolution.* Oxford, 1974. Jones's collected articles.

1414 —— (ed.). *Agriculture and economic growth in England 1650–1815.* 1967. Reprints of articles by various hands with long introduction linking earlier developments with those of the later eighteenth century.

1415 Mingay, Gordon Edmund. *British landed society in the eighteenth century.* 1963.

1416 —— (ed.). *The agricultural revolution: changes in agriculture, 1650–1880.* 1977. Documents, with an important introduction summarizing recent scholarship.

1417 Prothero, Rowland Edmund, Baron Ernle. *English farming, past and present.* 1912; 5th edn, 1936; reprinted, with an introduction by George Edwin Fussell and Oliver Ross McGregor, 1961. An increasingly outdated classic; important commentary by Eric Lionel Jones in *EcHR* 2nd ser., 15 (1962–3), 145–52. A useful bibliography of work on agricultural history to 1961 in the reprint, pp. xci–cxv.

1418 Thompson, Francis Michael Longstreth. *English landed society in the nineteenth century.* 1963.

3. Monographs

1419 Baker, Alan R. H. and Robin A. Butlin (eds.). *Studies of field systems in the British Isles.* Cambridge, 1973. Essays summarizing recent work; extends to the final breakup of the medieval patterns.

1420 Barnes, Donald Grove. *A history of the English corn laws, from 1660–1846.* 1930. Checklist of contemporary pamphlets, pp. 303–28.

1421 Bateman, John. *The great landowners of Great Britain and Ireland.* 4th edn, 1883; reprinted, with introduction by David Spring, Leicester, 1971. Based on the Return of Owners of Land (HC 1874, LXXII, Pt III); its value back to the end of the eighteenth century is discussed in (1418).

1422 Beastall, Tom William. *The agricultural revolution in Lincolnshire.* Lincoln, 1978. See also (1433) and (1456).

1423 —— *A north country estate: the Lumleys and Saundersons as landowners, 1600–1900.* 1975.

1424 Carter, Harold Burnell. *His Majesty's Spanish flock: Sir Joseph Banks and the merinos of George III of England.* Sydney, 1964.

1425 Colyer, Richard J. *The Welsh cattle drovers: agriculture and the Welsh cattle trade before and during the nineteenth century.* Cardiff, 1976.

1426 Crosby, Travis L. *English farmers and the politics of protection, 1815–1852.* Hassocks, Sussex, 1977.

1427 Darby, Henry Clifford. *The draining of the Fens.* Cambridge, 1940. To 1900.

1428 Evans, Eric J. *The contentious tithe: the tithe problem and English agriculture, 1750–1850.* 1976.

1429 Fussell, George Edwin. *The farmer's tools, 1500–1900: the history of British farm implements, tools and machinery before the tractor came.* 1952.

1430 Garnett, Frank Walls. *Westmoreland agriculture, 1800–1900.* Kendal, Cumbria, 1912.

1431   Gaut, Robert Charles. *A history of Worcestershire agriculture and rural evolution.* Worcester, 1939.

1432   Gonner, Sir Edward Carter Kersey. *Common land and inclosure.* 1912; reprinted, with introduction by Gordon Edmund Mingay, 1966. Old standard, whose interpretation of the course and effects of enclosure has been largely confirmed by recent work.

1433   Grigg, David Brian. *The agricultural revolution in south Lincolnshire.* Cambridge, 1966. See also (1422) and (1456).

1434   Harris, Alan Henry. *The rural landscape of the East Riding of Yorkshire, 1700–1850: a study in historical geography.* 1961.

1435   Harvey, John Hooper. *Early gardening catalogues: with complete reprints of lists and accounts of the 16th–19th centuries.* 1972.

1436   Harvey, Nigel. *A history of farm buildings in England and Wales.* Newton Abbot, Devon, 1970. See also (1514).

1437   Hoskins, William George. *The Midland peasant: the economic and social history of a Leicestershire village.* 1957. The famous study of Wigston Magna.

1438   Howell, David W. *Land and people in nineteenth-century Wales.* 1977.

1439   Hudson, Kenneth. *Patriotism with profit: British agricultural societies in the eighteenth and nineteenth centuries.* 1972.

1440   Johnson, Arthur Henry. *Disappearance of the small landowner.* Oxford, 1909; reprinted, with an introduction by Joan Thirsk, 1963. Argues that the small landowner had already declined drastically in numbers by 1700.

1441   Jones, Eric Lionel. *Seasons and prices: the role of the weather in English agricultural history.* 1964. Chronological survey of seasons, 1728–1911.

1442   Kerr, Barbara. *Bound to the soil: a social history of Dorset, 1750–1918.* 1968. Study of nine Dorset parishes.

1443   Maguire, William Alexander. *The Downshire estates in Ireland 1801–1845: the management of Irish landed estates in the early nineteenth century.* Oxford, 1972.

1444   Mingay, Gordon Edmund. *Enclosure and the small farmer in the age of the industrial revolution.* 1968. Brief but excellent.

1445   Orwin, Charles Stewart and Christabel Susan (Lowry) Orwin. *The open fields.* Oxford, 1938; 2nd edn, Oxford, 1954. Classic.

1446   Parker, Robert Alexander Clarke. *Enclosures in the eighteenth century.* (Historical Association, London. Aids for Teachers, 7.) 1966.

1447   Payne, Ernest Oscar. *Property in land in south Bedfordshire, 1750–1832.* (Bedfordshire Record Society, 23.) Streatley, Beds., 1946. Detailed survey of changes in land ownership in ten villages.

1448   Peacock, Alfred James. *Bread or blood: a study of the agrarian riots in East Anglia in 1816.* 1965.

1449   Perkins, J. A. *Sheep farming in eighteenth- and nineteenth-century Lincolnshire.* Grimsby, Lincs., 1977.

1450   Riches, Naomi. *The agricultural revolution in Norfolk.* Chapel Hill, NC, 1937; 2nd edn, with a new bibliographical note by William Henry Chaloner, 1967. Major reinterpretation of the chronology of agrarian change.

1451   Russell, Sir Edward John. *A history of agricultural science in Great Britain, 1620–1954.* 1966.

1452   Shrimpton, Colin. *The landed society and the farming community of Essex in the late eighteenth and early nineteenth centuries.* New York, 1977.

1453   Spring, David. *The English landed estate in the nineteenth century: its administration.* Baltimore, Md, 1963. Primarily concerned with the Bedford and Graham estates.

1454   Tate, William Edward. *A domesday of English enclosure acts and awards.* Ed. Michael E. Turner. Reading, 1978. A comprehensive collection of all of Turner's lists and analyses of these documents.

1455   —— *The English village community and the enclosure movement.* 1967. American title: *The enclosure movement.* Comprehensive account from the earliest times.

1456   Thirsk, Joan. *English peasant farming: the agrarian history of Lincolnshire from Tudor to recent times.* 1957. See also (1422) and (1433).

1457   Trow-Smith, Robert. *A history of British livestock husbandry, 1700–1900.* 1959. Useful bibliography.

1458   Turner, Michael E. *English parliamentary enclosure.* Folkestone, Kent, 1980.

Comprehensive account, with special emphasis on Buckinghamshire; incorporates a series of earlier articles.

1459 Ward, John Trevor. *East Yorkshire landed estates in the nineteenth century.* (East Yorkshire Local History Society Publications, 23.) York, 1967.

1460 Ward, John Trevor and Richard George Wilson (eds.). *Land and industry in the industrial revolution.* Newton Abbot, Devon, 1971. Important essays on the industrial activities of the landed classes.

1461 Wilkinson, Olga. *The agricultural revolution in the East Riding of Yorkshire.* (East Yorkshire Local History Society Publications, 5.) York, 1956.

1462 Yelling, James A. *Common field and enclosure in England, 1450–1850.* 1977. Concerned with types and methods of enclosure from the point of view of historical geography rather than with effects or even with chronology.

4. Biographies

1463 Arnold, Ralph. *A yeoman of Kent: an account of Richard Hayes, 1725–1790, and of the village of Cobham in which he lived and farmed.* 1949. Primarily mid-eighteenth century.

1464 Gazley, John Gerow. *The life of Arthur Young, 1741–1820.* Philadelphia, Pa, 1973. For Young's writings, see (1404) and (1407–10).

1465 Mitchison, Rosalind. *Agricultural Sir John: the life of Sir John Sinclair of Ulbster, 1754–1835.* 1962.

1466 Parker, Robert Alexander Clarke. *Coke of Norfolk: a financial and agricultural study, 1707–1842.* Oxford, 1975. Major revision of Coke's place in agricultural history; much on the First Earl of Leicester's innovations in the earlier eighteenth century and on family finances as well as on agriculture.

1467 Pawson, Henry Cecil. *Robert Bakewell, pioneer livestock breeder.* 1957.

1468 Stirling, Anna Maria Diana Wilhelmina (Pickering). *Coke of Norfolk and his friends.* 1908, 2 vols. Still important for its letters 1777–1837, but without value for its account of Coke's place in the history of agriculture.

5. Articles

1469 Baack, Bennett D. and Robert Paul Thomas. 'The enclosure movement and the supply of labour during the industrial revolution', *JEurEcH*, 3 (1974), 401–23. See also (1473) and (1479).

1470 Beckett, J. V. 'English landownership in the later seventeenth and eighteenth centuries: the debate and the problems', *EcHR* 2nd ser., 30 (1977), 567–81. Special emphasis on the land market and patterns of landownership in Cumbria.

1471 Beresford, Maurice Warwick. 'The commissioners of enclosures', *EcHR* 1st ser., 16 (1945–6), 130–40; reprinted in Walter Edward Minchinton (ed.), *Essays in agrarian history.* Newton Abbot, Devon, 1968, ii, pp. 89–102. Favourable to the commissioners.

1472 Canadine, David. 'The landowner as millionaire: the finances of the dukes of Devonshire, *c.* 1800 – *c.* 1926', *AgHR*, 25 (1977), 77–97.

1473 Chambers, Jonathan David. 'Enclosure and labour supply in the industrial revolution', *EcHR* 2nd ser., 5 (1952–3), 319–43; reprinted in Eric Lionel Jones (ed.), *Agriculture and economic growth in England, 1650–1815.* 1967, pp. 94–127. Population growth, not agrarian change, the source of the new labour supply. For criticism, see (1469) and (1479).

1474 Clarkson, L. A. 'The English bark trade, 1660–1830', *AgHR*, 22 (1974), 136–52.

1475 Clay, Christopher. 'Marriage, inheritance and the rise of large estates in England, 1660–1815', *EcHR* 2nd ser., 21 (1968), 503–18.

1476 —— 'The price of freehold land in the later seventeenth and eighteenth centuries', *EcHR* 2nd ser., 27 (1974), 173–89.

1477 Collins, E. J. T. 'Migrant labour in British agriculture in the nineteenth century', *EcHR* 2nd ser., 29 (1976), 38–59.

1478 Crafts, N. F. R. 'Determinants of the rate of parliamentary enclosure', *ExEcH* 2nd ser., 14 (1977), 227–49. Econometric.

1479 —— 'Enclosure and labour supply revisited', *ExEcH* 2nd ser., 15 (1978), 172–83. Econometric criticism of (1473); see also (1469).

1480   Fairlie, Susan. 'The nineteenth-century corn law reconsidered', *EcHR* 2nd ser., 18 (1965), 562–75.

1481   Fussell, George Edwin. 'Animal husbandry in eighteenth-century England', *AgH*, 11 (1937), 96–116, 189–214.

1482   —— 'The evolution of field drainage', *Bath and West Country Society Journal* 6th ser., 4 (1929–30), 59–72. Discusses most of the sources on the subject.

1483   Fussell, George Edwin and Constance Goodman. 'Crop husbandry in eighteenth-century England', *AgH*, 15 (1941), 202–16; 16 (1942), 41–63.

1484   Gould, J. D. 'Agricultural fluctuations and the English economy in the eighteenth century', *JEcH*, 22 (1962), 313–33.

1485   Habakkuk, Sir John. 'Economic functions of English landowners in the seventeenth and eighteenth centuries', *ExEcH* 1st ser., 6 (1953–4), 92–102; reprinted in Walter Edward Minchinton (ed.), *Essays in agrarian history*. Newton Abbot, Devon, 1968, i, pp. 187–201.

1486   —— 'The English land market in the eighteenth century', in John Selwyn Bromley and E. H. Kossman (eds.), *Britain and the Netherlands*, 1 (1960), pp. 154–73. Established the idea of an effective end to the land market, a view only recently being questioned; see especially (1470), (1475), (1476) and (1489).

1487   Henderson, H. C. K. 'Agriculture in England and Wales in 1801', *Geographical Journal*, 118 (1952), 338–45. General discussion of the replies to the government's inquiries of 1801; for other general discussions of this source, see (1488), (1504) and (1522).

1488   —— 'The 1801 crop returns: geographical distribution', *Transactions of the Leicestershire Archaeological Society*, 27 (1951), pp. 100–2. See also (1487), (1504) and (1522).

1489   Holderness, B. A. 'The English land market in the eighteenth century: the case of Lincolnshire', *EcHR* 2nd ser., 27 (1974), 557–76. Sees a relatively fluid land market.

1490   —— 'Landlord's capital formation in East Anglia, 1750–1870', *EcHR* 2nd ser., 25 (1972), 434–47.

1491   —— '"Open" and "Close" parishes in England in the eighteenth and nineteenth centuries', *AgHR*, 20 (1972), 126–39. Important distinction for the social condition of individual villages.

1492   Hueckel, Glenn. 'English farming profits during the Napoleonic Wars, 1793–1815', *ExEcH* 2nd ser., 13 (1976), 331–45.

1493   Hughes, Edward. 'The eighteenth-century estate agent', in Henry Alfred Cronne, et al. (eds.), *Essays in British and Irish history in honour of James Eadie Todd*. 1949, pp. 185–99. See also (1506).

1494   Hunt, H. G. 'Agricultural rent in south-east England, 1788–1825', *AgHR*, 7 (1959), 98–108.

1495   —— 'Landownership and enclosure, 1750–1830', *EcHR* 2nd ser., 11 (1958–9), 497–505.

1496   John, Arthur Henry. 'Farming in wartime: 1793–1815', in Eric Lionel Jones and Gordon Edmund Mingay (eds.), *Land, labour and population in the industrial revolution*. 1967, pp. 28–47.

1497   Large, David. 'The wealth of the greater Irish landowners, 1750–1815', *Irish Historical Studies*, 15 (1966–7), 21–47.

1498   Macdonald, Stuart. 'The diffusion of knowledge among Northumberland farmers, 1780–1815', *AgHR*, 27 (1979), 30–39. How the new ideas spread; good case study.

1499   —— 'The progress of the early threshing machine', *AgHR*, 23 (1975), 63–71. Criticized by N. E. Fox, with a reply by Macdonald, *AgHR*, 26 (1978), 26–33.

1500   Martin, J. M. 'The cost of parliamentary enclosure in Warwickshire', *University of Birmingham Historical Journal*, 9 (1963–4), 144–62; reprinted in Eric Lionel Jones (ed.), *Agriculture and economic growth in England, 1650–1815*. 1967, pp. 128–51. Emphasizes high and increasing cost, in contrast to (1520).

1501   —— 'Landownership and the land tax returns', *AgHR*, 16 (1966), 96–103. Defence of their value in determining changes in landownership, in partial reply to (1507).

1502   —— 'Members of Parliament and enclosure: a reconsideration', *AgHR*, 27 (1979), 101–9.

1503   —— 'The small landowner and parliamentary enclosure in Warwickshire', *EcHR*

2nd ser., 32 (1979), 328–43. Mostly eastern Feldon region; finds some decline in numbers, but mostly among the non-occupier owners.

1504 Minchinton, Walter Edward. 'Agricultural returns and the government during the Napoleonic Wars', AgHR, 1 (1953), 29–43; reprinted in Walter Edward Minchinton (ed.), Essays in agrarian history. Newton Abbot, Devon, 1968, ii, pp. 103–20. Discusses the inquiries of 1795 and 1800 as well as the crop returns of 1801. See also (1487), (1488) and (1522).

1505 Mingay, Gordon Edmund. 'The "agricultural revolution" in English history: a reconsideration', AgH, 37 (1963), 123–33; reprinted in Walter Edward Minchinton (ed.), Essays in agrarian history. Newton Abbot, Devon, 1968, ii, pp. 9–28.

1506 —— 'The eighteenth-century land steward', in Eric Lionel Jones and Gordon Edmund Mingay (eds.), Land, labour and population in the industrial revolution. 1967, pp. 3–27. See also (1493).

1507 —— 'The land tax assessments and the small landowner', EcHR 2nd ser., 17 (1964–5), 381–8. Criticizing the weight usually put on them in determining changes in landownership. Criticized in (1501).

1508 —— 'The large estate in eighteenth-century England', in First International Conference of Economic History: contributions... Stockholm, 1960. Paris and The Hague, 1960, pp. 367–83.

1509 Molland, R. 'Agriculture, c. 1793 – c. 1870', in VCH Wiltshire, Vol. 4, ed. by Elizabeth Crittall. 1959, pp. 65–91. Earlier developments are described by Eric Kerridge, ibid., pp. 43–64; together provide a model county study.

1510 O'Brien, Patrick Karl, D. Heath and Caglar Keyder. 'Agricultural efficiency in Britain and France, 1815–1914', JEurEcH, 6 (1977), 339–91.

1511 Perkins, J. A. 'Tenure, tenant right, and agricultural progress in Lindsey, 1780–1850', AgHR, 23 (1975), 1–22.

1512 Philpot, Gordon. 'Enclosure and population growth in eighteenth-century England', ExEcH 2nd ser., 12 (1975), 29–46. Criticized in (1530). See also (1528) and (1533).

1513 Richards, Eric. '"Leviathan of Wealth": West Midland agriculture, 1800–50', AgHR, 22 (1974), 97–117. Leveson-Gower estates.

1514 Robinson, John Martin. 'Model farm buildings of the age of improvement', Architectural history, 19 (1976), 17–31. See also (1436).

1515 Rowe, David John. 'The Culleys, Northumberland farmers, 1767–1813', AgHR, 19 (1971), 156–74.

1516 Sexauer, Benjamin. 'English and French agriculture in the late eighteenth century', AgH, 50 (1976), 491–505. Comparison, incorporating recent revisionary work on French agrarian development.

1517 Spring, David. 'English landowners and nineteenth-century industrialism', in John Trevor Ward and Richard George Wilson (eds.), Land and industry: the landed estate and the industrial revolution. Newton Abbot, Devon, 1971, pp. 16–62.

1518 Spring, Eileen. 'Landowners, lawyers and land law reform in nineteenth-century England', American Journal of Legal History, 21 (1977), 40–59. See also (290).

1519 —— 'The settlement of land in nineteenth-century England', American Journal of Legal History, 8 (1964), 209–23.

1520 Tate, William Edward. 'The cost of parliamentary enclosure in England (with special reference to the county of Oxford)', ExHR 2nd ser., 5 (1952–3), 258–65. Cost not as great as often thought. See also (1500).

1521 —— 'Oxfordshire enclosure commissioners, 1737–1856', JMH, 23 (1951), 137–45. Favourable to the commissioners.

1522 Thomas, David. 'The acreage returns of 1801: a test of accuracy', Bulletin of the Board of Celtic Studies, 18 (1959–60), 379–83. See also (1487), (1488) and (1504).

1523 Thompson, Francis Michael Longstreth. 'English great estates in the 19th century, 1790–1914', in First International Conference of Economic History: contributions... Stockholm, 1960. Paris and The Hague, 1960, pp. 385–97.

1524 —— 'Land and politics in England in the nineteenth century', TRHS 5th ser., 15 (1965), 23–44.

1525 —— 'The land market in the nineteenth century', Oxford Economic Papers NS, 9 (1957), 285–308; reprinted in Walter Edward Minchinton (ed.), Essays in agrarian history, Newton Abbot, Devon, 1968, ii, pp. 29–54.

1526 —— 'Landownership and economic growth in England in the eighteenth century', in Eric Lionel Jones and S. J. Woolf (eds.), *Agrarian change and economic development: the historical problems*, 1969, pp. 41–60.

1527 —— 'The second agricultural revolution, 1815–1880', *EcHR* 2nd ser., 21 (1968), 62–77.

1528 Tomaske, John A. 'Enclosures and population movements in England, 1700–1830: a methodological comment', *ExEcH* 2nd ser., 8 (1970–1), 223–7. Criticism of (1533); see also (1512) and (1530).

1529 Trueman, B. E. S. 'Corporate estate management: Guy's Hospital agricultural estates, 1726–1815', *AgHR*, 28 (1980), 31–44.

1530 Turner, Michael E. 'Parliamentary enclosure and population change in England, 1750–1830', *ExEcH* 2nd ser., 13 (1976), 463–8. Reply to (1512); further comment by Philpot, *ibid.* pp. 469–71. See also (1528) and (1533).

1531 Ward, John Trevor. 'The saving of a Yorkshire estate: George Lane Fox and the Bramham estate', *Yorkshire Archaeological Journal*, 42 (1967–70), 63–71.

1532 Wasson, E. A. 'The third Earl Spencer and agriculture, 1818–45', *AgHR*, 26 (1978), 89–99.

1533 White, Lawrence J. 'Enclosures and population movements in England, 1700–1830', *ExEcH* 2nd ser., 6 (1968–9), 175–86. The beginnings of this debate; see (1512), (1528) and (1530).

1534 Wilkes, A. R. 'Adjustments in arable farming after the Napoleonic Wars', *AgHR*, 28 (1980), 90–103.

X. SCIENCE AND TECHNOLOGY

For specialized bibliographies, lists and catalogues, see (10), (13), (45), (46), (50), (57), (63), (129) and (177). For military medicine, see also (1750), (1786), (1801), (1802), (1839), (1864), (1865), (1868), (1869), (1874), (1879) and (1885).

1. Printed sources

1535 Beaglehole, John Cawte (ed.). *The journals of Captain James Cook on his voyages of discovery.* Cambridge, 1955–67, 3 vols. For Cook's biography, see (1640).

1536 Brown, Sanborn Conner (ed.). *Collected works of Count Rumford.* Cambridge, Mass., 1968–70, 5 vols. For Rumford's biography, see (1643).

1537 Dalton, John, *A new system of chemical philosophy.* Manchester, 1808–27, 2 vols. Main work in which his theories were systematically expounded; no collected works, but see (1556). For Dalton's biography, see (1625); and for studies of his work, see (1584), (1598) and (1625).

1538 Davy, John (ed.). *The collected works of Sir Humphry Davy ... with a life.* 1839–40, 9 vols. For Davy's biography, see (1653); for studies of his work, see (1599) and (1722).

1539 Dawson, Warren Royal (comp.). *The Banks letters: a calendar of the manuscript correspondence of Sir Joseph Banks preserved in the British Museum, the British Museum (Natural History), and other collections in Great Britain.* 1958. Supplemented in *Bulletin of the British Museum (Natural History)*, Historical Series 3, 2 (1962), 41–70; 3 (1965), 71–93. Principal scientific correspondence of the period. For Banks's biography, see (1646).

1540 Faraday, Michael. *Experimental researches in electricity.* 1839–55, 3 vols. Reprinted papers; no collected works, but see (1543). For Faraday's correspondence, see (1557); for his biography, see (1672); for studies of his work, see (1605) and (1688).

1541 Herschel, Sir William. *The scientific papers of Sir William Herschel ... including early papers hitherto unpublished: collected and edited under the direction of a joint committee of the Royal Society and the Royal Astronomical Society.* 1912, 2 vols. For other documents concerning the Herschels, see (1547); for biographies, see (1637), (1645) and (1667); for studies, see (1698) and (1707).

1542 Hutton, James. *Theory of the earth, with proofs and illustrations.* 1795, 2 vols; a third vol., ed. Sir Archibald Geikie, 1899, contains additional chapters planned for the original; the first two vols. reprinted, New York, 1959. Three earlier pamphlets and papers by Hutton, together with John Playfair's biography of him, were edited by Victor Ambrose Eyles and George Willard White, Darien, Conn., 1970. For Hutton's biography, see (1639).

1543 Jeffreys, Alan Edward (comp.). *Michael Faraday: a list of his lectures and published writings.* 1960. See also (1540).

1544 Jenner, Edward. *An inquiry into the causes and effects of variolae vaccinae.* 1798. Announcing the discovery of vaccination. See also (1615), (1674) and (1733); for Jenner's biography, see (1651).

1545 King-Hele, Desmond George (ed.). *The essential works of Erasmus Darwin.* 1968. For Darwin's biography, see (1655).

1546 Lindsay, Jack (ed.). *Autobiography of Joseph Priestley.* Bath, 1970. For Priestley's writings, see also (1552), (1555), (1903) and (2265); for his biography, see (1654).

1547 Lubbock, Constance Anne (Herschel), Lady (ed.). *The Herschel chronicle: the life-story of William Herschel and his sister, Caroline Herschel.* Cambridge, 1933. Compiled from journals, letters and autobiographical fragments. See also (1541).

1548 Lyell, Sir Charles. *Principles of geology.* 1830–3, 3 vols; 2nd edn, 1832–3, 3 vols. and many subsequent editions. Completed demolition of Mosaic theories of cosmology and geology. For biographies of Lyell, see (1638) and (1673).

1549 Massingham, Harold John (ed.). *The writings of Gilbert White of Selborne.* 1938, 2 vols. A selection. For White's biography, see (1656).

1550 Maxwell, James Clerk, et al. (eds.). *The scientific papers of ... Henry Cavendish.* Cambridge, 1921, 2 vols. For Cavendish's biography, see (1641); for studies of his work, see (1684) and (1699).

1551 Palmer, Sir James Frederick (ed.). *The works of John Hunter, FRS, with notes.* 1835–7, 4 vols. For biographies, see (1650) and (1661).

1552 Passmore, John Arthur (ed.). *Priestley's writings in philosophy, science and politics.* New York, 1965. A selection. See also (1555) and (1718).

1553 Robinson, Eric and Douglas McKie (eds.). *Partners in science: letters of James Watt and Joseph Black.* 1970.

1554 Robinson, Eric and Albert Edward Musson (eds.). *James Watt and the steam revolution: a documentary history.* 1969.

1555 Schofield, Robert Edwin (ed.). *A scientific autobiography of Joseph Priestley, 1733–1804: selected scientific correspondence.* Cambridge, Mass., 1966. See also (1552) and (1718).

1556 Smyth, Albert Leslie (comp.). *John Dalton, 1766-1844: a bibliography of works by and about him.* Manchester, 1966.

1557 Williams, Leslie Pearce (ed.). *The selected correspondence of Michael Faraday.* Cambridge, 1971, 2 vols. For Faraday's works, see (1540) and (1543); for studies, see (1605) and (1688); for his biography, see (1672).

2. Surveys

1558 Butt, John and Ian Donnachie. *Industrial archaeology in the British Isles.* 1979. Most recent survey.

1559 Cardwell, Donald Stephen Lowell. *The organization of science in England.* 1957; rev. edn. 1972.

1560 Chaplin, Thomas Hancock Arnold. *Medicine in England during the reign of George III.* 1919; reprinted, New York, 1970.

1561 Dampier, Sir William Cecil (formerly Dampier-Whetham). *A history of science and its relations with philosophy and religion.* 4th edn, reprinted with a postscript by I. Bernard Cohen, Cambridge, 1961.

1562 Derry, Thomas Kingston and Trevor Illtyd Williams. *A short history of technology from earliest times to AD 1900.* Oxford, 1960. See also (1572).

1563 Habakkuk, Sir John. *American and British technology in the nineteenth century: the search for labour-saving inventions.* Cambridge, 1962.

1564 King, Lester Snow. *The medical world of the eighteenth century.* Chicago, Ill., 1958. Not limited to England.

1565 Landes, David S. *The unbound Prometheus: technological change and industrial development in western Europe from 1750 to the present.* 1969. The case for technological change as the principal cause of economic development.

1566   Musson, Albert Edward and Eric Robinson. *Science and technology in the industrial revolution*. Manchester, 1969.

1567   Musson, Albert Edward (ed.). *Science, technology and economic growth in the eighteenth century*. 1972. Reprinted articles by various hands with a long introduction.

1568   Poynter, Frederick Noël Lawrence (ed.). *The evolution of medical practice in Britain*. 1961.

1569   Rowland, K. T. *Eighteenth-century inventions*. Newton Abbot, Devon, 1974.

1570   Schofield, Robert Edwin. *Mechanism and materialism: British natural philosophy in an age of reason*. Princeton, NJ, 1970.

1571   Singer, Charles Joseph and Edgar Ashworth Underwood. *A short history of medicine*. 2nd edn, New York, 1962. General history; chapter four discusses the eighteenth and early nineteenth centuries; extensive bibliographies.

1572   Singer, Charles Joseph, et al. (eds.). *A history of technology*. Oxford, 1954–8, 5 vols. Vol. 4: *The industrial revolution, c. 1750 – c. 1850*. See also (1562).

1573   Wolf, Abraham. *A history of science: technology and philosophy in the eighteenth century*. 1938; 2nd edn, rev. by Douglas McKie, 1952.

3. Monographs

1574   Armytage, Walter Harry Green. *The rise of the technocrats: a social history*. 1965.

1575   —— *A social history of engineering*. Cambridge, Mass., 1961.

1576   Bennion, Elizabeth. *Antique medical instruments*. 1979. Lavishly illustrated.

1577   Berman, Morris. *Social change and scientific organization: The Royal Institution, 1799–1844*. Ithaca, NY, 1978.

1578   Bishop, George Daniel. *Physics teaching in England from early times up to 1850*. 1961.

1579   Burstall, Aubrey Frederic. *A history of mechanical engineering*. 1963.

1580   Burton, Anthony. *The canal builders*. 1972.

1581   Cannon, Susan Faye. *Science in culture: the early Victorian period*. New York, 1978. Much on the first three decades of the nineteenth century.

1582   Cardwell, Donald Stephen Lowell. *From Watt to Clausius: the rise of thermodynamics in the early industrial age*. 1971.

1583   —— *Steam power in the eighteenth century: a case study in the application of science*. 1963.

1584   —— (ed.). *John Dalton and the progress of science*. Manchester, 1968. Essays by various hands. For other Dalton references, see (1537).

1585   Chenevix Trench, Charles Pocklington. *The royal malady*. 1964. See also (1604).

1586   Clark, Sir George and A. M. Cooke. *A history of the Royal College of Physicians of London*. Oxford, 1964–72, 3 vols. Vol. 2 (by Clark) covers from the late seventeenth century to 1858. See also (1659) and (1732).

1587   Clow, Archibald and Nan Louise Clow. *The chemical revolution: a contribution to social technology*. 1952. Important; valuable bibliography.

1588   Cope, Sir Zachary. *The Royal College of Surgeons of England: a history*. 1959.

1589   Cossons, Neil. *The iron bridge: symbol of the industrial revolution*. Bradford-on-Avon, Wilts., 1979.

1590   Creighton, Charles. *A history of epidemics in Britain*. Cambridge, 1891, 2 vols.; reprinted, 1965, 2 vols., with additional material by David Edward Charles Eversley, Edgar Ashworth Underwood and Lynda Ovenall. Basic on the subject.

1591   Daumas, Maurice. *Les Instruments scientifiques aux xvii⁷ et xviii⁷ siècles*. Paris, 1953; English trans. by Harry Holland, New York, 1977.

1592   Dickinson, Henry Winram. *A short history of the steam engine*. Cambridge, 1939; 2nd edn, with introduction by Albert Edward Musson, 1963.

1593   Dickinson, Henry Winram and Rhys Jenkins. *James Watt and the steam engine*. Oxford, 1927. Very technical.

1594   Donovan, Arthur L. *Philosophical chemistry in the Scottish enlightenment: the doctrines and discourses of William Cullen and Joseph Black*. Edinburgh, 1975.

1595   Gage, Andrew Thomas. *A history of the Linnean Society of London*. 1938.

1596   Gillispie, Charles Coulston. *Genesis and geology: a study in the relations of scientific thought, natural theology, and scientific opinion in Great Britain, 1790–1850*. 1951. Valuable bibliography.

1597   Glass, Hiram Bentley, et al. (eds.). *Forerunners of Darwin 1745–1859*. Baltimore, Md, 1959.

1598   Greenaway, Frank. *John Dalton and the atom*. 1966. For other Dalton references, see (1537).

1599   Gregory, Joshua Craven. *The scientific achievement of Sir Humphry Davy*. 1930. For other Davy references, see (1538).

1600   Hills, Richard Leslie. *Power in the industrial revolution*. Manchester, 1970.

1601   Hunt, Thomas Cecil (ed.). *The Medical Society of London, 1773–1973*. 1972.

1602   Kirby, Richard Shelton and Philip Gustave Laurson. *The early years of modern civil engineering*. New Haven, Conn., 1932.

1603   Lyons, Sir Henry George. *The Royal Society, 1660–1940: a history of its administration under its charters*. Cambridge, 1944. See also (1622).

1604   Macalpine, Ida and Richard Alfred Hunter. *George III and the mad business*. 1969. Much on eighteenth century psychiatry as well as on the case of the King. See also (1585).

1605   Martin, Thomas. *Faraday's discovery of electro-magnetic induction*. 1949. For other Faraday references, see (1540).

1606   Morris, Robert John. *Cholera 1832: the social response to an epidemic*. 1976. See also (1611).

1607   Newman, Charles. *The evolution of medical education in the nineteenth century*. 1957.

1608   Olson, Richard. *Scottish philosophy and British physics, 1750–1880: a study in the foundations of the Victorian scientific style*. Princeton, NJ, 1975.

1609   Parry, Noel and Jose Parry. *The rise of the medical profession: a study of collective social mobility*. 1976.

1610   Parry-Jones, William Llewellyn. *The trade in lunacy: a study of private mad-houses in England in the eighteenth and nineteenth centuries*. 1971.

1611   Pelling, Margaret. *Cholera, fever, and English medicine 1825–65*. Oxford, 1978. See also (1606).

1612   Porter, Roy S. *The making of geology: earth science in Britain, 1660–1815*. Cambridge, 1977.

1613   Pugsley, Sir Alfred Grenville (ed.). *The works of Isambard Kingdom Brunel: an engineering approach*. 1976. See also (1665).

1614   Raistrick, Arthur. *Quakers in science and industry: being an account of the Quaker contribution to science and industry during the 17th and 18th centuries*. New York, 1950; reprinted, Newton Abbot, Devon, 1968.

1615   Razzell, Peter E. *Edward Jenner's cowpox vaccine: the history of a medical myth*. Firle, Sussex, 1977. See also (1544), (1651), (1674) and (1733).

1616   Ritterbush, Philip C. *Overtures to biology: the speculations of eighteenth-century naturalists*. New Haven, Conn., 1964. Much on English scientists; extensive bibliography.

1617   Ruddock, Ted. *Arch bridges and their builders, 1735–1835*. Cambridge, 1979.

1618   Schofield, Robert Edwin. *The Lunar Society of Birmingham: a social history of provincial science and industry in eighteenth-century England*. Oxford, 1963.

1619   Schonland, Sir Basil Ferdinand Jamieson. *The atomists (1805–1933)*. Oxford, 1968.

1620   Spratt, Hereward Philip. *The birth of the steamboat*. 1958.

1621   Steeds, William. *A history of machine tools, 1700–1910*. Oxford, 1969.

1622   Stimson, Dorothy. *Scientists and amateurs: a history of the Royal Society*. New York, 1948. See also (1603).

1623   Tann, Jennifer. *The development of the factory*. 1970. Plans from the Boulton and Watt papers of all sorts of factories; primarily concerned with technological developments.

1624   Taylor, Eva Germaine Rimmington. *The mathematical practitioners of Hanoverian England, 1714–1840*. 1966.

1625   Thackray, Arnold. *John Dalton: critical assessments of his life and science*. Cambridge, Mass., 1972. Collected and revised articles. For other Dalton references, see (1537).

1626   Underwood, Edgar Ashworth. *A history of the Worshipful Society of Apothecaries of London. Vol. 1: 1671–1815*. Abstracted and arranged from the notes of Cecil Wall ... by Hector Charles Camron ... revised, annotated, and edited by Edgar Ashworth Underwood. 1963.

1627   Von Tunzelmann, G. N. *Steam power and British industrialization to 1860*. Oxford, 1978. De-emphasizes the importance of steam power.

1628   Wall, Cecil. *The history of the Surgeons' Company, 1745–1800*. 1937.

1629   Watkins, George. *The stationary steam engine*. Newton Abbot, Devon, 1968.

1630　——— *The textile mill engine.* Newton Abbot, Devon, 1970.
1631　Whitaker, Sir Edmund Taylor. *A history of the theories of aether and electricity.* 1910; rev. and enlarged edn, 1951, 2 vols.
1632　White, John Henry. *The history of the phlogiston theory.* 1932. See also (1709).
1633　Williams, Guy R. *The age of agony: the art of healing, c. 1700–1800.* 1975.
1634　Wood, Sir Henry Trueman Wright. *A history of the Royal Society of Arts.* 1913; rev., abridged and brought up to date by George Kenneth Menzies, 1935. Concerned with technology, not the fine arts.
1635　Woodward, John Hunn. *To do the sick no harm: a study of the British voluntary hospital system to 1875.* 1974.
1636　Woolf, Harry. *The transits of Venus: a study of eighteenth-century science.* Princeton, NJ, 1959.

4. Biographies

1637　Armitage, Angus. *William Herschel.* 1962. See also (1667).
1638　Bailey, Sir Edward Battersby. *Charles Lyell.* 1962. See also (1548) and (1673).
1639　——— *James Hutton: the founder of modern geology.* Amsterdam, 1967. See also (1542).
1640　Beaglehole, John Cawte. *The life of Captain James Cook.* 1974. For Cook's journals, see (1535).
1641　Berry, Arthur J. *Henry Cavendish: his life and scientific work.* 1960. See also (1550).
1642　Boucher, Cyril Thomas Goodman. *John Rennie, 1761–1821: the life and work of a great engineer.* Manchester, 1963.
1643　Brown, Sanborn Conner. *Benjamin Thompson, Count Rumford.* Cambridge, Mass., 1979. See also (1536).
1644　Burton, Anthony. *Josiah Wedgwood: a biography.* 1976. See also (1119), (1355–8), (1677) and (1700).
1645　Buttman, Gunther. *The shadow of the telescope: a biography of John Herschel.* Trans. B. E. J. Pagel. Guildford, Surrey, 1974.
1646　Cameron, Hector Charles. *Sir Joseph Banks, KB, FRS:* the *autocrat of the philosophers.* 1952; reprinted, Sydney, 1966. Best biography. For Banks's correspondence, see (1539).
1647　Clements, Paul. *Marc Isambard Brunel.* Harlow, Essex, 1970.
1648　Dickinson, Henry Winram. *James Watt, craftsman and engineer.* Cambridge, 1936.
1649　——— *Matthew Boulton.* Cambridge, 1937.
1650　Dobson, Jessie. *John Hunter.* Edinburgh, 1969. See also (1551) and (1661).
1651　Drewitt, Frederic George Dawtrey. *The life of Edward Jenner.* 1931; 2nd edn, enlarged, 1933. See also (1544), (1615), (1674) and (1733).
1652　Gibb, Sir Alexander. *The story of Telford: the rise of civil engineering.* 1935. See also (1666).
1653　Hartley, Sir Harold B. *Humphry Davy.* 1966. See also (1538).
1654　Holt, Anne. *A life of Joseph Priestley.* 1931. For Priestley's writings, see (1546), (1552), (1555), (1903) and (2265).
1655　King-Hele, Desmond George. *Doctor of revolution: the life and genius of Erasmus Darwin.* 1977. King-Hele published an earlier biography in 1963. For Darwin's writings, see (1545).
1656　Lockley, R. M. *Gilbert White.* 1954. Best biography. For White's writings, see (1549).
1657　McNeil, Ian. *Joseph Bramah: a century of invention, 1749–1851.* Newton Abbot, Devon, 1968.
1658　Mair, Craig. *A star for seamen: the Stevenson family of engineers.* 1978. Builders of lighthouses from c. 1800.
1659　Munk, William. *The roll of the Royal College of Physicians of London, comprising biographical sketches of all the eminent physicians whose names are recorded in the annals.* 2nd edn, rev. and enlarged, 1878, 3 vols; continued in G. H. Brown, *Lives of the Fellows of the Royal College of Physicians of London 1826–1925.* 1955. See also (1586) and (1732).
1660　Oldham, Frank. *Thomas Young, FRS, philosopher and physician.* 1933; new edn, with Alexander Wood, Cambridge, 1954. Young was also a pioneer Egyptologist. See also (1730).
1661　Oppenheimer, Jane Marion. *New aspects of John and William Hunter.* New York, 1946. See also (1650).

1662 Patterson, Elizabeth C. *John Dalton and the atomic theory: the biography of a natural philosopher*. Garden City, NY, 1970. For other Dalton references, see (1537).

1663 Quill, Humphrey. *John Harrison: the man who found longitude*. New York, 1966.

1664 Ramsay, Sir William. *The life and letters of Joseph Black*. 1918.

1665 Rolt, Lionel Thomas Caswell. *Isambard Kingdom Brunel: a biography*. 1957. See also (1613).

1666 —— *Thomas Telford*. 1958. See also (1652).

1667 Sidgwick, John Benson. *William Herschel, explorer of the heavens*. 1953. See also (1637).

1668 Skeat, William C. *George Stephenson: the engineer and his letters*. 1973.

1669 Smiles, Samuel. *Industrial biography: iron-workers and tool-makers*. 1863; new edn by Lionel Thomas Caswell Rolt, 1967. In several instances, the only biographical studies.

1670 —— *Men of invention and industry*. 1884. In many instances, the only biographical studies of the subjects.

1671 Trevithick, Francis. *Life of Richard Trevithick, with an account of his inventions*. 1872. Locomotive pioneer.

1672 Williams, Leslie Pearce. *Michael Faraday: a biography*. 1965. For other Faraday references, see (1540).

1673 Wilson, Leonard Gilchrist. *Charles Lyell: the years to 1841: the revolution in geology*. New Haven, Conn., 1972. See also (1548) and (1638).

5. Articles

1674 Baxby, Derrick. 'Edward Jenner, William Woodville, and the origin of the vaccina virus', *JHMed*, 34 (1979), 234–62. See also (1544) and (1615).

1675 Beekman, Fenwick. 'The rise of British surgery in the eighteenth century', *Annals of Medical History* NS, 9 (1937), 549–66.

1676 Buckley, Roger N. 'The destruction of the British army in the West Indies, 1793–1815: a medical history', *Journal of the Society for Army Historical Research*, 56 (1978–9), 79–92.

1677 Chaldecott, John A. 'Josiah Wedgwood (1730–95): scientist', *British Journal For the History of Science*, 8 (1975), 1–16. See also (1644).

1678 Childs, St Julian R. 'Sir George Baker and the dry belly-ache', *BHMed*, 44 (1970), 213–30. Lead poisoning.

1679 Clay, Reginald Stanley and Thomas H. Court. 'English instrument making in the eighteenth century', *Transactions of the Newcomen Society*, 16 (1935–6), 45–54.

1680 Curtin, Philip D. 'Epidemiology and the slave trade', *Political Science Quarterly*, 83 (1968), 160–216. Principally concerned with the West Indies and the diseases of the British army there in the late eighteenth century.

1681 Daniels, Norman. 'Thomas Reid's discovery of a non-Euclidian geometry', *Philosophy of Science*, 39 (1972), 219–34. Discovered in 1764.

1682 Davies, Alun C. 'The life and death of a scientific instrument: the marine chronometer, 1770–1920', *Annals of Science*, 35 (1978), 509–25.

1683 Donovan, Arthur L. 'British chemistry and the concept of science in the eighteenth century', *Albion*, 7 (1975), 131–44.

1684 Dorling, Jon. 'Henry Cavendish's deduction of the electrostatic inverse square law from the result of a single experiment', *Studies in the History and Philosophy of Science*, 4 (1973–4), 327–48.

1685 Dukes, Cuthbert E. 'London medical societies in the 18th century', *Proceedings of the Royal Society of Medicine*, 53 (1960), 699–706.

1686 Gilbert, Keith Reginald. 'Henry Maudslay, 1771–1831', *Transactions of the Newcomen Society*, 44 (1971–2), 49–62. Engineer.

1687 Goodfield-Toulmin, June. 'Some aspects of English physiology, 1780–1840', *Journal of the History of Biology*, 2 (1969), 283–320. On the development of scientific knowledge and conflicts with the religious view of man.

1688 Guralnick, Stanley M. 'The contexts of Faraday's electro-chemical laws', *Isis*, 70 (1979), 59–75.

1689 Hall, A. Rupert. 'What did the industrial revolution owe to science?', in Neil McKendrick (ed.), *Historical perspectives: studies in English thought and society in honour of J. H. Plumb*. 1974, pp. 129–51. Concludes that it did not owe very much.

1690   Hankins, Thomas L. 'Triplets and triads: Sir William Rowan Hamilton on the metaphysics of mathematics', *Isis*, 68 (1977), 175–93.

1691   Harris, John Raymond. 'The employment of steam power in the eighteenth century', *History* NS, 52 (1967), 133–48.

1692   Hartog, Sir Philip J. 'The newer views of Priestley and Lavoisier', *Annals of Science*, 5 (1941–7), 1–56.

1693   Inkster, Ian. 'The development of a scientific community in Sheffield, 1790–1850: a network of people and interests', *Transactions of the Hunter Archaeological Society*, 10 (1973), 99–131.

1694   —— 'Science and society in the metropolis: a preliminary examination of the social and institutional context of the Askesian Society of London, 1796–1807', *Annals of Science*, 34 (1977), 1–32. Informal scientific society.

1695   Jeremy, David J. 'Damming the flood: British government efforts to check the outflow of technicians and machinery, 1780–1843', *BusHR*, 51 (1977), 1–34.

1696   Kanefsky, John and John Robey. 'Steam engines in 18th-century Britain: a quantitative assessment', *Technology and Culture*, 21 (1980), 161–86.

1697   Kett, Joseph F. 'Provincial medical practice in England, 1730–1818', *JHMed*, 19 (1964), 17–29.

1698   Lovell, Sir Bernard. 'Herschel's work on the structure of the universe', *Notes and Records of the Royal Society of London*, 33 (1978–9), 57–75.

1699   McCormmack, Russell. 'Henry Cavendish: a study of rational empiricism in eighteenth-century natural philosophy', *Isis*, 60 (1969), 293–306.

1700   McKendrick, Neil. 'The role of science in the industrial revolution: a study of Josiah Wedgwood as a scientist and industrial chemist', in Mikulas Teich and Robert Young (eds.), *Changing perspectives in the history of science: essays in honour of Joseph Needham*. 1973, pp. 274–319. See also (1644).

1701   Mathias, Peter. 'Skills and the diffusion of innovations from Britain in the eighteenth century', *TRHS* 5th ser., 25 (1975), 93–113; reprinted in Mathias's *The transformation of England*. New York, 1979, pp. 21–44.

1702   —— 'Swords and ploughshares: the armed forces, medicine, and public health in the late eighteenth century', in J. M. Winter (ed.), *War and economic development: essays in memory of David Joslin*. Cambridge, 1975, pp. 73–90; reprinted in Mathias's *The transformation of England*. New York, 1979, pp. 265–85.

1703   —— 'Who unbound Prometheus? Science and technical change, 1600–1800', in Mathias's *The transformation of England*. New York, 1979, pp. 45–71.

1704   Musson, Albert Edward. 'Industrial motive power in the United Kingdom, 1800–70', *EcHR* 2nd ser., 29 (1976), 415–39.

1705   Musson, Albert Edward and Eric Robinson. 'The early growth of steam power', *EcHR* 2nd ser., 11 (1958–9), 418–39.

1706   Ochs, Sidney. 'The early history of nerve regeneration beginning with Cruickshank's observations in 1776', *MedH*, 21 (1977), 261–74.

1707   Ogilvie, Marilyn Bailey. 'Caroline Herschel's contributions to astronomy', *Annals of Science*, 32 (1975), 149–61.

1708   Orange, A. D. 'The origins of the British Association for the Advancement of Science', *British Journal for the History of Science*, 6 (1972–3), 152–76.

1709   Partington, James Riddick and Douglas McKie. 'Historical studies on the phlogiston theory', *Annals of Science*, 2 (1937), 361–404; 3 (1938), 1–58, 337–51; 4 (1939), 113–49. See also (1632).

1710   Porter, Roy S. 'Gentlemen and geology: the emergence of a scientific career, 1660–1920', *HJ*, 21 (1978), 809–36. Mostly concerned with this period.

1711   Posner, E. 'Eighteenth-century health and social services in the pottery industry of North Staffordshire', *MedH*, 18 (1974), 138–45.

1712   Reed, Howard Sprague. 'Jan Ingenhouz, plant physiologist . . .', *Chronica Botanica*, 2 (1949), 285–393. Discovery of photosynthesis.

1713   Rees, Gareth. 'Copper sheathing: an example of technological diffusion in the English merchant fleet', *Journal of Transport History* NS, 1 (1971), 85–94.

1714   Risse, Guenter B. 'The Brownian system of medicine: its theoretical and practical implications', *Cliomedica*, 5 (1970), 45–51. System created by a Scottish doctor which was very influential on the continent.

1715   Robinson, Eric. 'The early diffusion of steam power', *JEcH*, 34 (1974), 91–107.

1716   Rolleston, Sir Humphry. 'The early history of: I. Human anatomy in London; II.

Morbid anatomy and pathology in Great Britain', *Annals of Medical History* 3rd ser., 1 (1939), 203–38. Much on the eighteenth century.

1717 Schofield, R. B. 'Bagshaw v. The Leeds to Liverpool Canal Company: a study in engineering history, 1790–99', *Bulletin of the John Rylands Library*, 59 (1976–7), 188–225.

1718 Schofield, Robert Edwin. 'The scientific background of Joseph Priestley', *Annals of Science*, 13 (1957), 148–63. See also (1552) and (1555).

1719 Shapin, Steven A. 'The Pottery Philosophical Society, 1819–1835: an examination of the cultural uses of provincial science', *Science Studies*, 2 (1972), 311–36.

1720 Shapin, Steven A. and Arnold Thackray. 'Prosopography as a research tool in the history of science: the British scientific community, 1700–1900', *History of Science*, 12 (1974), 1–28.

1721 Shaw, A. Batty. 'The oldest medical societies in Great Britain', *MedH*, 12 (1968), 232–44. Those founded before 1850.

1722 Siegfried, Robert. 'The mind of Humphry Davy', *Proceedings of the Royal Institution of Great Britain*, 43 (1970), 1–21. For other Davy references, see (1538).

1723 Sigsworth, Eric Milton. 'Gateways to death? Medicine, hospitals and mortality, 1700–1850', in Peter Mathias (ed.), *Science and society, 1600–1900*. Cambridge, 1972, pp. 97–110.

1724 Skempton, A. W. and Joyce Brown. 'John and Edward Troughton, mathematical instrument makers', *Notes and Records of the Royal Society of London*, 27 (1972–3), 233–62. With an appendix on dating Troughton instruments.

1725 Smith, Crosbie. '"Mechanical philosophy" and the emergence of physics in Britain, 1800–1850', *Annals of Science*, 33 (1976), 3–29.

1726 Spector, Benjamin. 'Jeremy Bentham 1748–1832: his influence upon medical thought and legislation', *BHMed*, 37 (1963), 25–42.

1727 Stephens, Michael D. and Gordon W. Roderick. 'Science, self-improvement and the first industrial revolution', *Annals of Science*, 31 (1974), 463–70.

1728 Tann, Jennifer. 'Fuel saving in the process industries during the industrial revolution: a study in technological diffusion', *BusH*, 15 (1973), 149–59.

1729 Tann, Jennifer and M. J. Breckin. 'The international diffusion of the Watt engine 1775–1825', *EcHR* 2nd ser., 31 (1978), 541–64.

1730 Turner, D. M. 'Thomas Young on the eye and vision', in Edgar Ashworth Underwood (ed.), *Science, medicine and history*. 1953, ii, pp. 243–55.

1731 Van Zwanenberg, David. 'The Suttons and the business of inoculation', *MedH*, 22 (1978), 71–82. Popularization of inoculation.

1732 Waddington, Ivan. 'The struggle to reform the Royal College of Physicians, 1767–1771: a sociological analysis', *MedH*, 17 (1973), 107–26. See also (1586).

1733 Wells, Lloyd Allan. '"Why not try the experiment?": the scientific education of Edward Jenner', *Proceedings of the American Philosophical Society*, 118 (1974), 135–45. See also (1651).

1734 Williams, Leslie Pearce. 'The physical sciences in the first half of the nineteenth century: problems and sources', *History of Science*, 1 (1962), 1–15.

1735 Wilson, Leonard Gilchrist. 'Fevers and science in early nineteenth-century medicine', *JHMed*, 33 (1978), 386–407.

XI. MILITARY AND NAVAL HISTORY

For specialized bibliographies, lists and catalogues, see (1), (6), (23), (62), (110) and (149). For military administration, see also (253), (261), (281), (318), (331), (337), (338), (344), (345), (360) and (362); and for additional material on military medicine, see (1676), (1680) and (1702).

1. Printed sources

1736 Army. *A list of the general and field officers as they rank in the Army*. 1754–1868. After 1814, *The monthly army list*. Gives officers by regiment as well as listing general officers.

1737 Baynham, Henry (ed.). *From the lower deck: the old Navy, 1780–1840*. 1969. Anthology of autobiographical writings.

1738   Bonner-Smith, David (ed.). *Letters of Admiral of the Fleet the Earl of St Vincent whilst first lord of the Admiralty 1801–4.* (Navy Records Society, 55; 61.) 1922–7, 2 vols.

1739   Bonner-Smith, David and Michael Arthur Lewis (comps.). *The commissioned sea officers of the Royal Navy, 1660–1815.* 1954, 3 vols.

1740   Bromley, John Selwyn (ed.). *The manning of the Royal Navy: selected public pamphlets, 1693–1873.* (Navy Records Society, 119.) 1976.

1741   Clark, William Bell, et al. (eds.). *Naval documents of the American Revolution.* Washington, DC, 1964–. From British and American archives; seven vols. published so far, covering events to the beginning of 1777.

1742   Colledge, James Joseph (comp.). *Ships of the Royal Navy: an historical index.* Newton Abbot, Devon, 1969–70, 2 vols.

1743   Corbett, Sir Julian Stafford (ed.). *Fighting instructions 1530–1816.* (Navy Records Society, 29.) 1905. Supplemented by his edition of *Signals and instructions, 1776–1794, with addenda to Vol. XXIX.* (Navy Records Society, 35.) 1908.

1744   Corbett, Sir Julian Stafford and Sir Herbert William Richmond (eds.). *Private papers of George, second Earl Spencer, first lord of the Admiralty, 1794–1801.* (Navy Records Society, 46; 48; 58; 59.) 1913–24, 4 vols.

1745   Firth, Sir Charles Harding (ed.). *Naval songs and ballads.* (Navy Records Society, 33.) 1908. One of many similar collections.

1746   Gurwood, John (ed.). *The despatches and general orders of … the Duke of Wellington … from 1799 to 1815.* 1834–9, 13 vols. *Supplementary despatches, correspondence, and memoranda ….* Ed. Arthur Richard Wellesley, 2nd Duke of Wellington. 1858–72, 14 vols. *Despatches, correspondence, and memoranda … from 1818 to 1832.* Ed. Arthur Richard Wellesley, 2nd Duke of Wellington. 1867–80, 8 vols. For Wellington's biography, see also (561).

1747   Hughes, Edward (ed.). *The private correspondence of Admiral Lord Collingwood.* (Navy Records Society, 98.) 1957. See also (1860).

1748   Jackson, Sir Thomas Sturges (ed.). *Logs of the great sea fights, 1794–1805.* (Navy Records Society, 16; 18.) 1899–1900, 2 vols.

1749   Laughton, Sir John Knox (ed.). *Letters and papers of Charles Lord Barham … 1758–1813.* (Navy Records Society, 32; 38; 39.) 1907–11, 3 vols. Barham was the most important figure after Anson in eighteenth century naval administration.

1750   Lloyd, Christopher (ed.). *The health of seamen: selections from the works of Dr James Lind, Sir Gilbert Blane, and Dr Thomas Trotter.* (Navy Records Society, 107.) 1965.

1751   Maurice, Sir John Frederick (ed.). *The diary of Sir John Moore.* 1904, 2 vols. For biographies, see (1851) and (1852).

1752   Naish, George Prideaux Brabant (ed.). *Nelson's letters to his wife and other documents, 1785–1831.* (Navy Records Society, 100.) 1958.

1753   Nicolas, Sir Nicholas Harris (ed.). *The dispatches of … Lord Nelson.* 1845–6, 7 vols. For biographies, see (1838), (1848), (1850), (1858) and (1861).

1754   Palmer, Roy (ed.). *The rambling soldier: life in the lower ranks, 1750–1900, through soldiers' songs and writings.* Harmondsworth, Middx, 1977.

1755   Ryan, Anthony Nicholas (ed.). *The Saumarez papers: selections from the Baltic correspondence of Vice-Admiral Sir James Saumarez, 1808–1812.* (Navy Records Society, 110.) 1968.

1756   Siborne, Herbert Taylor (ed.). *Waterloo letters.* 1891. Selections from a collection now in the British Library.

1757   Willcox, William Bradford (ed.). *The American rebellion: Sir Henry Clinton's narrative of his campaigns, 1775–1782, with an appendix of original documents.* New Haven, Conn., 1954. See also (1863).

2. Surveys

1758   Barnett, Correlli Douglas. *Britain and her army, 1509–1970: a military, political and social survey.* 1970.

1759   Fortescue, Sir John William. *History of the British army.* 1899–1930, 13 vols. and 6 atlases. Standard, but not very satisfactory; very full on this period.

1760   Glover, Michael. *The Peninsular War, 1807–1814: a concise military history.* Newton Abbot, Devon, 1974.

1761   Low, Charles Rathbone. *History of the Indian navy (1613–1863).* 1877, 2 vols.

1762   Mackesy, Piers. *The war for America, 1775–1783*. 1964. Best account from a British perspective.

1763   Marcus, Geoffrey Jules. *Heart of oak : a survey of British sea power in the Georgian era*. 1975.

1764   —— *A naval history of England*. Vol. 1 : *The formative centuries*. 1961. Vol. 2 : *The age of Nelson : the Royal Navy, 1793–1815*. 1971. Good general history.

1765   Oman, Sir Charles William Chadwick. *A history of the Peninsular War*. Oxford, 1902–30, 7 vols. Standard.

1766   Rogers, Hugh Cuthbert Basset. *The British army of the eighteenth century*. 1977.

1767   Sheppard, Eric William. *A short history of the British army*. 1926; 4th edn, 1950.

1768   Warner, Oliver Martin Wilson. *The British Navy : a concise history*. 1975.

3. Monographs

1769   Albion, Robert Greenhalgh. *Forests and sea power : the timber problem of the Royal Navy, 1652–1862*. Cambridge, Mass., 1926; reprinted, Hamden, Conn., 1965.

1770   Bartlett, Christopher John. *Great Britain and sea power, 1815–1853*. Oxford, 1963.

1771   Bennett, Geoffrey Martin. *The battle of Trafalgar*. 1977. See also (1816) and (1833).

1772   Bond, Gordon C. *The great expedition : the British invasion of Holland in 1809*. Athens, Ga, 1979. First detailed study in a century of scholarship.

1773   Brett-James, Anthony. *Life in Wellington's army*. 1972.

1774   Bullocke, John Greville. *Sailor's rebellion : a century of naval mutinies*. 1938. Events 1707–97.

1775   Claver, Scott. *Under the lash : a history of corporal punishment in the British armed forces, including a digest of the report of the Royal Commission, 1835–36, and the first reprint of 'Certain immoral practices in His Majesty's Navy' (1821)*. 1954.

1776   Clowes, Geoffrey Swinford Laird. *Sailing ships : their history and development*. 4th edn, 1952–3, 2 vols. Standard.

1777   Creswell, John. *British admirals of the eighteenth century : tactics in battle*. 1972.

1778   Crowhurst, Patrick. *The defence of British trade, 1689–1815*. Folkestone, Kent, 1977. Defence against privateering, principally in the Channel.

1779   Curtis, Edward Ely. *The organization of the British army in the American Revolution*. New Haven, Conn., 1926.

1780   Davies, David William. *Sir John Moore's Peninsular campaign, 1808–1809*. The Hague, 1974.

1781   Davies, Godfrey. *Wellington and his army*. Oxford, 1954. Concerned with internal affairs of the Army rather than with military operations.

1782   Desbrière, Edouard. *1793–1805 : projets et tentatives de débarquement aux Iles Britanniques*. Paris, 1900–2, 4 vols.

1783   Dugan, James. *The great mutiny*. New York, 1966. Good study of naval mutiny of 1797; see also (1787).

1784   Fortescue, Sir John William. *The British army, 1783–1802*. 1905. Concerned with organization.

1785   Fuller, John Frederic Charles. *Sir John Moore's system of training*. 1925.

1786   Garrison, Fielding Hudson. *Notes on the history of military medicine*. Washington, DC, 1922. Basic for the subject.

1787   Gill, Conrad. *The naval mutinies of 1797*. Manchester, 1913. Classic account. See also (1783).

1788   Glover, Michael. *Britannia sickens : Sir Arthur Wellesley and the Convention of Cintra*. 1970.

1789   —— *Wellington as military commander*. 1968. Important assessment.

1790   —— *Wellington's army in the Peninsular, 1808–14*. Newton Abbot, Devon, 1977.

1791   Glover, Richard Gilchrist. *Peninsular preparation : the reform of the British army, 1795–1809*. Cambridge, 1963.

1792   —— (ed.). *Britain at bay : defence against Bonaparte, 1803–14*. 1973. Documents with a long introduction.

1793   Graham, Gerald Sandford. *Empire of the North Atlantic : the maritime struggle for North America*. Toronto, 1958.

1794   —— *Great Britain in the Indian Ocean : a study of maritime enterprise, 1810–1850*. Oxford, 1967.

1795   —— *The politics of naval supremacy : studies in British maritime supremacy*. Cambridge, 1965.

1796   Gruber, Ira Demsey. *The Howe brothers and the American Revolution*. New York, 1972.
1797   Horsman, Reginald. *The war of 1812*. 1969. Excellent.
1798   Horward, Donald D. *The battle of Bussaco: Massena vs Wellington*. Tallahassee, Fla, 1965. Extensive use of French as well as English sources.
1799   Jones, Edwyn Henry Stuart. *An invasion that failed: the French expedition to Ireland, 1796*. Oxford, 1950. From the point of view of a professional seaman.
1800   —— *The last invasion of Britain*. Cardiff, 1950. French landing in Pembrokeshire, 1797.
1801   Keevil, John J., Christopher Lloyd and Jack Leonard Sagar Coulter. *Medicine and the Navy, 1200–1900*. 1957–63, 4 vols. Vol. 3 (by Lloyd and Coulter): 1714–1815; Vol. 4 (by Lloyd and Coulter): 1815–1900.
1802   Laffin, John. *Surgeons in the field*. 1970. Military medicine.
1803   Lewis, Michael Arthur. *A social history of the Navy, 1793–1815*. 1960. *The Navy in transition, 1814–1864: a social history*. 1965.
1804   Lloyd, Christopher. *Nelson and sea power*. 1973.
1805   —— *The Nile campaign: Nelson and Napoleon in Egypt*. Newton Abbot, Devon, 1973.
1806   —— *St Vincent and Camperdown*. 1963.
1807   McGuffie, Tom Henderson. *The siege of Gibraltar, 1779–1783*. 1965.
1808   Mackesy, Piers. *The war in the Mediterranean, 1803–1810*. 1957.
1809   Mahan, Alfred Thayer. *The influence of sea power upon the French Revolution and Empire, 1793–1815*. 1892, 2 vols; 14th edn, 1919. Classic.
1810   Oman, Sir Charles William Chadwick. *Wellington's army, 1809–1814*. 1913. Excellent on organization, daily life and psychology.
1811   Parkinson, Cyril Northcote. *Britannia rules: the classic age of naval history 1793–1815*. 1977.
1812   —— *War in the eastern seas, 1793–1815*. 1954.
1813   Patterson, Alfred Temple. *The other Armada: the Franco-Spanish attempt to invade Britain in 1779*. Manchester, 1960.
1814   Perrin, William Gordon. *British flags, their early history, and their development at sea*. Cambridge, 1922. Important work of reference.
1815   Pope, Dudley. *The black ship*. 1963. Mutiny on the *Hermione* in the West Indies, 1797.
1816   —— *England expects*. 1959. American title: *Decision at Trafalgar*. Philadelphia, Pa, 1960. See also (1771) and (1833).
1817   —— *The great gamble*. 1972. Battle of Copenhagen, 1801; very full. See also (1833).
1818   Porter, Whitworth and Sir Charles Moore Watson. *History of the Corps of Royal Engineers*. 1889–1915, 3 vols.
1819   Prebble, John. *Mutiny: Highland regiments in revolt, 1743–1804*. 1975.
1820   Presnail, James. *Chatham: the story of a dockyard town and the birthplace of the British navy*. Chatham, Kent, 1952.
1821   Richmond, Sir Herbert William. *The navy in India, 1763–1783*. 1931.
1822   —— *Statesmen and sea power*. Oxford, 1946. Principally concerned with the Napoleonic period.
1823   Rodger, Alexander B. *The War of the Second Coalition, 1798–1801; a strategic commentary*. Oxford, 1964. Better on the military than on the naval side.
1824   Rose, John Holland. *Lord Hood and the defence of Toulon*. Cambridge, 1922.
1825   Savory, Sir Reginald. *His Britannic Majesty's Army in Germany during the Seven Years' War*. Oxford, 1966.
1826   Shy, John W. *Toward Lexington: the role of the British Army in the coming of the American Revolution*. Princeton, NJ, 1965.
1827   Smyth, Sir John George. *Sandhurst: the history of the Royal Military Academy, Woolwich, the Royal Military College, Sandhurst, and the Royal Military Academy, Sandhurst, 1741–1961*. 1961.
1828   Stout, Neil R. *The Royal Navy in America, 1760–1775: a study of enforcement of British colonial policy in the era of the American Revolution*. Annapolis, Md, 1973.
1829   Strachan, Hew. *British military uniforms, 1768–1796: the dress of the British army from official sources*. 1975.
1830   Syrett, David. *Shipping and the American War, 1775–83: a study of British transport organization*. 1970.
1831   Ward, Stephen George Peregrine. *Wellington's headquarters: a study of the administrative problems in the Peninsular, 1809–1814*. 1957.

1832 Warner, Oliver Martin Wilson. *The glorious first of June*. 1961. Naval battle of 1 June 1794.
1833 —— *Nelson's battles*. 1965. The Nile, Copenhagen and Trafalgar, incorporating his previously published studies of the first two. See also (1771), (1816) and (1817).
1834 —— *The sea and the sword: the Baltic, 1630–1945*. 1965.
1835 Weller, Jac. *Wellington in India*. 1972. *Wellington in the Peninsular, 1808–1814*. 1962. *Wellington at Waterloo*. 1967.
1836 Young, Peter and James Philip Lawford. *Wellington's masterpiece: the battle and campaign of Salamanca*. 1972.

4. Biographies

1837 Anglesey, George Charles Henry Victor Paget, 7th Marquess of. *One-Leg: the life and letters of Henry William Paget, first Marquess of Anglesey, KG, 1768–1854*. 1961. Commanded the cavalry in the Peninsular and at Waterloo; politically important after the wars.
1838 Bennett, Geoffrey Martin. *Nelson the commander*. 1972. See also (1753), (1848), (1850), (1858) and (1861).
1839 Blanco, Richard L. *Wellington's surgeon-general: Sir James McGrigor*. Durham, NC, 1974.
1840 Brett-James, Anthony. *General Graham, Lord Lynedoch*. 1959. Important Peninsular general.
1841 Burne, Alfred Higgins. *The noble Duke of York: the military life of Frederick, Duke of York and Albany*. 1949.
1842 Haswell, Jock (pseud. of Chetwynd John Drake Haswell). *The first respectable spy: the life and times of Colquhoun Grant, Wellington's head of intelligence*. 1969.
1843 Howson, Gerald. *Burgoyne of Saratoga: a biography*. New York, 1979.
1844 James, Sir William Milbourne. *Old Oak: the life of John Jervis, Earl of St Vincent*. 1950.
1845 Kennedy, Ludovic Henry Coverley. *Nelson's band of brothers*. 1951. American title: *Nelson's captains*. New York, 1951.
1846 Lloyd, Christopher. *Lord Cochrane: seaman, radical, liberator: a life of Thomas, Lord Cochrane, 10th Earl of Dundonald*. 1947.
1847 Mackeness, George. *The life of Vice-Admiral William Bligh*. Sydney, 1931, 2 vols; rev. edn, Sydney, 1951. Best life of the commander of the *Bounty*.
1848 Mahan, Alfred Thayer. *The life of Nelson, the embodiment of the sea power of Great Britain*. 1897; reprinted, New York, 1968, 2 vols. Only full biography by a professional sailor; still valuable.
1849 Mason, Michael Henry. *Willoughby the immortal: an account of the life of Rear-Admiral Sir Nesbit Willoughby*. Oxford, 1969.
1850 Oman, Carola Mary Anima. *Nelson*. 1947. Best life. She also published a much briefer *Lord Nelson*. 1954; reprinted, Hamden, Conn., 1968.
1851 —— *Sir John Moore*. 1953. See also (1751) and (1852).
1852 Parkinson, Roger. *Moore of Corunna*. 1976. See also (1751) and (1851).
1853 Pocock, Tom. *Remember Nelson: the life of Captain Sir William Hoste*. 1977.
1854 Russell of Liverpool, Edward Frederick Langley Russell, Baron. *Knight of the sword: the life and letters of Admiral Sir Sidney Smith*. 1964.
1855 Shankland, Peter. *Byron of the Wager*. 1975.
1856 Spinney, David. *Rodney*. 1969.
1857 Thoumine, Reginald Harold. *Scientific soldier: a life of General Le Marchant, 1766–1812*. 1968. A pioneer of officer training.
1858 Walder, David. *Nelson: a biography*. New York, 1978. Most comprehensive since (1850).
1859 Warner, Oliver Martin Wilson. *Emma Hamilton and Sir William*. 1960.
1860 —— *The life and letters of Vice-Admiral Lord Collingwood*. 1968. See also (1747).
1861 —— *Nelson*. 1975. Good brief life. Warner published an earlier biography, *A portrait of Lord Nelson*, 1959.
1862 Wickwire, Franklin B. and Mary Wickwire. *Cornwallis: the American adventure*. Boston, Mass., 1970. *Cornwallis: the imperial years*. Chapel Hill, NC, 1980. English title of the first volume: *Cornwallis and the War of Independence*. 1971.
1863 Willcox, William Bradford. *Portrait of a general: Sir Henry Clinton in the War of*

Independence. New York, 1964. Of major importance for the general military history of the war as well. See also (1757).

5. Articles

1864 Blanco, Richard L. 'The development of British military medicine, 1793–1814', *Military Affairs*, 38 (1974), 4–10.

1865 —— 'The soldier's friend: Sir Jeremiah Fitzpatrick, inspector of health for land forces', *MedH*, 20 (1976), 402–21.

1866 Broomfield, J. H. 'The Keppel–Palliser affair, 1778–79', *Mariner's Mirror*, 47 (1961), 195–207.

1867 Condon, Mary Ellen. 'Living conditions on board troopships during the war against revolutionary France, 1793–1802', *Journal of the Society for Army Historical Research*, 49 (1971), 14–19.

1868 Crowe, Kate Elizabeth. 'Thomas, Baron Catherwood, and the medical department of Wellington's army, 1809–1814', *MedH*, 20 (1976), 22–40.

1869 —— 'The Walcheren expedition and the new Army Medical Board: a reconsideration', *EHR*, 88 (1973), 770–85.

1870 Duffy, Michael. '"A particular service": the British government and the Dunkirk expedition of 1793', *EHR*, 91 (1976), 529–54.

1871 Emsley, Clive. 'Political disaffection and the British Army in 1792', *BIHR*, 48 (1975), 230–45.

1872 Frey, Sylvia R. 'The common British soldier in the late eighteenth century: a profile', *Societas*, 5 (1975), 117–31.

1873 —— 'Courts and cats: British military justice in the eighteenth century', *Military Affairs*, 43 (1979), 5–11.

1874 Geggus, David. 'Yellow fever in the 1790's: the British army in occupied Saint Dominique', *MedH*, 23 (1979), 38–58.

1875 Gilbert, Arthur N. 'Law and honour among eighteenth-century British army officers', *HJ*, 19 (1976), 75–87.

1876 —— 'Military and civilian justice in eighteenth-century England: an assessment', *JBS*, 17, 2 (1978), 41–65.

1877 —— 'The regimental courts martial in the eighteenth century', *Albion*, 8 (1976), 50–66.

1878 Haas, James M. 'The royal dockyards: the earliest visitations and reform, 1749–1778', *HJ*, 13 (1970), 191–215.

1879 Hughes, R. E. 'James Lind and the cure of scurvy: an experimental approach', *MedH*, 19 (1975), 342–51. Discussion continued by H. V. Wyatt, *ibid.* 20 (1976), 433–8, including a reply by Hughes.

1880 Hutt, Maurice. 'The British government's responsibility for the "divided command" of the expedition to Quiberon, 1795', *EHR*, 76 (1961), 479–89.

1881 Knight, R. J. B. 'The introduction of copper sheathing into the Royal Navy, 1779–1786', *Mariner's Mirror*, 59 (1973), 299–309.

1882 ——'Sandwich, Middleton and dockyard appointments', *Mariner's Mirror*, 57 (1971), 175–92.

1883 McGuffie, Tom Henderson. 'The significance of military rank in the British army between 1790 and 1820', *BIHR*, 30 (1957), 207–24.

1884 —— 'The stone ships expedition against Boulogne, 1804', *EHR*, 64 (1949), 488–502.

1885 —— 'The Walcheren expedition and the Walcheren fever', *EHR*, 62 (1947), 191–202.

1886 Piechowiak, A. B. 'The Anglo-Russian expedition to Holland in 1799', *Slavonic and East European Review*, 41 (1962), 182–95.

1887 Robson, Eric. 'Purchase and promotion in the British army in the eighteenth century', *History* NS, 36 (1951), 57–72.

1888 Webb, Paul L. C. 'The naval aspect of the Nootka Sound crisis', *Mariner's Mirror*, 61 (1975), 133–54.

1889 ——'The rebuilding and repair of the fleet, 1783–93', *BIHR*, 50 (1977), 194–209.

XII. RELIGIOUS HISTORY

For specialized bibliographies, lists and catalogues, see (16), (17), (48), (53), (55), (56), (99), (128), (132) and (151).

1. Printed sources

1890   Beresford, John Baldwin (ed.). *The diary of a country parson: the Rev. James Woodforde (1758–1802)*. 1924–31, 5 vols; reprinted, New York, 1968, 5 vols.

1891   Cook, Michael (ed.). *The diocese of Exeter in 1821: Bishop Carey's replies to querries before visitation*. Vol. 1: *Cornwall*. (Devon and Cornwall Record Society NS, 3.) Exeter, 1958. Vol. 2: *Devon*. (Devon and Cornwall Record Society NS, 4.) Exeter, 1960.

1892   Curnock, Nehemiah (ed.). *The journal of the Rev. John Wesley . . . enlarged from original Mss, with notes from unpublished diaries*. 1909–16, 8 vols.; reprinted, 1938, 8 vols. The standard edition; there are numerous abridgments, most based on one made by Curnock.

1893   Fletcher, John William. *The works of the Rev. John Fletcher . . . containing Mr Benson's life of . . . Fletcher*. 2nd edn, 1814–19, 9 vols. Numerous subsequent editions. Fletcher was the theologian of the Wesleyan movement.

1894   Flindall, Roy Philip (ed.). *The Church of England, 1815–1948: a documentary history*. 1972. Prints 105 documents.

1895   Hughes, Edward (ed.). 'The bishops and reform, 1831–3: some fresh correspondence', *EHR*, 56 (1941), 459–90. Documents.

1896   —— (ed.). *The letters of Spencer Cowper, Dean of Durham, 1746–74*. (Surtees Society, 165.) Durham, 1956.

1897   *Minutes of the Methodist Conference*. 1812–55, 12 vols. Minutes of the conferences, 1744–1854.

1898   More, Hannah. *Works*. 1801, 8 vols.; new edn, 1830, 11 vols.; and many other editions. See also (2001) and (2007).

1899   Nye, Robert (ed.). *The English sermon*. Vol. 3: *1750–1850*. Manchester, 1976.

1900   Ransome, Mary (ed.). *The state of the bishopric of Worcester, 1782–1808*. (Worcestershire Historical Society NS, 6.) Birmingham, 1968.

1901   —— (ed.). *Wiltshire returns to the bishop's visitation querries, 1782*. (Wiltshire Record Society, 27.) Devizes, Wilts., 1973.

1902   Royle, Edward (ed.). *The infidel tradition from Paine to Bradlaugh*. 1976. Selections.

1903   Rutt, John Towell (ed.). *The theological and miscellaneous works of Joseph Priestley*. 1817–32, Twenty-six vols. in twenty-five. For works on science and politics, see (1546), (1552), (1555) and (2265).

1904   Telford, John (ed.). *The letters of the Rev. John Wesley*. 1931, 8 vols.

1905   Thompson, David Michael (ed.). *Nonconformity in the nineteenth century*. 1972. Documents.

1906   Ward, William Reginald (ed.). *The early correspondence of Jabez Bunting, 1820–1829*. (Camden Society 4th ser., 11.) 1972. *Early Victorian Methodism: the correspondence of Jabez Bunting, 1830–58*. Oxford, 1976.

1907   Watson, Richard. *Anecdotes of the life of Richard Watson, Bishop of Llandaff: written by himself at different intervals, and revised in 1814*. 1817; 2nd edn, 1818, 2 vols. One of the most versatile and 'liberal' of the late eighteenth century bishops.

1908   Wesley, John. *The works of the Rev. John Wesley*. 1860–8, 14 vols. A 'representative collection', ed. Albert C. Outler, New York, 1964.

2. Surveys

1909   Abbey, Charles John and John Henry Overton. *The English Church in the eighteenth century*. 1878, 2 vols., rev. and abridged edn in one vol., 1887; reprinted, 1926.

1910   Carpenter, Spencer Cecil. *Eighteenth-century Church and people*. 1959.

1911   Chadwick, William Owen. *The Victorian Church*. Vol. 1: *1829–59*. 1966; 3rd edn, 1979.

1912   Cragg, Gordon Robertson. *The Church and the age of reason, 1648–1789*. Harmondsworth, Middx, 1960.

1913   Davies, Horton. *Worship and theology in England*. Vol. 3: *From Watts and Wesley to Maurice, 1690–1850*. Princeton, NJ, 1961.

1914   Gilbert, Alan D. *Religion and society in industrial England : Church, chapel and social change, 1740–1914*. 1976.

1915   Hudson, Cyril Edward and Maurice Bennington Reckitt. *The Church and the world*. 1938–40, 3 vols. Vol. 3: *Church and society in England from 1800*, 1940, is by Reckitt.

1916   Norman, Edward Robert. *Church and society in England, 1770–1970 : a historical study*. Oxford, 1976.

1917   Overton, John Henry and Frederic Relton. *The English Church, from the accession of George I to the end of the eighteenth century (1714–1800)*. 1906; another edn, 1924. Good survey.

1918   Sykes, Norman. *Church and state in England in the XVIIIth century*. Cambridge, 1934; reprinted, Hamden, Conn., 1962. Best book on the eighteenth century Church.

3. Monographs

1919   Addison, William George. *Religious equality in modern England, 1714–1914*. 1944.

1920   Armstrong, Anthony. *The Church of England, the Methodists and society, 1700–1850*. 1973.

1921   Aveling, J. C. Hugh. *The handle and the axe : the Catholic recusants in England from Reformation to Emancipation*. 1976. See also (1927).

1922   Barlow, Richard Burgess. *Citizenship and conscience : a study in the theory and practice of religious toleration in England during the eighteenth century*. Philadelphia, Pa, 1962.

1923   Barth, John Robert. *Coleridge and Christian doctrine*. Cambridge, Mass., 1969. See also (2294).

1924   Best, Geoffrey Francis Andrew. *Temporal pillars : Queen Anne's Bounty, the Ecclesiastical Commissioners, and the Church of England*. Cambridge, 1964.

1925   Binfield, Clyde. *So down to prayers : studies in English nonconformity, 1780–1920*. 1977.

1926   Bolam, C. Gordon, et al. *The English Presbyterians : from Elizabethan puritanism to modern Unitarianism*. 1968.

1927   Bossy, John. *The English Catholic community, 1570–1850*. 1975. Major revisionary study. See also (1921).

1928   Bowmer, J. C. *Pastor and people : a study of church and ministry in Wesleyan Methodism from the death of John Wesley (1791) to the death of Jabez Bunting (1858)*. 1975.

1929   Bridenbaugh, Carl. *Mitre and sceptre : transatlantic faiths, ideas, personalities and politics, 1689–1775*. New York, 1962.

1930   Brockett, Allan. *Nonconformity in Exeter, 1650–1875*. Manchester, 1962. Good local study.

1931   Brose, Olive Johnson. *Church and Parliament : the reshaping of the Church of England, 1828–60*. Stanford, Calif., 1959. See also (1967).

1932   Brown, Ford Keeler. *Fathers of the Victorians : the age of Wilberforce*. Cambridge, 1961. Very critical of the evangelicals and especially of the Claphamites.

1933   Butler, Charles. *Historical memoirs of the English, Irish, and Scottish Catholics, since the Reformation*. 3rd edn, corr. and rev., 1822, 4 vols. The most comprehensive work and very useful for facts.

1934   Canton, William. *A history of the British and Foreign Bible Society*. 1904–10, 5 vols.

1935   Carwardine, Richard. *Transatlantic revivalism : popular evangelicalism in Britain and America, 1790–1865*. Westport, Conn., 1978.

1936   Cell, George Croft. *The rediscovery of John Wesley*. New York, 1935. Study of Wesley's theology; emphasis on the Calvinist elements.

1937   Church, Richard William. *The Oxford Movement : twelve years, 1833–1845*. 1891; 3rd edn, 1892; reprinted, Hamden, Conn., 1966. See also (1949).

1938   Clarke, William Kemp Lowther. *Eighteenth-century piety*. 1944.

1939   —— *A history of the SPCK*. 1959. The Society for Promoting Christian Knowledge.

1940   Cnattingius, Hans Jacob. *Bishops and societies : a study of Anglican colonial and missionary expansion, 1698–1850*. 1952.

1941   Colligan, James Hay. *The Arian movement in England*. Manchester, 1913.

1942   Cowherd, Raymond Gibson. *The politics of English dissent : the religious aspects of liberal and humanitarian reform movements from 1815 to 1848*. New York, 1956.

1943   Currie, Robert, Alan D. Gilbert and Lee Horsley. *Churches and churchgoers: patterns of church growth in the British Isles since 1700.* Oxford, 1977.

1944   Davies, Ebenezer Thomas. *Religion in the industrial revolution in South Wales.* Gardiff, 1965.

1945   Davies, Rupert Eric and Ernest Gordon Rupp (eds.). *A history of the Methodist Church in Great Britain.* 1965. Scholarly essays by various hands.

1946   Edwards, Maldwyn Lloyd. *After Wesley: a study of the social and political influence of Methodism in the middle period (1791–1849).* 1935; new edn, 1948.

1947   —— *John Wesley and the eighteenth century: a study of his social and political influence.* 1933; rev. edn, 1955.

1948   Elliott-Binns, Leonard. *The early evangelicals: a religious and social study.* 1954.

1949   Faber, Geoffrey. *Oxford apostles: character study of the Oxford Movement.* 1933; 2nd edn, 1936; reprinted, Harmondsworth, Middx, 1954. See also (1937).

1950   Garrett, Clarke. *Respectable folly: millenarians and the French Revolution in France and England.* Baltimore, Md, 1975. See also (1952) and (1976).

1951   Gloyn, Cyril Keenard. *The Church in the social order: a study of Anglican social theory from Coleridge to Maurice.* Forest Grove, Oreg., 1942. See also (1981).

1952   Harrison, John Fletcher Clewes. *The second coming: popular millenarianism, 1780–1850.* New Brunswick, NJ, 1979. British and American. See also (1950) and (1976).

1953   Henriques, Ursula Ruth Quixano. *Religious toleration in England, 1787–1833.* 1961.

1954   Howse, Ernest Marshall. *Saints in politics: the 'Clapham Sect' and the growth of freedom.* 1952. Sympathetic.

1955   Ingham, Kenneth. *Reformers in India, 1793–1833: an account of the work of Christian missionaries on behalf of social reform.* Cambridge, 1956.

1956   Jones, Robert Tudur. *Congregationalism in England, 1662–1962.* 1962. Standard.

1957   Jones, Rufus Matthew. *The later periods of Quakerism.* 1921, 2 vols. Standard account of the period 1725–1900.

1958   Kent, John Henry Somerset. *The age of disunity.* 1966. Divisions within Methodism.

1959   Lawson, Albert Brown, *John Wesley and the Christian ministry: the sources and development of his opinions and practice.* 1963.

1960   Lincoln, Anthony Handley. *Some political and social ideas of English dissent, 1763–1800.* Cambridge, 1938. Excellent.

1961   Loane, Marcus Lawrence. *Oxford and the evangelical succession.* 1950. *Cambridge and the evangelical succession.* 1952. Studies of religious leaders.

1962   Lyles, Albert M. *Methodism mocked: the satiric reaction to Methodism in the eighteenth century.* 1960.

1963   McClatchey, Diana. *Oxfordshire clergy, 1777–1869: a study of the Established Church and of the role of its clergy in local society.* Oxford, 1960.

1964   McLachlan, Herbert. *The Unitarian movement in the religious life of England.* Vol. 1: *Its contribution to thought and learning, 1700–1900.* 1934.

1965   Mathew, David. *Catholicism in England, 1535–1935: portrait of a minority: its culture and tradition.* 1936; 3rd edn, 1955. Excellent survey.

1966   Mathews, Horace Frederick. *Methodism and the education of the people, 1791–1851.* 1949.

1967   Mathieson, William Law. *English church reform, 1815–40.* 1923. Less thorough than (1931) but more on the early period.

1968   Mineka, Francis Edward. *The dissidence of dissent: the Monthly Repository, 1806–1838, under the editorship of Robert Aspland, W. J. Fox, R. H. Horne, and Leigh Hunt: with a chapter of religious periodicals, 1700–1875.* Chapel Hill, NC, 1944. Of major importance for non-conformist religious thought.

1969   Overton, John Henry. *The evangelical revival in the eighteenth century.* 1882; many reprints to 1907. Standard account.

1970   Ravitch, Norman. *Sword and mitre: government and episcopate in France and England in the age of aristocracy.* The Hague, 1966.

1971   Reardon, Bernard Morris Gavin. *Religious thought in the nineteenth century.* Cambridge, 1966.

1972   Reynolds, John Stewart. *The evangelicals at Oxford, 1735–1871: a record of an unchronicled movement.* Oxford, 1953.

1973   Roth, Cecil. *A history of the Jews in England.* Oxford, 1941; 3rd edn, rev., Oxford, 1964. See also (918).

1974   Routley, Erik Reginald. *English religious dissent.* Cambridge, 1960. Good general survey.

1975 Royle, Edward. *Victorian infidels: the origins of the British secularist movement, 1791–1866.* Manchester, 1974. See also (2013).

1976 Sandeen, Ernest Robert. *The roots of fundamentalism: British and American millenarianism, 1800–1930.* Chicago, Ill., 1970. See also (1950) and (1952).

1977 Scully, Francis Michael. *L'Évolution de l'opinion anglaise sur les rapports entre l'église établie d'Angleterre et l'état à l'époque des réformes, 1829–39.* Paris, 1938.

1978 Sellers, Ian. *Nineteenth-century nonconformity.* 1977.

1979 Semmel, Bernard. *The Methodist revolution.* New York, 1973. Argues that Wesleyan doctrine was 'liberal' and progressive, not repressive. Extensive bibliography. See also (2025).

1980 Smyth, Charles Hugh Egerton. *Simeon and church order: a study of the origins of the evangelical revival in Cambridge in the 18th century.* Cambridge, 1940.

1981 Soloway, Richard Allen. *Prelates and people: ecclesiastical social thought in England, 1783–1852.* 1969. See also (1951).

1982 Stock, Eugene. *The history of the Church Missionary Society.* 1899–1916, 4 vols. Standard on the missionary work of the evangelicals.

1983 Stromberg, Roland N. *Religious liberalism in eighteenth-century England.* 1954.

1984 Thompson, Henry Paget. *Into all lands: the history of the Society for the Propagation of the Gospel in Foreign Parts, 1701–1950.* 1951.

1985 Thompson, Kenneth Alfred. *Bureaucracy and church reform: the organizational response of the Church of England to social change, 1800–1965.* Oxford, 1970.

1986 Townsend, William John, et al. (eds.). *A new history of Methodism.* 1909, 2 vols.

1987 Underwood, Alfred Clair. *A history of the English Baptists.* 1947.

1988 Ward, Bernard Nicolas. *The dawn of the Catholic revival in England, 1781–1803.* 1909, 2 vols. *The eve of Catholic emancipation: being a history of the English Catholics during the first thirty years of the nineteenth century.* 1911–12, 3 vols. *The sequel to Catholic emancipation: the story of the English Catholics continued down to the re-establishment of their hierarchy in 1850.* 1915, 2 vols. Best account.

1989 Ward, William Reginald. *Religion and society in England, 1790–1850.* 1972.

1990 Warne, Arthur. *Church and society in eighteenth-century Devon.* Newton Abbot, Devon, 1969.

1991 Watts, Michael. R. *The dissenters: from the Reformation to the French Revolution.* Oxford, 1978–. Attempt at a comprehensive account, assimilating much of the recent research on the various denominations.

1992 Wearmouth, Robert Featherstone. *Methodism and the common people of the eighteenth century.* 1945. Exaggerated.

1993 —— *Methodism and the working-class movements of England, 1800–1850.* 1937; 2nd edn, 1947.

1994 Williams, Bill. *The making of Manchester Jewry, 1740–1875.* Manchester, 1976.

4. Biographies

1995 Ayling, Stanley. *John Wesley.* 1979. Good account.

1996 Green, Vivian Hubert Howard. *John Wesley.* 1964. Brief biography.

1997 Hennell, Michael. *John Venn and the Clapham Sect.* 1958.

1998 Jackson, Thomas (ed.). *The lives of the early Methodist preachers, chiefly written by themselves.* 1837–8, 3 vols.; 3rd edn, with additions, 1865–6, 6 vols.

1999 Jebb, Heneage Horsley. *A great bishop of one hundred years ago: being a sketch of the life of Samuel Horsley.* 1909. Important cleric, bishop and intellectual.

2000 Jessup, Ronald. *Man of many talents: an informal biography of James Douglas 1753–1819.* 1975. Divine, antiquary, artist and character.

2001 Jones, Mary Gwladys. *Hannah More.* 1952. Best biography. For her works, see (1898).

2002 Knutsford, Margaret Joan (Trevelyan), Viscountess. *Life and letters of Zachary Macaulay.* 1900. Letters 1791–1838; a leading Claphamite.

2003 Martin, Brian W. *John Keble: priest, professor and poet.* 1976. Best recent biography.

2004 Meacham, Standish. *Henry Thornton of Clapham 1760–1815.* Cambridge, Mass., 1964. Leading Claphamite and banker.

2005 Morris, Henry. *The life of Charles Grant.* 1904. Claphamite; also an important figure in the East India Company.

2006 Petre, Maude Dominica Mary. *The ninth Lord petre: or, pioneers of Roman Catholic emancipation.* 1928. Leading Catholic layman during later eighteenth century.

2007 Roberts, William. *Memoirs of the life and correspondence of Mrs Hannah More.* 1834, 4 vols. Letters 1773–1828, much mangled but the only texts in most cases. See also (1898).

2008 Seymour, Aaron Crossley Hobart. *The life and times of Selina, Countess of Huntingdon.* 1839, 2 vols. Foundress of Lady Huntingdon's connection of Calvinist Methodists.

2009 Simon, John Smith. *John Wesley and the religious societies.* 1921; 2nd edn, 1955. *John Wesley and the Methodist societies.* 1923; 3rd edn, 1952. *John Wesley and the advance of Methodism.* 1925; 2nd edn, 1955. *John Wesley: the master builder.* 1927; 2nd edn, 1955. *John Wesley: the last phase.* 1934. Together, the most comprehensive modern biography.

2010 Tyerman, Luke. *The life and times of the Rev. John Wesley, MA, founder of the Methodists.* 1870–1, 3 vols.; 6th edn, 1890, 3 vols. Old standard life; still useful for facts.

2011 Venn, John. *Annals of a clerical family.* 1904. The Venns; useful biographical approach to a dynasty of prominent evangelicals.

2012 Webster, Alan Brunskill. *Joshua Watson: the story of a layman, 1771–1855.* 1954. Leader of the pre-Tractarian High Church party.

2013 Williams, Gwyn Alfred. *Roland Detrosier: a working-class infidel, 1800–1834.* (Bothwick Papers, 28.) York, 1965. See also (1975).

5. Articles

2014 Balda, Wesley D. 'Ecclesiastics and enthusiasts: the evangelical emergence in England, 1760–1800', *Historical Magazine of the Protestant Episcopal Church,* 49 (1980), 221–31.

2015 Barlow, Richard Burgess. 'Anti-subscription and the clerical petition movement in the Church of England', *Historical Magazine of the Protestant Episcopal Church,* 30 (1961), 35–49.

2016 Best, Geoffrey Francis Andrew. 'The evangelicals and the Established Church in the early nineteenth century', *Journal of Theological Studies* NS, 10 (1959), 63–78.

2017 —— 'The protestant constitution and its supporters, 1800–1829', *TRHS* 5th ser., 8 (1958), 105–27. Anti-Catholicism.

2018 —— 'The Whigs and the Church establishment in the age of Grey and Holland', *History* NS, 45 (1960), 103–18.

2019 Cone, Carl B. 'Newington Green: a study of a dissenting community', *Catholic Historical Review,* 54 (1968–9), 1–16. Dr Price's chapel.

2020 Elliott, Charles M. 'The ideology of economic growth: a case study', in Eric Lionel Jones and Gordon Edmund Mingay (eds.), *Land, labour and population in the industrial revolution.* 1967, pp. 78–99. No evidence for a direct connection between Methodism or any other dissenting group, except possibly the Unitarians, and the 'new' economic ethic.

2021 —— 'The political economy of English dissent, 1780–1840', in Ronald Maxwell Hartwell (ed.), *The industrial revolution.* Oxford, 1970, pp. 144–66.

2022 Harland, Lowell B. 'Theology of eighteenth-century hymns', *Historical Magazine of the Protestant Episcopal Church,* 48 (1979), 167–93.

2023 Harris, P. R. 'The English College, Douai, 1750–1794', *Recusant History,* 10 (1969–70), 79–95.

2024 Hey, David G. 'The pattern of nonconformity in South Yorkshire, 1660–1851', *Northern History,* 8 (1973), 86–118.

2025 Itzkin, Elissa S. 'The Halévy thesis – a working hypothesis? English revivalism: antidote for revolution and radicalism, 1789–1815', *Church History,* 44 (1975), 47–56. See also (1979), (2026), (2027), (2041), (2045) and (2047) for other contributions to this debate.

2026 Kent, John Henry Somerset. 'Methodism and revolution', *Methodist History,* 12, 4 (1973–4), 136–44. For other references to this debate, see (2025).

2027 Kiernan, V. 'Evangelicalism and the French Revolution', *PP,* 1 (1952), 44–56. Sees the evangelical movement as wholly reactionary.

2028 Linker, R. W. 'The English Roman Catholics and emancipation', *Journal of Ecclesiastical History,* 27 (1976), 151–80.

2029 MacDonagh, Oliver Ormond Gerard Michael. 'The politicization of the Irish Catholic bishops, 1800–1850', *HJ,* 18 (1975), 37–53.

2030 Mather, Frederick Clare. 'Church, Parliament and penal laws: some Anglo-Scottish interactions in the eighteenth century', *EHR*, 92 (1977), 540–72. Concerned with the relief of the Scottish episcopalians 1788–92. See also (619).

2031 Meacham, Standish. 'The evangelical inheritance', *JBS*, 3, 1 (1963), 88–104.

2032 Mews, Stuart. 'Reason and emotion in working-class religion, 1794–1824', in Derek Baker (ed.), *Schism, heresy and religious protest*. Cambridge, 1972, pp. 365–82.

2033 Mills, Frederick V., Sr. 'The internal Anglican controversy over an American episcopate, 1763–1775', *Historical Magazine of the Protestant Episcopal Church*, 44 (1975), 257–76.

2034 Morgan, David T. '"The dupes of designing men": John Wesley and the American Revolution', *Historical Magazine of the Protestant Episcopal Church*, 44 (1975), 121–31. One of the better of many articles on this subject.

2035 O'Neill, James E. 'The British quarterlies and the religious question, 1802–1829', *Catholic Historical Review*, 52 (1966–7), 350–71. Catholic emancipation.

2036 Prochaska, Franklyn K. 'Public worship: an eighteenth-century debate', *Transactions of the Unitarian Historical Society*, 15 (1971–2), 1–14.

2037 Richey, Russell E. 'Effects of toleration on eighteenth-century dissent', *Journal of Religious History*, 9 (1974–5), 350–63.

2038 —— 'Joseph Priestley: worship and theology', *Transactions of the Unitarian Historical Society*, 15 (1972–3), 41–53, 98–104.

2039 —— 'The origins of British radicalism: the changing rationale for dissent', *ECS*, 7 (1973–4), 179–92.

2040 Rule, Philip C. 'Coleridge's reputation as a religious thinker, 1816–1972', *Harvard Theological Review*, 67 (1974), 289–320.

2041 Semmel, Bernard. 'The Halévy thesis: Methodism and revolution', *Encounter*, 37 (1971), 44–55; reprinted as 'Elie Halévy, Methodism and revolution', in Semmel's translation of Halévy's articles on the origins of Methodism, *The birth of methodism in England*. Chicago, Ill., 1971. For other references to this debate, see (2025).

2042 Short, K. R. M. 'The English Indemnity Acts, 1726–1867', *Church History*, 42 (1973), 366–76. The usually annual acts forgiving violations of the religious tests.

2043 Soloway, Richard Allan. 'Episcopal perspectives and religious revivalism in England, 1784–1851', *Historical Magazine of the Protestant Episcopal Church*, 40 (1971), 27–61.

2044 Spring, David. 'The Clapham Sect: some social and political aspects', *Victorian Studies*, 5 (1961–2), 35–48.

2045 Stigant, P. 'Wesleyan methodism and working-class radicalism in the North, 1792–1821', *Northern History*, 6 (1971), 98–116. See also (2025).

2046 Sykes, Norman. 'The Duke of Newcastle as ecclesiastical minister', *EHR*, 57 (1942), 59–84.

2047 Walsh, John D. 'Elie Halévy and the birth of Methodism', *TRHS* 5th ser., 25 (1975), 1–20. Comprehensive discussion. For other references to this debate, see (2025).

2048 Ward, William Reginald. 'The Baptists and the transformation of the [Baptist] Church, 1780–1830', *Baptist Quarterly* NS, 25 (1973–4), 167–84.

2049 —— 'The legacy of John Wesley: the pastoral office in Britain and America', in Anne Whiteman, et al. (eds.), *Statesmen, scholars and merchants*. Oxford, 1973, pp. 323–50. The controversy surrounding the organization of the Wesleyan connection and its relations with the Establishment.

2050 —— 'The religion of the people and the problem of control, 1790–1830', in G. J. Cuming and Derek Baker (eds.), *Popular belief and practice*. Cambridge, 1972, pp. 237–57.

2051 —— 'The tithe question in England in the early nineteenth century', *Journal of Ecclesiastical History*, 16 (1965), 67–81.

XIII. FINE ARTS

For specialized bibliographies, lists and catalogues, see (38), (66), (96), (111), (114) and (152).

1. Printed sources

2052 Barry, James. *The works of James Barry, containing his correspondence from France and Italy with Mr Burke, his lectures on painting* . . . . 1809, 2 vols.

2053 Beckett, Ronald Brymer (ed.). *Correspondence of John Constable.* (Suffolk Record Society Publications, 4; 6; 8; 10–12.) Ipswich, Suffolk, 1962–3, 6 vols. Supplemented by Leslie Parris, et al. (eds.), *John Constable: further documents and correspondence.* (Suffolk Record Society Publications, 18.) Ipswich, Suffolk, 1975.

2054 Binyon, Robert Laurence (comp.). *British Museum catalogue of drawings by British artists and artists of foreign origin working in Great Britain, preserved in the Department of Prints and Drawings in the British Museum.* 1878–1907, 4 vols. A new edition is in progress.

2055 Graves, Algernon. *The British Institution 1806–1867: a complete dictionary of contributors and their work.* 1908; reprinted, 1969.

2056 —— *The Royal Academy of Arts: a complete dictionary of all work exhibited at the Royal Academy from 1769 to 1804.* 1905–6, 8 vols.

2057 —— *The Society of Artists of Great Britain, 1760–1791: the Free Society of Artists, 1761–1783: a complete dictionary of contributors and their work from the foundation of the societies to 1791.* 1907; reprinted, Bath, 1969.

2058 Graves, Algernon and W. V. Cronin. *A history of the works of Sir Joshua Reynolds.* 1899–1901, 4 vols. Full documentation.

2059 Greig, James (ed.). *The Farington diary, 1793–1821.* 1922–8, 8 vols. Major source of gossip about the art world. The first six volumes of a new, more complete, but unannotated edition, ed. Kenneth John Garlick and Angus MacIntyre, New Haven, Conn., 1978–.

2060 Hilles, Frederick Whitley (ed.). *Letters of Sir Joshua Reynolds.* Cambridge, 1929.

2061 Pevsner, Sir Nikolaus Bernhard Leon, et al. *The buildings of England.* Harmondsworth, Middx, 1951–74. Second editions of some of the volumes; brief descriptions of most surviving buildings of the period.

2062 Physick, John Frederick. *Designs for English sculpture 1680–1860.* 1969.

2063 Pope, William Bissell (ed.). *The diary of Benjamin Robert Haydon.* Cambridge, Mass., 1960–3, 5 vols. Much on early nineteenth century art world.

2064 Repton, Humphry. *The red books of Humphry Repton.* 1976, 4 vols. Principal source for late eighteenth century landscape design.

2065 Reynolds, Sir Joshua. *The works of Sir Joshua Reynolds . . . to which is prefixed, an account of the life and writings of the author.* 1797, 2 vols; 5th edn, corr., 1819, 3 vols. The best edition of the *Discourses* is by R. P. Wark, San Marino, Calif., 1959.

2066 Smith, John Thomas. *Nollekins and his times, comprehending a life of that sculptor and memoirs of several contemporary artists* . . . . 1828, 2 vols.; new edn by George Walter Stonier, 1945. A minor classic, frequently reprinted.

2067 Woodhall, Mary (ed.). *The letters of Thomas Gainsborough.* New York, 1963.

2. Surveys

2068 Boase, Thomas Sherrer Ross. *English art, 1800–1870.* (Oxford history of English art, 10.) Oxford, 1959.

2069 Burke, Joseph. *English art, 1714–1800.* (Oxford history of English art, 9.) Oxford, 1976.

2070 Edwards, Herbert Cecil Ralph and Leonard Gerald Gwynne Ramsay (eds.). *The connoisseur period guide to the houses, decorations, furnishings and chattels of the classic periods. The late Georgian period, 1760–1810.* 1956; *The Regency period, 1810–1830.* 1958; *The early Victorian period, 1830–60.* 1958. Chapters by various experts on all the fine and decorative arts. The individual period guides were reprinted in a single volume, New York, 1968.

2071 Girouard, Mark. *Life in the English country house: a social and architectural history.* New Haven, Conn., 1978. From the middle ages to the twentieth century; lavishly illustrated.

2072 Herrmann, Luke. *British landscape painting of the eighteenth century.* 1973. Both oils and watercolours.

2073 Summerson, Sir John Newenham. *Architecture in Britain, 1530–1830.* Harmondsworth, Middx, 1953; 5th edn, 1969. Best introduction.

2074 Turnor, Christopher Reginald. *Nineteenth-century architecture in Britain.* 1950.

2075 Walker, Ernest. *A history of music in England*. Oxford, 1907; 3rd edn, rev. and enlarged by Sir Jack Allan Westrup, Oxford, 1952.
2076 Waterhouse, Ellis Kirkham. *Painting in Britain, 1530 to 1790*. Harmondsworth, Middx, 1953; 4th edn, Harmondsworth, Middx, 1978.
2077 Whinney, Margaret Dickens. *Sculpture in Britain, 1530–1830*. Harmondsworth, Middx, 1964.
2078 Whitley, William Thomas. *Artists and their friends in England 1700–1799*. 1928, 2 vols. *Art in England, 1800–1820*. Cambridge, 1928. *Art in England, 1821–37*. Cambridge, 1930. General account of artists' lives, exhibitions and the like.
2079 Wilenski, Reginald Howard. *English painting*. 1933.
2080 Young, Percy Marshall. *A history of British music*. 1967.

3. Monographs

2081 Armstrong, Sir Walter. *Lawrence*. 1913; reprinted, New York, 1969. Standard older study. See also (2200).
2082 Atherton, Herbert A. *Political prints in the age of Hogarth: a study of the ideographic representation of politics*. Oxford, 1974. See also (464).
2083 Beard, Geoffrey W. *Georgian craftsmen and their work*. 1966. Second half on the Adam period.
2084 —— *The work of Robert Adam*. Edinburgh, 1978. Primarily on his architecture. See also (2110) and (2174).
2085 Blunt, Anthony Frederick. *The art of William Blake*. 1959. See also (2138) and (2139).
2086 Bolton, Arthur Thomas. *The architecture of Robert and James Adam, 1758–1794*. 1922, 2 vols. Some 700 illustrations, plans and drawings.
2087 Bradbury, Frederick. *History of old Sheffield plate, being an account of the origin, growth and decay of the industry*. 1912. Standard.
2088 Brand, Charles Peter. *Italy and the English romantics: the Italianate fashion in early nineteenth-century England*. Cambridge, 1957.
2089 Bronowski, Jacob. *William Blake and the age of revolution*. New York, 1965.
2090 Butlin, Martin and Evelyn Joll. *The paintings of J. M. W. Turner*. New Haven, Conn., 1977. Definitive catalogue raisonné. See also (2199), (2209) and (2228).
2091 Charleston, Robert Jesse (ed.). *English porcelain, 1745–1850*. 1965. Chapters on the different factories, with full bibliographies, by various authorities.
2092 Clarke, P. (ed.). *Georgian Dublin*. 1976.
2093 Clifford, Derek Plint. *A history of garden design*. 1962.
2094 Coleridge, Anthony. *Chippendale furniture*. 1968. Fully documented discussion of Chippendale's competitors as well; 420 illustrations.
2095 Craig, Maurice James. *Dublin, 1660–1860: a social and architectural history*. 1952.
2096 Croft-Murray, Edward. *Decorative painting in England, 1537–1837*. Vol. 2: *The eighteenth and early nineteenth centuries*. 1962–70.
2097 Crook, Joseph Mordaunt. *The Greek revival: neo-classical attitudes in British architecture, 1760–1870*. 1972.
2098 Culme, John. *Nineteenth-century silver*. 1977.
2099 Darcy, Cornelius P. *The encouragement of the fine arts in Lancashire, 1760–1860*. (Chetham Society 3rd ser., 24.) Manchester, 1976.
2100 Davis, Terence. *The architecture of John Nash: introduced with a critical essay by John Summerson*. 1960.
2101 Delieb, Eric. *The great silver manufactory: Matthew Boulton and the Birmingham silversmiths, 1760–1790*. 1971.
2102 Doherty, Terence. *The anatomical works of George Stubbs*. Boston, Mass., 1975. Supersedes all other editions and adds many further reproductions.
2103 Du Prey, Pierre de la Ruffinière. *John Soane's architectural education, 1753–1780*. New York, 1977. See also (2175).
2104 Edwards, Herbert Cecil Ralph and Margaret Jourdain. *Georgian cabinet-makers, c. 1700–1800*. 1944; 3rd edn, rev., 1955. Illustrated collection of documented furniture from both well- and lesser-known cabinet-makers.
2105 Ehrlich, Cyril. *The piano: a history*. 1976.
2106 Esdaile, Katherine Ada (McDowell). *English church monuments, 1510–1840*. Oxford, 1947.
2107 Fastnedge, Ralph. *Sheraton furniture*. 1962.

2108   Fawcett, Trevor. *The rise of English provincial art: artists, patrons and institutions outside London, 1800–1830.* Oxford, 1974.

2109   Fiske, Roger, *English theatre music in the eighteenth century.* 1973.

2110   Fleming, John. *Robert Adam and his circle, in Edinburgh and Rome.* 1962. Only to 1763, but fundamental for Adam. See also (2084) and (2174).

2111   Ganz, Paul Leonhard. *The drawings of Henry Fuseli.* 1949.

2112   Gardner, John Starkee. *English ironwork of the XVIIth and XVIIIth centuries: an account of the development of exterior smith-work.* 1911. With a list of English smiths.

2113   Gear, Josephine. *Masters or servants? A study of selected English painters and their patrons of the late eighteenth and early nineteenth centuries.* New York, 1977.

2114   Gilberg, Sir Walter. *Animal painters of England from the year 1650: a brief survey of their lives and works.* 1910–11, 3 vols. Basic study of the subject. See also (2178).

2115   Gloag, John. *Georgian grace: a social history of design from 1660 to 1830.* 1956; 3rd edn, 1967.

2116   Godden, Geoffrey Arthur. *British pottery and porcelain, 1780–1850.* 1963. Godden published an illustrated encyclopaedia of the subject in 1966.

2117   Grant, Maurice Harold. *A chronological history of the old English landscape painters (in oil) from the XVIth century to the XIXth century.* 1929, 2 vols; new edn, rev. and enlarged, Leigh-on-Sea, Essex, 1957–61, 8 vols.

2118   Guinness, Desmond and Julius Thomasdale Sadler, Jr. *The palladian style in England, Ireland and America.* 1976.

2119   Hammelmann, Hans. *Book illustrators in eighteenth-century England.* Ed. and completed by Thomas Sherrer Ross Boase. New Haven, Conn., 1975. See also (2163).

2120   Hardie, Martin. *Watercolour painting in Britain.* Ed. Dudley Snelgrove with Jonathan Mayne and Basil Taylor. Vol. 1: *The eighteenth century.* 1966; Vol. 2: *The romantic period.* 1967; Vol. 3: *The Victorian period.* 1968.

2121   Harris, Eileen. *The furniture of Robert Adam.* 1963. Best scholarly account.

2122   Hayes, John T. *The drawings of Thomas Gainsborough.* New Haven, Conn., 1971, 2 vols.

2123   —— *Gainsborough: paintings and drawings.* 1975. Contains the best selection of plates. See also (2225) and (2227).

2124   —— *Rowlandson: watercolours and drawings.* 1972. See also (2159).

2125   Honour, Hugh. *Chinoiserie: the vision of Cathay.* 1961.

2126   —— *Neo-Classicism.* Harmondsworth, Middx, 1968.

2127   Humphries, Charles and William Charles Smith. *Music publishing in the British Isles from the beginning to the middle of the nineteenth century: a dictionary of engravers, printers, publishers and music sellers, with a historical introduction.* 1954; 2nd edn, with supplement, Oxford, 1970.

2128   Hussey, Christopher Edward Clive. *English country houses.* Vol. 2: *Mid-Georgian, 1760–1806.* 2nd edn, 1963. *Late Georgian, 1800–1840.* 1958.

2129   —— *The picturesque: studies in a point of view.* 1927; new impression, 1967.

2130   Hutchison, Sidney Charles. *The history of the Royal Academy, 1768–1968.* 1968.

2131   Irwin, David G. *English neoclassical art: studies in inspiration and taste.* 1966. Extensive bibliography.

2132   Irwin, David G. and Francina Irwin. *Scottish painters at home and abroad 1700–1900.* 1975. Useful bibliography.

2133   Ison, Walter. *The Georgian buildings of Bath from 1700 to 1830.* 1941; reprinted, Bath, 1969. *The Georgian buildings of Bristol.* 1952.

2134   Jarrett, David. *The English landscape garden.* 1978.

2135   Jenkins, Frank. *Architect and patron: a survey of professional relations and practice in England from the sixteenth century to the present day.* 1961.

2136   Johnson, James William. *The formation of English neoclassical thought.* Princeton, NJ, 1967.

2137   Jourdain, Margaret. *Regency furniture, 1795–1830.* 1934; new edn, rev. and enlarged by Ralph Fastnedge, 1965. Standard.

2138   Keynes, Sir Geoffrey Langdon. *Blake studies: essays on his life and work.* Oxford, 1971. See also (2085) and (2155).

2139   —— *William Blake's engravings.* 1950.

2140   Klingender, Francis Donald. *Art and the industrial revolution.* 1947; new edn, rev. by Arthur Elton, 1968.

2141   Krumbhaar, Edward Bell. *Isaac Cruickshank: a catalogue raisonné with a sketch of his life and work.* Philadelphia, Pa, 1966.

2142 Lipking, Lawrence. *The ordering of the arts in eighteenth-century England*. Princeton, NJ, 1970.
2143 Mackerness, Eric David. *A social history of English music*. 1964. Relates music to social and economic background.
2144 Macquoid, Percy and Herbert Cecil Ralph Edwards. *The dictionary of English furniture from the middle ages to the late Georgian period*. 1924–7, 3 vols.; new edn, rev. and enlarged, 1954, 3 vols. Most important reference work on the subject.
2145 Malins, Edward Greenway. *English landscaping and literature 1660–1840*. 1966.
2146 —— *Lost desmesnes: Irish landscape gardening 1661–1845*. 1976.
2147 Manwaring, Elizabeth Wheeler. *Italian landscape in eighteenth-century England: a study chiefly of the influence of Claude Lorraine and Salvator Rosa on English taste 1700–1800*. New York, 1925.
2148 Marillier, Henry Currie. *Christie's 1766 to 1925*. 1926.
2149 Mee, John Henry. *The oldest music-room in Europe: a record of eighteenth-century enterprise at Oxford*. 1911.
2150 Morris, William Meredith. *British violin makers: a biographical dictionary of British makers of stringed instruments and bows and a critical description of their work*. 2nd edn, 1920.
2151 Morshead, Sir Owen Frederick. *Windsor Castle*. 2nd edn, rev., 1957.
2152 Musgrave, Clifford. *Royal Pavilion: an episode in the romantic*. Brighton, Sussex, 1951; rev. and enlarged edn, 1959; reprinted, 1964.
2153 Nettle, Reginald. *The orchestra in England: a social history*. 1946.
2154 Oman, Charles Chichele. *English domestic silver*. 6th edn, 1965. Standard.
2155 Paley, Morton D. and Michael Phillips (eds.). *William Blake: essays in honour of Sir Geoffrey Keynes*. Oxford, 1973. See also (2138).
2156 Patten, Robert L., et al. George Cruikshank. Double issue of the *Princeton University Library Chronicle*, 35 (1973–4).
2157 Pattullo, Nan. *Castles, houses and gardens of Scotland*. Edinburgh, 1967–74, 2 vols.
2158 Paulson, Ronald. *Emblem and expression: meaning in English art in the eighteenth century*. 1975.
2159 —— *Rowlandson: a new interpretation*. 1972. See also (2124).
2160 Port, Michael Harry. *Six hundred new churches: a study of the Church Building Commission, 1818–1856, and its church building activities*. 1961.
2161 Praz, Mario. *Conversation pieces: a survey of the informal group portrait in Europe and America*. University Park, Pa, 1971.
2162 —— *Gusto neoclassico*. Florence, 1940; trans. by Angus Davidson as *On neoclassicism*. 1969.
2163 Ray, Gordon Norton. *The illustrator and the book in England from 1790 to 1914*. New York, 1976. See also (2119).
2164 Reitlinger, Gerald. *The economics of taste: the rise and fall of picture prices, 1760–1960*. 1961–2, 2 vols.
2165 Richardson, Sir Albert Edward and Harold Donaldson Eberlein. *The smaller English house of the later Renaissance, 1660–1830: an account of its design, plans, and details*. 1911; new issue, 1933.
2166 Rosenau, Helen. *Social purpose in architecture: Paris and London compared, 1760–1800*. 1970.
2167 Rosenblum, Robert. *Transformations in late eighteenth-century art*. Princeton, NJ, 1970.
2168 Rotherberg, Jacob. '*Descensus ad terram*': the acquisition and reception of the Elgin Marbles. New York, 1977.
2169 Sitwell, Sacheverell. *Conversation pieces: a survey of English domestic portraits and their painters*. 1936.
2170 —— *Narrative pictures: a survey of English genre and its painters*. 1937.
2171 Smith, Bernard William. *European vision and the South Pacific: a study in the history of art and ideas*. Oxford, 1960. Useful bibliography.
2172 Sparrow, Walter Shaw. *A history of sporting painters*. 1931. Including biographical material on many painters.
2173 Stewart, Cecil. *The stones of Manchester*. 1956. The architecture of Manchester: an index of the principal buildings and their architects, 1800–1900. Manchester, 1956.
2174 Stillman, Damie. *The decorative work of Robert Adam*. 1966. See also (2084) and (2110).
2175 Stroud, Dorothy Nancy. *The architecture of Sir John Soane: with an introduction by Professor Henry-Russell Hitchcock*. 1961. See also (2103).

2176 Summerson, Sir John Newenham. *Georgian London*. 1945; 2nd edn, rev., 1962. Best book on architecture of London.
2177 Sumner, William Leslie. *The pianoforte*. 1966; 3rd edn, with corrections and additions, 1971.
2178 Taylor, Basil. *Animal painting in England from Baslow to Landseer*. 1955. See also (2114).
2179 Taylor, Gerald. *Silver*. 2nd edn., Harmondsworth, Middx, 1963. Useful bibliography.
2180 Thompson, Francis. *A history of Chatsworth*. 1949.
2181 Thorpe, William Arnold. *A history of English and Irish glass*. 1929, 2 vols.
2182 Walker, Stella A. *Sporting art: England 1700–1900*. 1972.
2183 Ward-Jackson, Peter. *English furniture designs of the eighteenth century*. 1958. Includes a bibliography of the major eighteenth century pattern books.
2184 Warrillow, Ernest Jones Dalzell. *History of Etruria ... 1760–1951*. Hanley, Staffs., 1952.
2185 Waterhouse, Ellis Kirkham. *Reynolds*. 1941. Illustrated catalogue raisonné rather than a biography; Waterhouse's *Reynolds*, 1973, is a more general account. See also (2206).
2186 —— *Three decades of British art, 1740–1770*. Philadelphia, Pa, 1965. Lectures.
2187 Weber, Wilbur. *Music and the middle class: the social structure of concert life in London, Paris and Vienna*. 1975. Covers period 1815–1848.
2188 Wedgwood, Josiah Clement, Baron Wedgwood. *Staffordshire pottery and its history*. 1913.
2189 Weibenson, Dora. *Sources of Greek Revival architecture*. University Park, Pa, 1969.
2190 Whiffen, Marcus. *Stuart and Georgian churches: the architecture of the Church of England outside London, 1603–1837*. 1948.
2191 Whiter, Leonard. *Spode: a history of the family, factory and wares from 1733 to 1833*. 1970.
2192 Woodbridge, Kenneth. *Landscape and antiquity: aspects of English culture at Stourhead 1718 to 1838*. 1970.
2193 Youngson, Alexander John. *The making of classical Edinburgh: 1750–1840*. Edinburgh, 1966.

4. Biographies

2194 Alberts, Roberts, C. *Benjamin West: a biography*. Boston, Mass., 1978.
2195 Chancellor, Edwin Beresford. *The lives of the British sculptors and those who have worked in England from the earliest days to Sir Francis Chantry*. 1911. Two-thirds on the eighteenth and early nineteenth centuries.
2196 Colvin, Howard Montagu (comp.). *A biographical dictionary of English architects, 1660–1840*. 1954.
2197 Constable, William George. *John Flaxman, 1755–1826*. 1927. Standard.
2198 Dale, Antony. *James Wyatt*. Oxford, 1936; rev. edn, Oxford, 1956.
2199 Finberg, Alexander Joseph. *The life of J. M. W. Turner, RA*. Oxford, 1939; 2nd edn, rev., Oxford, 1961. Standard life; see also (2090), (2209) and (2228).
2200 Garlick, Kenneth John. *Sir Thomas Lawrence*. 1954. Garlick also complied a catalogue of Lawrence's paintings, drawings and pastels for the Walpole Society (Publications, 35), Glasgow, 1964. See also (2081).
2201 Goldberg, Norman L. *John Crome, the Elder*. New York, 1978.
2202 Gunnis, Rupert. *Dictionary of British sculptors, 1660–1851*. 1953.
2203 Harris, John Frederick. *Sir William Chambers, Knight of the Polar Star*. 1970.
2204 Hill, Draper. *Mr Gillray, the caricaturist: a biography*. 1965. With a volume of reproductions, *Fashionable contrasts*. 1966.
2205 Hobhouse, Hermione. *Thomas Cubitt, master builder*. 1971.
2206 Hudson, Derek. *Sir Joshua Reynolds: a personal study*. 1958. Best short biography. See also (2058) and (2185).
2207 Key, Sydney J. *John Constable: his life and work*. 1948.
2208 Langley, Hubert. *Doctor Arne*. Cambridge, 1938.
2209 Lindsay, Jack. *J. M. W. Turner, his life and work: a critical biography*. 1966. See also (2090), (2199) and (2228).
2210 Linstrum, Derek. *Sir Jeffrey Wyatville: architect to the King*. Oxford, 1972.
2211 Mayne, Jonathan. *Thomas Girtin*. Leigh-on-Sea, Essex, 1949.
2212 Nicolson, Benedict. *Joseph Wright of Derby: painter of light*. 1968.

2213 Parker, Constance Anne. *Mr Stubbs the horse painter.* 1971.
2214 Peacock, Carlos. *Richard Parks Bonington.* 1980. See also (2219).
2215 Prown, Jules David. *John Singleton Copley.* Cambridge, Mass., 1966, 2 vols.
2216 Redgrave, Samuel. *A dictionary of artists of the English school from the middle ages to the nineteenth century: painters, sculptors, architects, engravers, and ornamentalists.* 1874; new edn, rev., 1970. Still the most useful work for quick reference.
2217 Routley, Erik Reginald. *The musical Wesleys.* 1968.
2218 Scholes, Percy Alfred. *The great Dr Burney: his life, his travels, his family and his friends.* Oxford, 1948, 2 vols.
2219 Shirley, Andrew. *Bonington.* 1941. Standard. See also (2214).
2220 Strickland, Walter George. *A dictionary of Irish artists.* Dublin, 1913, 2 vols. Useful work of reference.
2221 Stroud, Dorothy Nancy. *George Dance, architect, 1741–1825.* 1971.
2222 —— *Henry Holland: his life and architecture.* 1966.
2223 —— *Humphry Repton.* 1962.
2224 Ward, Thomas Humphry and William Roberts. *Romney: a biographical and critical essay with a catalogue raisonné of his works.* 1904, 2 vols.
2225 Waterhouse, Ellis Kirkham. *Gainsborough.* 1958; new edn, 1966. See also (2122), (2123) and (2227).
2226 Weekley, Montague. *Thomas Bewick.* 1953.
2227 Whitley, William Thomas. *Thomas Gainsborough.* 1915. Most full biography.
2228 Wilton, Andrew. *The life and work of J. M. W. Turner.* 1979. See also (2090), (2199) and (2209).

5. Articles

2229 Fox, Celina. 'The engravers' battle for professional recognition in early nineteenth-century London', *London Journal*, 2 (1976), 3–31.
2230 Gibbon, Michael. 'Stowe, Buckinghamshire: the house and garden buildings and their designers', *Architectural History*, 20 (1977), 31–44.
2231 Harris, John Frederick. 'English county-house guides 1740–1840', in Sir John Summerson (ed.), *Concerning architecture: essays on architectural writers and writings presented to Nikolaus Pevsner.* 1968, pp. 58–74.
2232 Hower, R. M. 'The Wedgwoods, ten generations of potters, part i, 1612–1795', *Journal of Economic and Business History*, 4 (1932), 281–313.
2233 Hunt, John Dixon. 'Emblem and expressionism in the eighteenth-century landscape garden', *ECS*, 4 (1970–1), 294–317.
2234 Mitchell, C. 'Benjamin West's "Death of General Wolfe" and the popular history piece', *Journal of the Warburg and Courtauld Intitute*, 7 (1944), 20–33.
2235 Pace, K. Claire. '"Strong contraries ... happy discord": some eighteenth-century discussions about landscape', *JHI*, 40 (1979), 141–55.
2236 Penny, N. B. 'The Whig cult of Fox in early nineteenth-century sculpture', *PP*, 70 (1976), 94–105.
2237 Rorabaugh, W. J. 'Politics and the architectural competition for the Houses of Parliament, 1834–1837', *Victorian Studies*, 17 (1973), 155–75.
2238 Stillman, Damie. 'British architects and Italian architectural competitions, 1758–1780', *Journal of the Society of Architectural Historians*, 32 (1973), 43–66.
2239 Symmons, Sarah. 'The spirit of despair: patronage, primitivism and the art of John Flaxman', *Burlington Magazine*, 117 (1975), 644–50.

XIV. INTELLECTUAL HISTORY

For specialized bibliographies, lists and catalogues, see (9), (26), (39), (60), (61) and (143). Religious thought is listed in Section XII.

1. Printed sources

2240 Bowring, Sir John (ed.). *The works of Jeremy Bentham.* Edinburgh, 1838–43, 11 vols. The new *Collected works of Jeremy Bentham*, general editor, James Henderson Burns,

1968–, has so far produced three volumes of Bentham's correspondence: 1752–88, ed. Timothy Lauro Squire Sprigge and Ian Ralph Christie, 1968–71; *An introduction to the principles of morals and legislation*, ed. James Henderson Burns and Herbert Lionel Adolphus Hart, 1970; *Of laws in general*, ed. Hart, 1970; and *A comment on the Commentaries* and *A fragment on government*, ed. Burns and Hart, 1977. Other writings not in Bowring are included in (2269) and (2288). For Bentham, see also (266), (339), (350), (2283), (2316), (2337), (2346), (2367), (2387), (2394), (2408), (2446), (2452), (2469), (2479), (2489) and (2490).

2241 Coburn, Kathleen, et al. (eds.). *The collected works of Samuel Taylor Coleridge*. Princeton, NJ, 1969–. In progress. For Coleridge, see also (1923), (2242), (2248), (2294), (2302), (2317), (2357), (2372), (2387) and (2427).

2242 Coburn, Kathleen (ed.). *The notebooks of Samuel Taylor Coleridge*. Princeton, NJ, 1957–. In progress, 3 vols. published so far. See (2241) for list of works on Coleridge.

2243 Curry, Kenneth (ed.). *New letters of Robert Southey*. New York, 1965, 2 vols. See also (2438).

2244 De Selincourt, Ernest (ed.). *The letters of William and Dorothy Wordsworth*. Oxford, 1935–9, 6 vols. These are being re-edited, with much additional material, by Chester L. Shaver, Oxford, 1967–.

2245 *Encyclopaedia britannica*. 1768–71, 3 vols.; 2nd edn, Edinburgh, 1778–83, 10 vols.; 3rd edn, Edinburgh, 1797–1801, 20 vols. For its history, see (2358).

2246 Godwin, William. *An enquiry concerning political justice, and its influence on general virtue and happiness*. 1793, 2 vols.; 3rd edn, 1798, 2 vols.; reprinted, with a critical introduction and notes by Francis Ethelbert Louis Priestley, Toronto, 1946, 3 vols.; another edition, with introduction by Isaac Kramnick, Harmondsworth, Middx, 1976. For Godwin, see also (2296), (2370), (2456), (2466) and (2507).

2247 Greig, John Young Thompson (ed.). *The letters of David Hume*. Oxford, 1932, 2 vols. For additional letters, see (2252). For Hume, see also (2290), (2329), (2405), (2422), (2447) and (2455).

2248 Griggs, Earl Leslie (ed.). *Collected letters of Samuel Taylor Coleridge*. Oxford, 1956–71, 6 vols. See (2241) for other Coleridge references.

2249 Hamilton, Sir William (ed.). *The collected works of Dugald Stewart*. Edinburgh, 1854–60, 11 vols.

2250 Hill, George Birkbeck and Lawrence Fitzroy Powell (eds.). *Boswell's Life of Johnson*. 1934–64, 6 vols. The edition for reference. Boswell's *Life* is still the best introduction to intelligent eighteenth century conversation.

2251 Howe, Percival Presland (ed.). *The complete works of William Hazlitt*. 1930–4, 21 vols. See also (2434).

2252 Klibansky, Raymond and Ernest Campbell Mossner (eds.). *New letters of David Hume*. Oxford, 1954. Ninety-eight new letters and twenty-seven more new in part since publication of (2247). For Hume, see also (2329), (2405), (2422), (2447) and (2455).

2253 Liebert, Herman W., et al. (eds.). *The Yale edition of the works of Samuel Johnson*. New Haven, Conn., 1958–. 11 vols. so far published.

2254 Lively, Jack and John Collwyn Rees (eds.). *Utilitarian logic and politics: James Mill's 'Essay on Government', Macaulay's critique, and the ensuing debate*. Oxford, 1978.

2255 Malthus, Thomas Robert. *An essay on the principle of population, as it affects the future improvement of society: with remarks on the speculations of Mr Godwin, M. Condorcet and other writers*. 1798; reprinted, 1926. 2nd edn, much enlarged and modified, as *An essay on the principle of population: or, a view of its past and present effects on human happiness*. 1803 and many subsequent editions. For Malthus, see also (2332), (2346), (2364), (2375), (2380), (2404), (2457), (2487) and (2509).

2256 Marchand, Leslie Alexis (ed.). *Byron's letters and journals*. 1973–. In progress; 10 vols. so far published. See also (2453).

2257 Murray, John (ed.). *The autobiographies of Edward Gibbon*. 1896. Prints all six texts as Gibbon left them. The usual version, in many editions, is the one prepared by Lord Sheffield in 1796; a new edition, prepared from the manuscripts by Georges Alfred Bonnard, as *Memoirs of my life*. 1966. For Gibbon, see also (2259), (2290), (2295), (2444), (2451) and (2486).

2258 Nichols, John (ed.). *Illustrations of the literary history of the eighteenth century*. 1817–58, 8 vols.; reprinted, New York, 1966, 8 vols. *Literary anecdotes of the eighteenth century*.

1812–16, 9 vols.; reprinted, New York, 1966, 9 vols. Most of the letters printed in these volumes concern antiquarian and scholarly matters rather than literature.

2259 Norton, Jane Elizabeth (ed.). *The letters of Edward Gibbon*. 1956, 3 vols. See (2257) for other Gibbon references.

2260 Owen, Robert. *The life of Robert Owen, written by himself*. 1857; ed. John Butt, 1971. For Owen, see also (866), (2344), (2435), (2443) and (2458).

2261 Paley, William. *The works of William Paley... with a life by Alexander Chalmers*. 1819, 5 vols.; new edn by Edmund Paley, 1830, 6 vols., and many subsequent editions. A leading popularizer of ideas. See also (2439).

2262 Parekh, Bhikhu C. (ed.). *Bentham's political thought*. New York, 1973. Useful collection of selections. See (2240) for other Bentham references.

2263 Peach, Bernard (ed.). *Richard Price and the ethical foundations of the American Revolution: selections from his pamphlets, with appendices....* Durham, NC, 1979. Long introduction. See also (2410).

2264 Pinney, Thomas (ed.). *The letters of Thomas Babington Macaulay*. Cambridge, 1974–. The first three volumes extend from 1807 to 1841. For Macaulay, see also (2254), (2339) and (2441).

2265 Priestley, Joseph. *An essay on the first principles of government, and on the nature of political, civil and religious liberty*. 1768; 2nd edn, with additions, 1771. Priestley's most important political pamphlet. For his writings on other subjects, see (1546), (1552), (1555) and (1903); for a biography, see (1654).

2266 Schuyler, Robert Livingston (ed.). *Josiah Tucker: a selection from his economic and political writings*. New York, 1931.

2267 Smith, Adam. *The Glasgow edition of the works and correspondence of Adam Smith*. Oxford, 1976–. This edition, still in progress, so far includes *The correspondence of Adam Smith*, ed. Ernest Campbell Mossner and Ian Simpson Ross, Oxford, 1977; *The wealth of nations*, ed. Roy Hutcheson Campbell and Andrew S. Skinner, Oxford, 1976, 2 vols.; the *Theory of moral sentiments*, ed. D. D. Raphael and Alec Lawrence Macfie, Oxford, 1976; and *Lectures in jurisprudence*, ed. Ronald L. Meek, et al., Oxford, 1978. There is also an edition of *The early writings of Adam Smith*, ed. J. Ralph Lindgren, New York, 1967, and various editions of his lecture notes. For Smith, see also (2349), (2365), (2389), (2402), (2403), (2428), (2429), 2459), (2460), (2462), (2465), (2471), (2477), (2503), (2506), (2512) and (2513).

2268 Sraffa, Piero and Maurice Herbert Dobb (eds.). *The works and correspondence of David Ricardo*. Cambridge, 1951–73, 11 vols. For Ricardo, see also (2291), (2396), (2401), (2464), (2483), (2491) and (2500).

2269 Stark, Werner (ed.). *Jeremy Bentham's economic writings*. 1952–4, 3 vols. Includes previously unpublished material not yet incorporated into the edition of Bentham's collected works. See (2240) for other Bentham references.

2270 White, Reginald James (ed.). *Political tracts of Wordsworth, Coleridge and Shelley*. Cambridge, 1953.

2271 Winch, Donald Norman (ed.). *James Mill: selected economic writings*. Chicago, 1966. Prints all of *Elements of political economy* (1821) and other writings. For Mill, see also (2254), (2299), (2338), (2393), (2433) and (2454).

2. Surveys

2272 Bowle, John. *Politics and opinion in the nineteenth century: an historical introduction*. 1954.

2273 Brinton, Clarence Crane. *English political thought in the nineteenth century*. 1933; 2nd edn, Cambridge, Mass., 1949; reprinted, New York, 1962.

2274 Cassirer, Ernst. *The philosophy of the enlightenment*. Eng. trans. by Fritz C. A. Kuchin and James P. Pettegrove. Princeton, NJ, 1951. First published, Tübingen, 1932.

2275 Deane, Phyllis. *The evolution of economic ideas*. Cambridge, 1978. From Adam Smith to the present.

2276 Laski, Harold Joseph. *Political thought in England from Locke to Bentham*. New York, 1920; many subsequent editions to 1955.

2277 Renwick, William Lindsay. *English literature, 1789–1815*. Oxford, 1963. (Oxford history of English literature, 9.)

2278 Somerville, David Churchill. *English thought in the nineteenth century*. 1929; 6th edn, 1950.

2279 Stephen, Sir Leslie. *History of English thought in the eighteenth century*. 1876, 2 vols.; 3rd edn, 1902, 2 vols.; reprinted, New York, 1949 and 1962, 2 vols.

2280 Taylor, Overton H. *A history of economic thought: social ideals and economic theories from Quesnay to Keynes*. New York, 1960. Much on England.

2281 Williams, Raymond. *Culture and society, 1780–1950*. 1958.

3. Monographs

2282 Aarsleff, Hans. *The study of language in England, 1780–1860*. Princeton, NJ, 1967; reprinted, Westport, Conn., 1979.

2283 Albee, Ernest. *A history of English utilitarianism*. 1902; reprinted, 1952.

2284 Bailyn, Bernard. *The ideological origins of the American Revolution*. Cambridge, Mass., 1967. Important for English political thought.

2285 Barker, Nicolas. *The Oxford University Press and the spread of learning, 1478–1978: an illustrated history*. Oxford, 1978.

2286 Barrell, Joseph. *Shelley and the thought of his time: a study in the history of ideas*. New Haven, Conn., 1947; reprinted, Hamden, Conn., 1967.

2287 Bate, Walter Jackson. *From classic to romantic: premises of taste in eighteenth-century England*. Cambridge, Mass., 1946; reprinted, New York, 1961.

2288 Baumgardt, David. *Bentham and the ethics of today, with Bentham manuscripts hitherto unpublished*. Princeton, NJ, 1952; reprinted, New York, 1966. Discussion of Bentham's moral philosophy. See (2240) for other Bentham references.

2289 Ben Israel, Hedva. *English historians on the French Revolution*. 1968.

2290 Black, John Bennett. *The art of history: a study of four great historians of the eighteenth century*. 1926. Voltaire, Hume, Robertson and Gibbon.

2291 Blaug, Mark. *Ricardian economics: a historical study*. New Haven, Conn., 1956. One of the most comprehensive studies of Ricardo; extensive bibliography. See (2268) for other Ricardo references.

2292 Bond, Donovan H. and William Reynolds McLeod (eds.). *Newsletters to newspapers: eighteenth-century journalism*. Morgantown, W. Va, 1977. Twenty-eight papers on the press in Britain and America.

2293 Bonwick, Colin C. *English radicals and the American Revolution*. Chapel Hill, NC, 1977.

2294 Boulger, James D. *Coleridge as religious thinker*. New Haven, Conn., 1961. See also (1923) and (2241) for other Coleridge references.

2295 Bowersock, Glen, John Leonard Clive and Stephen Richards Graubard (eds.). *Edward Gibbon and the Decline and Fall of the Roman Empire*. Cambridge, Mass., 1977. Twenty essays on the bicentenary of the publication of the first volume. See (2257) for other Gibbon references.

2296 Brailsford, Henry Noel. *Shelley, Godwin and their circle*. 1913; 2nd edn, 1951; reprinted, Hamden, Conn., 1969.

2297 Brinton, Clarence Crane. *The political ideas of the English romantics*. 1933; 2nd edn, Cambridge, Mass., 1949; reprinted, New York, 1962.

2298 Bryson, Gladys. *Man and society: the Scottish inquiry of the eighteenth century*. Princeton, NJ, 1945; reprinted, New York, 1968.

2299 Burston, Wyndham Hedley. *James Mill on philosophy and education*. 1973. See (2271) for other Mill references.

2300 Burton, Kenneth George. *The early newspaper press in Berkshire (1723–1855)*. Reading, Berks., 1954. Model study of the local press.

2301 Bury, John Bagnall. *The idea of progress: an inquiry into its origins and growth*. 1920; reprinted, Chicago, Ill., 1948 and New York, 1955.

2302 Calleo, David Patrick. *Coleridge and the idea of the modern state*. New Haven, Conn., 1966. See (2241) for other Coleridge references.

2303 Camerson, David R. *The social thought of Rousseau and Burke: a comparative study*. 1973. See (382) for other Burke references.

2304 Canavan, Francis Patrick. *The political reason of Edmund Burke*. Durham, NC, 1960. See (382) for other Burke references.

2305 Cannan, Edwin. *A history of theories of production and distribution in English political economy from 1776 to 1848*. 1891; 3rd edn, 1917; reprinted, 1953.

2306 Chapman, Gerald Wester. *Edmund Burke, the practical imagination*. Cambridge, Mass., 1967. Excellent brief study. See (382) for other Burke references.

2307 Chitnis, Anand C. *The Scotch enlightenment: a social history.* 1976.

2308 Clark, Sir Kenneth McKenzie Clark, Baron. *The Gothic revival: an essay in the history of taste.* 1928; 3rd edn, 1962; reprinted, New York, 1970.

2309 Clarke, Martin Lowther. *Classical education in Britain, 1500–1900.* Cambridge, 1959.

2310 —— *Greek studies in England, 1700 to 1830.* Cambridge, 1945.

2311 Clifford, James Lowry (ed.). *Man versus society in eighteenth-century Britain: six points of view.* 1968. Essays by John Harold Plumb, Jacob Viner, Gordon Robertson Cragg, Rudolph Wittkower, Paul Henry Lang and Bertrand Harris Bronson.

2312 Clive, John Leonard. *Scotch reviewers: the Edinburgh Review, 1802–1815.* Cambridge, Mass., 1957.

2313 Cobban, Alfred Bert Carter. *Edmund Burke and the revolt against the eighteenth century: a study of the political and social thinking of Burke, Worsworth, Coleridge, and Southey.* 1929; 2nd edn, 1960. See (382) for other Burke references.

2314 Colbourne, H. Trevor. *The lamp of experience: Whig history and the intellectual origins of the American Revolution.* Chapel Hill, NC, 1965.

2315 Cole, George Douglas Howard. *A history of socialist thought.* Vol. 1: *The forerunners, 1789–1850.* 1953.

2316 Collins, Arthur Simons. *Authorship in the days of Johnson: being a study of the relations between author, patron, publisher, and public, 1726–1780.* 1927. *The profession of letters: a study of the relations of author to patron, publisher and public, 1780–1832.* 1928.

2317 Colmer, John Anthony. *Coleridge, critic of society.* Oxford, 1959. See (2241) for other Coleridge references.

2318 Cragg, Gordon Robertson. *Reason and authority in the eighteenth century.* Cambridge, 1964.

2319 Curran, James, George Boyce and Pauline Wingate (eds.). *Newspaper history from the 17th century to the present day.* 1978. Nineteen essays on social, economic and political pressures which have influenced development of the English press.

2320 Dickinson, H. T. *Liberty and property: political ideology in 18th century Britain.* 1977. Incorporates important earlier articles on the subject.

2321 Dorson, Richard Mercer. *The British folklorists: a history.* 1968. Useful bibliography.

2322 Drescher, Seymour. *Tocqueville and England.* Cambridge, Mass., 1964.

2323 Elder, Dominic. *The common man philosophy of Thomas Paine: a study of the political ideas of Paine.* South Bend, Ind., 1951. Careful analysis. See (389) for other Paine references.

2324 Esdaile, Arundell James Kennedy. *The British Museum Library: a short history and survey.* Introduction by Sir Frederick Kenyon. 1946.

2325 Evans, Joan. *A history of the Society of Antiquaries.* Oxford, 1956.

2326 Everett, Charles Warren. *The education of Jeremy Bentham.* New York, 1931. To 1792. See (2240) for other Bentham references.

2327 Fetter, Frank Whitson. *Development of British monetary orthodoxy, 1797–1875.* Cambridge, Mass., 1965.

2328 Fletcher, Frank Thomas Herbert. *Montesquieu and English politics (1750–1800).* 1939.

2329 Forbes, Duncan. *Hume's philosophical politics.* Cambridge, 1975. Best study of the subject. See (2247) for other Hume references.

2330 Freeman, Michael. *Edmund Burke and the critique of political radicalism.* Oxford, 1980. See (382) for other Burke references.

2331 Gibb, Mildred Ann and Frank Beckwith. *The Yorkshire Post: two centuries.* Leeds, 1954.

2332 Glass, David Victor (ed.). *Introduction to Malthus.* 1953. Essays by various hands. See (2255) for other Malthus references.

2333 Godley, Alfred Denis. *Oxford in the eighteenth century.* 1908.

2334 Gooch, George Peabody. *History and historians in the nineteenth century.* 1913; 2nd edn, 1920; reprinted, 1952. Chaps. 15–17 discuss early nineteenth century British historians.

2335 Greene, Donald Johnson. *The politics of Samuel Johnson.* New Haven, Conn., 1960. Produced a long controversy, principally with Peter James Stanlis.

2336 Haig, Robert Lewis. *The Gazetteer, 1735–1797: a study in the eighteenth-century English newspaper.* Carbondale, Ill., 1960.

2337 Halévy, Élie. *The growth of philosophic radicalism.* Trans. Mary Morris. 1928; new edn, with bibliography by Charles Warren Everett, 1949; reprinted, Boston, Mass.,

1955. First published as *La Formation du radicalisme philosophique*. Paris, 1901–4, 3 vols. Classical study of the subject.

2338 Hamburger, Joseph. *James Mill and the art of revolution*. New Haven, Conn., 1963. See (2271) for other Mill references.

2339 —— *Macaulay and the Whig tradition*. Chicago, Ill., 1976. See (2264) for other Macaulay references.

2340 Handover, Phyllis Margaret. *A history of the London Gazette, 1665–1965*. 1965.

2341 Harris, Ronald Walter. *Political ideas, 1760–1792*. 1963.

2342 —— *Reason and nature in the eighteenth century, 1714–1780*. 1968.

2343 —— *Romanticism and the social order, 1780–1830*. 1969.

2344 Harrison, John Fletcher Clewes. *Robert Owen and the Owenites in Britain and America: the quest for a new moral world*. 1969. See (2260) for other Owen references.

2345 Heckscher, Elie Filip. *Mercantilism*. Trans. Mendel Shapiro. 1935, 2 vols.; rev. edn, 1955, 2 vols. First published, Stockholm, 1931.

2346 Himmelfarb, Gertrude. *Victorian minds*. New York, 1968. Essays on Burke, Bentham, Malthus and J. S. Mill among others.

2347 Hindle, Wilfrid. *The Morning Post, 1772–1937: portrait of a newspaper*. 1937.

2348 Hipple, Walter John. *The beautiful, the sublime and the picturesque in eighteenth-century British aesthetic theory*. Carbondale, Ill., 1957. See also (2369).

2349 Hollander, Samuel. *The economics of Adam Smith*. 1973. Criticized by Laurence S. Moss in *HPolEc*, 8 (1976), 564–74. See (2267) for other Smith references.

2350 Hollis, Patricia. *The pauper press: a study in working-class radicalism of the 1830s*. 1970.

2351 Howell, Wilbur Samuel. *Eighteenth-century British logic and rhetoric*. Princeton, NJ, 1971.

2352 Kaufman, Paul. *The community library: a chapter in English social history*. (Transactions of the American Philosophical Society NS, 57 [1967], Pt 7.) Philadelphia, Pa, 1967.

2353 Kelly, Gary. *The English Jacobin novel, 1780–1805*. Oxford, 1976.

2354 Kelly, Thomas. *Early public libraries: a history of public libraries in Great Britain before 1850*. 1966.

2355 Kettler, David. *The social and political thought of Adam Ferguson: an intellectual and the emergence of modern society*. Columbus, Ohio, 1965.

2356 Kliger, Samuel. *The Goths in England: a study in seventeenth- and eighteenth-century thought*. Cambridge, Mass., 1952.

2357 Knights, Ben. *The idea of the clerisy in the nineteenth century*. Cambridge, 1978. The idea was Coleridge's.

2358 Kogan, Herman. *The great EB: the story of the Encyclopaedia Britannica*. Chicago, Ill., 1958.

2359 Kovacevic, Ivanka. *Fact into fiction: English literature and the industrial scene, 1750–1850*. Leicester, 1975.

2360 Lehmann, William Christian. *Henry Home, Lord Kames, and the Scottish enlightenment: a study in national character and in the history of ideas*. The Hague, 1971.

2361 Leonard, Sterling Andrus. *The doctrine of correctness in English usage, 1700–1800*. Madison, Wis., 1929.

2362 Lovejoy, Arthur Oncken. *Essays in the history of ideas*. Baltimore, Md, 1947; reprinted, Baltimore, Md, 1962. Collected essays, most of them concerned with this period.

2363 —— *The great chain of being: a study of the history of an idea*. Cambridge, Mass., 1936; reprinted, 1953.

2364 McCleary, George Frederick. *The Malthusian population theory*. 1953. See (2255) for other Malthus references.

2365 Macfie, Alec Lawrence. *The individual in society: papers on Adam Smith*. 1967. See (2267) for other Smith references.

2366 Mallet, Sir Charles Edward. *A history of the University of Oxford*. Oxford, 1924–7, 3 vols.; reprinted, New York, 1968. Vol. 3: *Modern Oxford*. Standard; from the beginning of the seventeenth century.

2367 Manning, David John. *The mind of Jeremy Bentham*. 1968. Good introduction. See (2240) for other Bentham references.

2368 Mansfield, Harvey Claflin. *Statesmanship and party government: a study of Burke and Bolingbroke*. Chicago, Ill., 1965. See (382) for other Burke references.

2369 Monk, Samuel Holt. *The sublime: a study of critical theories in XVIIIth century England*. New York, 1935; reprinted, Ann Arbor, Mich., 1960. See also (2348).

2370 Monro, David Hector. *Godwin's moral philosophy: an interpretation of William Godwin.* 1953. See (2246) for other Godwin references.

2371 [Morison, Stanley]. *The history of the Times.* 1935–52, 4 vols. Vol. 1: '*The Thunderer*' *in the making, 1785–1841.* 1935.

2372 Muirhead, John Henry. *Coleridge as philosopher.* 1930; reprinted, 1954. See (2241) for other Coleridge references.

2373 Nesbitt, George Lyman. *Benthamite reviewing: the first twelve years of the Westminster Review, 1824–1836.* New York, 1934.

2374 Neuburg, Victor E. *Popular literature: a history and guide from the beginning of printing to the year 1897.* Harmondsworth, Middx, 1977.

2375 Nickerson, Jane Soames. *Homage to Malthus.* Port Washington, NY, 1975. See (2255) for other Malthus references.

2376 Nicolson, Marjorie Hope. *Mountain gloom and mountain glory: the development of the aesthetics of the infinite.* Ithaca, NY, 1959.

2377 O'Brien, Denis Patrick. *The classical economists.* Oxford, 1975. Good introduction.

2378 Ogilvie, Robert Maxwell. *Latin and Greek: a history of the influence of the classics on English life, from 1600 to 1918.* 1964.

2379 O'Gorman, Frank. *Edmund Burke: his political philosophy.* 1973. See (382) for other Burke references.

2380 Paglin, Morton. *Malthus and Lauderdale: the anti-Ricardian tradition.* New York, 1961. See (2255) for other Malthus references.

2381 Pankhurst, Richard Keir Pethick. *The Saint-Simonians, Mill and Carlyle: a preface to modern thought.* 1957.

2382 Parkin, Charles. *The moral basis of Burke's political thought.* Cambridge, 1956. Good brief analysis. See (382) for other Burke references.

2383 Peardon, Thomas Preston. *The transition in English historical writing, 1760–1830.* New York, 1933.

2384 Pier, Bernhard. *William Robertson als historiker und geschichtsphilosoph.* Radbod, 1929.

2385 Plamenatz, John Petrov. *The English utilitarians.* 1949; 2nd edn, rev., Oxford, 1958.

2386 Pocock, John Greville Agard. *Politics, language and time: essays on political thought and history.* 1972.

2387 Preyer, Robert. *Bentham, Coleridge and the science of history.* Bochum-Langendreer, 1958.

2388 Reed, Joseph Wayne. *English biography in the early nineteenth century, 1801–1838.* New Haven, Conn., 1966. For earlier biographical writing, see (2407).

2389 Reisman, D. A. *Adam Smith's sociological economics.* 1976. See (2267) for other Smith references.

2390 Robbins, Caroline. *The eighteenth-century commonwealth man: studies in the transmission, development and circumstance of English liberal thought from the restoration of Charles II until the war with the thirteen colonies.* Cambridge, Mass., 1959.

2391 Robbins, Lionel Charles Robbins, Baron. *The theory of economic policy in English classical political economy.* 1952.

2392 Roberts, Sydney Castle. *A history of the Cambridge University Press, 1521–1921.* Cambridge, 1921.

2393 Robson, John M. and Michael Laine (eds.). *James and John Stuart Mill: papers of the Centenary Conference.* Toronto, 1976. See (2271) for other James Mill references.

2394 Rosenblum, Nancy L. *Bentham's theory of the modern state.* Cambridge, Mass., 1978. See (2240) for other Bentham references.

2395 Ross, Ian Simpson. *Lord Kames and the Scotland of his day.* Oxford, 1972.

2396 St Clair, Oswald. *A key to Ricardo.* 1957. See (2268) for other Ricardo references.

2397 Schilling, Bernard Nicholas. *Conservative England and the case against Voltaire.* New York, 1950. Good account of the growing conservatism of later eighteenth century attitudes.

2398 Schwartz, Richard B. *Samuel Johnson and the new science.* Madison, Wis., 1971.

2399 Sen, Samar Ranjan. *The economics of Sir James Steuart.* 1957.

2400 Shine, Hill and Helen Chadwick Shine. *The Quarterly Review under Gifford: identification of contributors, 1809–1824.* Chapel Hill, NC, 1949.

2401 Shoup, Carl Sumner. *Ricardo on taxation.* New York, 1960. See (2268) for other Ricardo references.

2402 Skinner, Andrew S. *A system of social science: papers relating to Adam Smith.* Oxford,

1979. Collected essays stressing the unity of Smith's thought. See (2267) for other Smith references.

2403 Skinner, Andrew S. and Thomas Wilson (eds.). *Essays on Adam Smith*. Oxford, 1975. Thirty papers by various authorities on most aspects of Smith's thought. See (2267) for other Smith references.

2404 Smith, Kenneth. *The Malthusian controversy*. 1951; reprinted, New York, 1978. See (2255) for other Malthus references.

2405 Smith, Norman Kemp. *The philosophy of David Hume: a critical study of its origins and central doctrines*. 1941; reprinted, 1949. The best introduction. See (2247) for other Hume references.

2406 Stanlis, Peter James. *Edmund Burke and the natural law*. Ann Arbor, Mich., 1958; reprinted, Ann Arbor, Mich., 1965. Overly polemical, but one of the more important studies. See (382) for other Burke references.

2407 Stauffer, Donald Alfred. *The art of biography in eighteenth-century England: with a bibliographical supplement*. Princeton, NJ, 1941, 2 vols. Continued in (2388).

2408 Stephen, Sir Leslie. *The English utilitarians*. 1900, 3 vols.; reprinted, 1950, 3 vols.

2409 Stokes, Eric. *The English utilitarians and India*. Oxford, 1959.

2410 Thomas, David Oswald. *The honest mind: the thought and work of Richard Price*. Oxford, 1977. Best study of his ideas. See also (2263).

2411 Thomas, William. *The philosophic radicals: nine studies in theory and practice 1817–1841*. Oxford, 1980.

2412 Tinker, Chauncey Brewster. *Nature's simple plan: a phase of radical thought in the mid-eighteenth century*. Princeton, NJ, 1922.

2413 Tucker, Graham Shardalow Lee. *Progress and profits in British economic thought, 1650–1850*. Cambridge, 1960.

2414 Vicinus, Martha. *The industrial muse: a study of nineteenth-century British working-class literature*. 1974.

2415 Ward, William Reginald. *Georgian Oxford: university politics in the eighteenth century*. Oxford, 1958.

2416 Webb, Robert Kiefer. *The British working-class reader, 1790–1848: literacy and social tension*. 1955.

2417 Wellek, René. *A history of modern criticism: 1750–1950*. Vol. 1: *The later eighteenth century*. New Haven, Conn., 1955. Vol. 2: *The romantic age*. New Haven, Conn., 1955. Vol. 3: *The age of transition*. New Haven, Conn., 1966.

2418 —— *Immanuel Kant in England, 1793–1838*. Princeton, NJ, 1931.

2419 —— *The rise of English literary history*. Chapel Hill, NC, 1941; rev. edn, New York, 1966.

2420 Werkmeister, Lucyle. *The London daily press, 1772–1792*. Lincoln, Nebr., 1963. See also (495) and (2421).

2421 —— *A newspaper history of England, 1792–1793*. Lincoln, Nebr., 1967. See also (495) and (2420).

2422 Wexler, Victor G. *David Hume and the history of England*. Philadelphia, Pa, 1979. See (2247) for other Hume references.

2423 Wickwar, William Hardy. *The struggle for freedom of the press, 1819–1832*. 1928. The early unstamped radical press.

2424 Wiener, Joel H. *The war of the unstamped: the movement to repeal the British newspaper tax, 1830 to 1836*. Ithaca, NY, 1969.

2425 Wilkins, Burleigh Taylor. *The problem of Burke's political philosophy*. Oxford, 1967. See (382) for other Burke references.

2426 Willey, Basil. *The eighteenth-century background: studies on the idea of nature in the thought of the period*. 1940; reprinted, New York, 1953.

2427 —— *Nineteenth-century studies: Coleridge to Matthew Arnold*. 1949; reprinted, 1955.

2428 Wilson, Thomas and Andrew S. Skinner (eds.). *The market and the state: essays in honour of Adam Smith*. Oxford, 1976. Essays by various hands. See (2267) for other Smith references.

2429 Winch, Donald Norman. *Adam Smith's politics: an essay in historiographical revision*. Cambridge, 1978. See (2267) for other Smith references.

2430 —— *Classical political economy and colonies*. 1965.

2431 Winstanley, Denys Arthur. *Unreformed Cambridge: a study of certain aspects of the University in the eighteenth century*. Cambridge, 1935; reprinted, New York, 1977.

2432   Wyld, Henry Cecil Kennedy. *A history of modern colloquial English*. 1920; 3rd edn, 1937. Important for eighteenth century pronunciation.

4. Biographies

2433   Bain, Alexander. *James Mill: a biography*. 1882. Strong on his philosophy; written by a philosopher. See (2271) for other Mill references.
2434   Baker, Herschel Clay. *William Hazlitt*. Cambridge, Mass., 1962. See also (2251).
2435   Butt, John (ed.). *Robert Owen, prince of cotton spinners: a symposium*. Newton Abbot, Devon, 1971. Collection of essays by various hands. See (2260) for other Owen references.
2436   Cameron, Kenneth Neill. *The young Shelley: genesis of a radical*. 1951.
2437   Cannon, Garland Hampton. *Oriental Jones: a biography of Sir William Jones, 1746–1794*. Bombay, 1964. An important orientalist and judge in India. Cannon has also edited Jones's correspondence, 2 vols., Oxford, 1970.
2438   Carnall, Geoffrey. *Robert Southey and his age: the development of a conservative mind*. Oxford, 1960. See also (2243).
2439   Clarke, Martin Lowther. *Paley: evidences for the man*. 1974. See also (2261).
2440   —— *Richard Porson: a biographical essay*. Cambridge, 1937. Major Greek scholar.
2441   Clive, John Leonard. *Macaulay: the shaping of the historian*. New York, 1973. See (2264) for other Macaulay references.
2442   Cloyd, Emily L. *James Burnett, Lord Monboddo*. Oxford, 1972.
2443   Cole, George Douglas Howard. *The life of Robert Owen*. 1925; 2nd edn, 1930; 3rd edn, with introduction by Dame Margaret Cole, Hamden, Conn., 1966. See (2260) for other Owen references.
2444   De Beer, Sir Gavin Rylands. *Gibbon and his world*. 1968. See (2257) for other Gibbon references.
2445   Derry, Warren. *Dr Parr: a portrait of the Whig Dr Johnson*. Oxford, 1966.
2446   Everett, Charles Warren. *Jeremy Bentham*. 1966. See (2240) for other Bentham references.
2447   Greig, John Young Thompson. *David Hume*. 1931. Standard. See (2247) for other Hume references.
2448   Halévy, Elie. *Thomas Hodgskin*. Paris, 1903; trans. Arthur John Taylor, 1956. Early socialist who influenced Marx.
2449   Hay, Carla H. *James Burgh: spokesman for reform in Hanoverian England*. Washington, DC, 1979.
2450   Lehmann, William Christian. *John Millar of Glasgow, 1735–1801*. Cambridge, 1960. Includes a reprint of Millar's *Origins of the distinctions of ranks* from the 3rd (1779) edition.
2451   Low, David Morrice. *Edward Gibbon, 1737–1794*. 1937. Among the best biographies. See (2257) for other Gibbon references.
2452   Mack, Mary Peter. *Jeremy Bentham: an odyssey of ideas, 1748–1792*. 1962. Controversial, but the most detailed study. See (2240) for other Bentham references.
2453   Marchand, Leslie Alexis. *Byron: a biography*. New York, 1957, 3 vols. Standard. See also (2256).
2454   Mazlish, Bruce. *James and John Stuart Mill: father and son in the nineteenth century*. New York, 1975. A psychobiography. See (2271) for other James Mill references.
2455   Mossner, Ernest Campbell. *The life of David Hume*. 1954; 2nd edn, Oxford, 1980. Standard. See (2247) for other Hume references.
2456   Paul, Charles Kegan. *William Godwin: his friends and contemporaries*. 1876, 2 vols. Standard. See (2246) for other Godwin references.
2457   Petersen, William. *Malthus*. Cambridge, Mass., 1979. Extensive bibliography. See (2255) for other Malthus references.
2458   Pollard, Sidney and John Salt (eds.). *Robert Owen, prophet of the poor*. 1971. Essays by various hands. See (2260) for other Owen references.
2459   Rae, John. *Life of Adam Smith*. 1895; reprinted, New York, 1965, with Jacob Viner's 'Guide to John Rae's Life of Adam Smith' as an introduction. Basic biography. See (2267) for other Smith references.
2460   Recktenwald, Horst Claus. *Adam Smith: sein leben und sein werke*. Munich, 1976. See (2267) for other Smith references.

2461 Rudkin, Olive Durant. *Thomas Spence and his connections.* 1927; reprinted, New York, 1966.
2462 Scott, William Robert. *Adam Smith as student and professor, with unpublished documents.* Glasgow, 1937. See (2267) for other Smith references.
2463 Shea, Donald F. *The English Ranke: John Lingard.* New York, 1969.
2464 Weatherall, D. *David Ricardo: a biography.* The Hague, 1976. See (2268) for other Ricardo references.
2465 West, E. G. *Adam Smith.* New Rochelle, NY, 1969. See (2267) for other Smith references.
2466 Woodcock, George. *William Godwin: a biographical study.* 1946. See (2246) for other Godwin references.

5. Articles

2467 Abrams, Meyer Howard. 'English romanticism: the spirit of the age', in Northrop Frye (ed.), *Romanticism reconsidered.* New York, 1963, pp. 26–72.
2468 Avery, Margaret. 'Toryism in the age of the American Revolution: John Lind and John Shebbeare', *Historical Studies*, 18 (1978), 24–36. Pamphleteers.
2469 Bartle, G. F. 'Jeremy Bentham and John Bowring: a study of the relationship between Bentham and the editor of his *Collected Works*', *BIHR*, 36 (1963), 27–35. See (2240) for other Bentham references.
2470 Bernstein, John Andrew. 'Adam Ferguson and the idea of progress', *Studies in Burke and His Time*, 19 (1978), 99–118.
2471 Berry, Christopher J. 'Adam Smith's *Considerations* on language', *JHI*, 35 (1974), 130–8. See (2267) for other Smith references.
2472 Blaug, Mark. 'The classical economists and the Factory Acts: a re-examination', *Quarterly Journal of Economics*, 72 (1958), 211–26; reprinted in Alfred William Coats (ed.), *The classical economists and economic policy.* 1971, pp. 104–22.
2473 Checkland, Sydney George. 'Growth and progress: the nineteenth-century view in Britain', *EcHR* 2nd ser., 12 (1959–60), 49–62.
2474 Christian, William. 'The moral economics of Tom Paine', *JHI*, 34 (1973), 367–80. See (389) for other Paine references.
2475 Christie, Ian Ralph. 'British newspapers in the later Georgian age', in his *Myth and reality in late-eighteenth-century British politics and other papers.* 1970, pp. 311–33.
2476 —— 'James Perry of the *Morning Chronicle*, 1756–1821', in his *Myth and reality in late-eighteenth-century British politics and other papers.* 1970, pp. 334–58.
2477 Coats, Alfred William. 'Adam Smith: the modern re-appraisal', *Renaissance and Modern Studies*, 6 (1962), 25–48. See (2267) for other Smith references.
2478 —— 'The classical economists and the labourer', in Eric Lionel Jones and Gordon Edmund Mingay (eds.), *Land, labour and population in the industrial revolution.* 1967, pp. 100–30; reprinted in Coats's (ed.), *The classical economists and economic policy.* 1971, pp. 144–79. Argues that they were more sympathetic to the labourer than is usually assumed.
2479 Dinwiddy, John Rowland. 'Bentham's transition to political radicalism, 1809–10', *JHI*, 36 (1975), 683–700. See (2240) for other Bentham references.
2480 Dreyer, Frederick. 'Burke's religion', *Studies in Burke and His Time*, 17 (1976), 199–212. See (382) for other Burke references.
2481 —— 'The genesis of Burke's *Reflections*', *JMH*, 50 (1978), 462–79. On the immediate background. See (382) for other Burke references.
2482 Fetter, Frank Whitson. 'Economic controversy in the British reviews, 1802–1850', *Economica* NS, 32 (1965), 424–37. Fetter has also published a series of articles on the authorship of the economic articles in various reviews during the first half of the century: the *Edinburgh, JPolEc*, 61 (1953), 232–59; the *Quarterly, JPolEc*, 66 (1958), 47–64, 154–70; the *Westminster, JPolEc*, 70 (1962), 570–96; and *Blackwood's, Scottish Journal of Political Economy*, 7 (1960), 85–107, 213–31.
2483 —— 'The rise and decline of Ricardian economics', *HPolEc*, 1 (1969), 67–84. See (2268) for other Ricardo references.
2484 Finer, Samuel Edward. 'The transmission of Benthamite ideas 1820–50', in Gillian Ray Sutherland (ed.), *Studies in the growth of nineteenth-century government.* 1972, pp. 11–32. Benthamite propagandizing, especially the Political Economy Club. See (2240) for other Bentham references.

2485 Firth, Sir Charles Harding. 'Modern history at Oxford, 1724–1841', *EHR*, 32 (1917), 1–21.

2486 Geanakoplos, Dino T. 'Edward Gibbon and Byzantine ecclesiastical history', *Church History*, 35 (1966), 170–85. See (2257) for other Gibbon references.

2487 Grampp, William Dyer. 'Malthus and his contemporaries', *HPolEc*, 6 (1974), 278–304. See (2255) for other Malthus references.

2488 —— 'Scots, Jews, and subversives among the dismal scientists', *JEcH*, 36 (1976), 543–71.

2489 Himmelfarb, Gertrude. 'Bentham scholarship and the Bentham "problem"', *JMH*, 41 (1969), 189–206. Review article on the first two volumes of his correspondence; very critical of Bentham. See (2240) for other Bentham references.

2490 ——'Bentham's utopia: the National Charity Company', *JBS*, 10, 1 (1970), 80–125. See (2240) for other Bentham references.

2491 Hollander, Samuel. 'Ricardo and the Corn Laws: a revision', *HPolEc*, 9 (1977), 1–47. See (2268) for other Ricardo references.

2492 Kettler, David. 'History and theory in the Scottish enlightenment', *JMH*, 48 (1976), 95–100.

2493 Kilcup, Rodney W. 'Burke's historicism', *JMH*, 49 (1977), 394–410. See (382) for other Burke references.

2494 Knox, Thomas R. 'Thomas Spence: the trumpet of jubilee', *PP*, 76 (1977), 75–98.

2495 Kramnick, Isaac. 'Religion and radicalism: English political theory in the age of revolution', *Political Theory*, 5 (1977), 605–34.

2496 Kriegel, Abraham D. 'Liberty and Whiggery in early nineteenth-century England', *JMH*, 52 (1980), 253–78.

2497 Lovejoy, Arthur Oncken. 'The meaning of romanticism for the historian of ideas', *JHI*, 2 (1941), 257–78.

2498 Maitland, Frederic William. 'A historical sketch of liberty and equality as ideals of English political philosophy from the time of Hobbes to the time of Coleridge', in Herbert Albert Laurens Fisher (ed.), *Collected papers of ... Maitland*. 1911, i, 1–161.

2499 Newman, Gerald. 'Anti-French propaganda and British liberal nationalism in the early nineteenth century: suggestions toward a general interpretation', *Victorian Studies*, 18 (1974–5), 385–418.

2500 Peake, Charles F. 'Henry Thornton and the development of Ricardo's economic thought', *HPolEc*, 10 (1978), 193–212. See (2268) for other Ricardo references.

2501 Pocock, John Greville Agard. 'Burke and the Ancient Constitution: a problem in the history of ideas', *HJ*, 3 (1960), 125–43. Argues that Burke's traditionalism is in the main line of English political thought. See (382) for other Burke references.

2502 Prochaska, Franklyn K. 'Thomas Paine's *The Age of Reason* revisited', *JHI*, 33 (1972), 561–76. See (389) for other Paine references.

2503 Recktenwald, Horst Claus. 'An Adam Smith renaissance *anno* 1976? The bicentenary output: a reappraisal of his scholarship', *Journal of Economic Literature*, 16 (1978), 56–83. See (2267) for other Smith references.

2504 Robbins, Caroline. 'The strenuous Whig: Thomas Hollis of Lincoln's Inn', *W&MQ* 3rd ser., 7 (1950), 406–53.

2505 Rothblatt, Sheldon. 'The student sub-culture and the examination system in early 19th-century Oxbridge', in Lawrence Stone (ed.), *The university in society*. Vol. 1: *Oxford and Cambridge from the 14th to the early 19th centuries*. Princeton, NJ, 1974, pp. 246–303.

2506 Samuelson, Paul A. 'A modern theorist's vindication of Adam Smith', *American Economic Review: Papers and Proceedings*, 67 (1977), 42–9. Econometric vindication. See (2267) for other Smith references.

2507 Scrivener, Michael H. 'Godwin's philosophy: a re-evaluation', *JHI*, 39 (1978), 615–26. See (2246) for other Godwin references.

2508 Soloway, Richard Allen. 'Reform or ruin: English moral thought during the first French Republic', *Review of Politics*, 25 (1963), 110–28.

2509 Spengler, Joseph John. 'Malthus's total population theory: a restatement and reappraisal', *Canadian Journal of Economics*, 11 (1945), 83–110, 234–64. One of the more important articles on the subject. See (2255) for other Malthus references.

2510 Thackray, Arnold. 'Natural knowledge in cultural context: the Manchester model', *AHR*, 79 (1974), 672–709.

2511 Tholfsen, Trygve R. 'The intellectual origins of mid-Victorian stability', *Political Science Quarterly*, 86 (1971), 57–91.

2512 West, E. G. 'Adam Smith's economics of politics', *HPolEc*, 8 (1976), 515–39. See (2267) for other Smith references.

2513 —— 'Scotland's resurgent economist: a survey of the new literature on Adam Smith', *Scottish Journal of Economics*, 45 (1978), 343–69. See (2267) for other Smith references.

2514 Withey, Lynne E. 'Catherine Macaulay and the uses of history: ancient rights, perfectionism, and propaganda', *JBS*, 16, 1 (1976), 59–83.

INDEX OF AUTHORS, EDITORS AND TRANSLATORS

Numbers are entry numbers

INDEX OF AUTHORS, ETC.